THE ANATOMY OF ARGUMENT

Barrie A. Wilson

UNIVERSITY
PRESS OF
AMERICA

LANHAM • NEW YORK • LONDON

13.50
-5

Copyright © 1980 by

University Press of America,™ Inc.

4720 Boston Way
Lanham, MD 20706

3 Henrietta Street
London WC2E 8LU England

All rights reserved

Printed in the United States of America

Library of Congress Cataloging in Publication Data
Wilson, Barrie A
   The anatomy of argument.

   Bibliography: p.
   1. Logic.   I. Title.
BC71.W55   160   80-5606
ISBN 0-8191-1211-9 (pbk.)

160
W746a

for

LINDA

who has "reasoned out" her position

and for

ANDREW

DOROTHY

JAMIE

DAVID

who have yet to "reason out" theirs

41370

iv

TABLE OF CONTENTS

PART TWO: ON EVALUATING ARGUMENTS

PREFACE

for the instructor

purpose of this text
- to provide a comprehensive introduction to the study of argument
- specifically, to provide a basic introductory text that both presents theory and develops skills in
  - argument identification
  - argument evaluation
  - argument preparation
  - argument presentation

features

(1) it focuses specifically on argument

Most texts (e.g. in logic, debate, rhetoric, speech communication, etc.) are designed simply to present the approach of one particular discipline as it relates to the study of argument. This situation has the following undesirable consequences:
- it presents the student with only a partial perspective on argument
- it undercuts the development of a systematic integrated framework for looking at arguments
- it frustrates the course director who wants to offer his students a balanced view of argument analysis
- it fails to meet current university curricular objectives which urgently demand, at the elementary levels, a more integrated and comprehensive approach to the study of argument in order to provide students with those skills needed for successful university study

This text seeks to overcome these problems by making its primary emphasis the study of argument as such. In so doing it of course incorporates contributions from specific disciplines (e.g. from logic, debate, rhetoric, etc.). It does so, however, within the compass of a larger perspective than simply the point of view of one discipline, and it does so, moreover, within the framework of a conceptual structure designed to be more appropriate to the systematic and comprehensive study of argument as a whole.

> (2) it partitions the study of argument
> into two main areas:
>> (I) argument identification
>> (II) argument evaluation

Part One of the text is concerned with argument identification. The student is introduced to the basic structural features of an argument and learns how to recognize arguments in what others have written.

Part Two of the text is concerned with argument evaluation. The student is introduced to 10 different aspects of argument assessment (including the concerns of symbolic logic, inductive logic, and debate and rhetoric studies) and learns how to comment on arguments critically.

It has been my experience in teaching the study of argument that it is important to spend a considerable amount of time at the outset helping students find out what the argument is before judging how good it is.

It has also been my experience that some of the interesting and important philosophical issues that occur in the study of argument are best left for classroom comment rather than for explicit treatment in the text. Classes differ markedly in their capacity for philosophical reflection and the latter may serve only to distract some students from the matter immediately at hand.

> (3) it also examines the preparation
> and presentation of arguments

Most texts simply teach students how to pick apart the arguments of others. This is inadequate, for, on this approach, the student very often comes away from the course not knowing how to structure his own line of reasoning in essays, reports, class presentations, discussions and confrontations in the public domain, etc. where he has to make arguments of his own.

This text, especially at the end of chapters 2, 3 and 4, and in chapter 12, provides opportunities in a cumulative and progressive manner for the student to gain experience in mastering this important aspect of argument study. It does so, moreover, with respect to both written and oral contexts.

      (4) it presents a new format for
          depicting arguments, one that
             (a) enables the structure of arguments
                to be "seen" and which
             (b) facilitates the systematic evaluation of arguments.

This new format is developed in chapter 2 and is used throughout the book. It uses space to help the student visualize structure and to differentiate tasks. The format allows the student specifically
    - to see the structure of the main
      argument (vertically)
    - to see the structure of the supporting
      arguments (horizontally)
    - to recognize when he is identifying
      and when he is evaluating an argument.

The format is easily mastered by the student and represents, in my teaching experience, a vastly superior format to those in other texts.

      (5) it develops argument evaluation
          systematically as a series of
          10 Steps

These 10 Steps are presented, one at a time, in Part Two of the text. This method allows the critical perspectives of symbolic logic, inductive reasoning, debate studies, "informal" logic (fallacies, language, etc.) and so on to be brought to bear upon the critical assessment of an argument in a systematic and integrated fashion.

This method also allows for a different way of
organizing a large number of fallacies--often
treated with little reference to systematic
classification, and, indeed, often without
explicit reference to actual arguments--and to
do so in a way that connects the study of fallacies
with other topics in the study of argument.

In addition, the systematic application of each
step to each argument helps overcome the tendency
I have noted in teaching for students to jump
right in with a blanket denial of the conclusion
of the argument (the "not-so" approach) rather
than to take the time to engage in a more diver-
sified and more demanding inspection of the main
structural elements of the argument presented.

    (6) it uses examples and exercises not
        likely soon to become outdated

Rather than being drawn from the political sector
(short longevity span), the arguments used in the
examples and exercises are drawn more from current
moral issues, consumer and business concerns, popular social scientific findings, religious positions,
etc. likely to have a longer lifespan in the arena
of interest and controversy.

Exercises are not simply concocted to illustrate
theoretical points but to reflect authentic arguments found in current controversies. To a large
extent they are taken from material likely to be
encountered at university or college level.

    (7) in sum, it is unique in the following
        respects:
          - in its comprehensive focus on
            argument as such, drawing on
            contributions from many disciplines
            in an integrated and balanced
            fashion
          - in its separation of tasks: argument
            identification first, then argument
            evaluation
          - in its format for identifying and
            evaluating arguments critically

Consider the following conversation:

> Ernie: I think people shouldn't be discrim-
> inated against simply for being homo-
> sexual, even if they are school teach-
> ers.
>
> Bert: Why?
>
> Ernie: Well, for a couple of reasons, I
> suppose. For one thing, people should
> not be forced into a cover-up life-
> style, having to protect their true
> identity for fear of losing their job.
> For another thing, there is no evidence
> to suggest that homosexuals are any
> more apt to become involved with stu-
> dents than are heterosexuals.

In this brief exchange, Ernie has made an argument.
An argument is offered when people back up a position with reasons. This Ernie has done. That is,
he has put forward a position, namely:

> People shouldn't be discriminated against
> simply for being homosexual, even if they
> are school teachers.

And he has defended it by offering reasons, as
follows:

> (1) People should not be forced into a cover-
> up lifestyle, having to protect their true
> identity for fear of losing their job.

and

> (2) There is no evidence to suggest that homo-
> sexuals are any more apt to become involv-
> ed with students than are heterosexuals.

This book presents a basic introduction to the
study of arguments. As such it has certain characteristics.

It is introductory. It provides you with a basic
survey of the subject material that belongs to the
study of argument. The book is intended for those

who like to reason and who want to learn how to do it more effectively. It doesn't purport to tell you the whole story about argumentation, but it does manage to cover a lot -- enough that should you become interested in the subject itself, you would be well equipped for more specialized studies.

It has three main objectives.

    (1) argument identification - to learn how to pick out arguments from the controversial contexts in which they are made.

    (2) argument preparation and presentation - to learn how to put across arguments of your own, both in written and oral situations.

    (3) argument evaluation - to learn how to judge arguments critically, looking at both their merits and defects.

Because of these objectives, the book is meant to be intensely practical. It isn't intended to be a mere theoretical study, teaching you that something is so. It is that, but it's meant to be much more. For this text to achieve its goals, it requires that you learn how to do something. Specifically it requires that you gain from this text important skills in argument identification, argument preparation and presentation, and argument evaluation.

Since the purpose of the text is practical, the study involves practice on your part. The desirable skills cannot be developed merely by reading the text: they are gained only by doing the assignments. Do the "Recall Quizzes" at the end of each chapter -- force yourself to bring to mind the points you have read. Do the exercises -- force yourself to apply the points you have read about. For you to realize the primary purposes of this text, for you in other words to gain these important skills, involves a willingness and a commitment on your part to enter into a sort of apprenticeship, to proceed step by step until you have mastered the various phases of this study.

The study, moreover, is <u>cumulative</u>: it builds carefully upon previous points. This means that each section must be carefully mastered before proceeding with the next. It is a book that must be worked through, section by section. It is not one that can be dipped into here and there.

The text adopts a <u>systematic</u> approach. For clarity in learning, we separate argument identification and argument evaluation.

> In <u>Part One</u> we start with <u>argument identification</u>. This is basic. Here you are introduced to the structure of simple arguments, then that of more complex arguments. More importantly, here you gain considerable experience in learning how to recognize and identify the structure of arguments people put forward.
>
> The text then moves on, in <u>Part Two</u>, to a consideration of <u>argument evaluation</u>. Here you learn, in a series of 10 steps, how to judge arguments critically. Each step focuses on a different aspect of an argument that needs critical inspection. Here you gain, step by step, considerable experience in picking apart arguments, learning how to spot weaknesses and strengths.
>
> In addition, at various stages along the way, opportunities are provided for gaining experience in <u>argument preparation and presentation</u>.

The study is an exceptionally <u>important and useful</u> one.

- it teaches fundamental skills in how to identify, criticize and present arguments.
- such skills are crucial in developing solid skills in rational decision-making and in avoiding the pitfalls of irrationality and brain-washing.

- such skills play a valuable role in a
  society such as ours that emphasizes
  citizen participation in political decision-
  making, where arguments are brought to bear
  upon different policies and weighed critically in our legislative and social forums.

- such skills are basic to good college and
  university work, as you read texts that
  present arguments, listen to lectures that
  put arguments forth, and as you have to
  write essays and reports that express and
  defend a point of view.

Finally, it is an interesting study, seeing the
moves people make as they struggle with opposing
points of view, learning how to spot alternative
options that may be present as people think
through issues or decide what to do, and learning
how to present your own position in a more organized and effective fashion.

PART ONE

ON IDENTIFYING ARGUMENTS

CHAPTER ONE

THE STRUCTURE OF ARGUMENT

1. Some Preliminaries About the Study of Argument

This text provides a broad basic introduction to the study of argument.

The word 'argument' is a technical term in this book. It does not mean what it so often means in popular usage. That is, it does not refer to a nasty, heated exchange between people who cannot agree. An argument is not a shouting match between persons who endlessly and pointlessly insist on their own point of view. Simply put, as used in this text,

>An argument is a position which is reasoned out, whether "heated" or not.

This represents a preliminary description of what an argument is. It'll be refined eventually in more technical language. But this simple account will do for now.

Suppose you hear someone expressing the following point of view:

>The government should enact legislation permitting euthanasia because people have the right to die with dignity and also because people ought to be able to choose for themselves whether to live or die.

This person is presenting a reasoned out position. The position is what he is advocating, namely:

>the government should enact legislation permitting euthanasia

Why should the government do this? The person gives two reasons:

>1. people have the right to die with dignity.
>2. people ought to be able to choose for themselves whether to live or die.

The person here has advocated a position, and

he has given reasons for that position. He has, in other words, made an argument.

As this example shows, an argument is a structured piece of reasoning. It has at least two basic ingredients:

1. a position put forward.
2. reasons which support that position.

The argument considered above is a skimpy one, and not too exciting. There are a lot of questions you would probably want the arguer to elaborate on. For example: under what conditions should euthanasia be permitted? What is the meaning of the phrase "the right to die with dignity"? Would euthanasia, if performed, serve to guarantee that right? And who decides - and when - in a particular case? And so on. These are legitimate questions to ask of the person advocating euthanasia. Even so, you should recognize, however, that the person has at least put forward an argument.

As we shall see, as arguers defend, elaborate on, and qualify the points they raise in support of a position, arguments can become quite complex and tangled....and certainly highly contentious! Part of the fun in the study of argument lies in sorting out the various strands in complex, tangled arguments and in learning how to come to grips with highly controversial matters.

This text presents an introduction to the study of "reasoned out" positions. Before beginning this study, however, there are a few general points about the nature of this study that you should carefully note:

(1) The study of argument may be divided into three main areas:

(a) <u>argument identification</u>

As has already been pointed out, an argument has a specific basic structure: (1) a position advocated along with (2) reasons which support that position. Argument identification is concerned

4

with the structural features of an argument. It involves (1) making clear what position the arguer is advancing, and (2) pointing out what reasons the arguer gives in support of his position. In this way, argument identification clarifies the structure of what a person says when he presents an argument.

Before arguments can be pulled apart, responded to, applauded, defended, or considered in relation to other arguments, etc., what the argument is has to be made clear. This is the essential task of argument identification.

Part One of this text is entitled: "On Identifying Arguments." It outlines the way in which the basic structural features of arguments can be depicted, not only the skimpy sort encountered above but also the more complex varieties that will be met as we progress in this study. In this section of the book, you should learn how to recognize arguments.

(b) argument evaluation

Not all reasoned out positions, however, are reasoned out well. Many arguments contain flaws of one sort or another. Before being accepted or rejected, arguments should be subjected to extensive critical scrutiny. This is the task of argument evaluation.

Argument evaluation looks at the structure and content of arguments critically. It examines where, why, and how arguments are defective. It also considers ways in which poor arguments may be improved.

Part Two of this text is entitled: "On Evaluating Arguments." It presents a series of 10 steps which look systematically at various important features of an argument that should be critically considered. By following these steps, you should learn how to judge arguments critically.

(c) argument preparation and presentation

It is not enough simply to be able to recognize
and judge critically the arguments that others
have made. It is also important for you to learn
how to make and present arguments of your own.
This represents a third area in the study of argument.

Argument preparation is concerned with ways in
which arguments can be put together in a clear
manner. Argument presentation suggests ways in
which arguments can be put across effectively, in
both written and oral contexts.

This area builds upon the first two areas. Skills
in argument preparation and presentation are developed out of a knowledge of argument structure and
the merits a good argument ought to have. At various places in the text opportunities are provided
for you to prepare and present an argument of your
own making. By doing this, you should learn how
to construct and put forward an argument of your
own.

As we see, then, there are these three areas in
the study of argument:

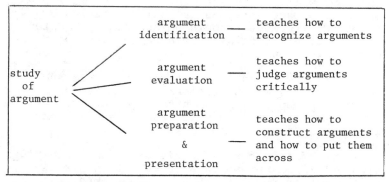

study of argument	argument identification	teaches how to recognize arguments
	argument evaluation	teaches how to judge arguments critically
	argument preparation & presentation	teaches how to construct arguments and how to put them across

As you can readily appreciate, the study of argument teaches fundamental skills in critical reasoning.

Some other general features of the study of argument are worth noting before the study begins:

(2) The study of argument may be approached from either of two different critical perspectives:
- (a) the <u>descriptive</u> approach - investigates what <u>people do</u> take into account when they accept <u>or</u> reject reasoned out positions.
- (b) the <u>normative</u> approach - investigates what <u>people ought to</u> take into account when they accept or reject reasoned out positions.

A descriptive approach to the study of argument would survey the many different factors that enter into a person's acceptance or rejection of a reasoned out position. No doubt many people do accept arguments that are poorly presented, inadequately constructed, and of dubious worth. It is beyond dispute that many people do in fact accept arguments that can be shot full-of-holes. It is also true that many people fail to accept arguments which are well constructed, expertly presented, and of considerable worth. That is, many people reject arguments which are air-tight.

Why people <u>do</u> accept or reject the arguments they do represents a descriptive approach to the study. It is an important study and can be found in the sociological or psychological consideration of argumentation. This is not, however, the approach that is adopted in this text.

This text studies argument from a normative perspective. That is, it investigates the features of an argument a person <u>ought to</u> consider if he wishes to accept or reject a reasoned out position <u>on a rational basis</u>. No one can compel an arguer or a person <u>reading</u> an argument to be rational. But <u>if one wants to be rational</u>, then a normative approach sets forth what must be considered by such a person.

(3) The study of argument is, moreover, one that is <u>about</u> arguments. It presents a framework for <u>looking</u> at arguments. It investigates the structure, merits, and the preparation and presentation

of arguments. Its focus is on arguments as arguments, regardless of the particular side or point of view the argument favors and regardless of the popularity of the position being argued for.

The study of argument does not advocate any particular position on the various issues about which people argue. You should not approach the study of argument expecting to find out what is true about such issues as euthanasia, genetic planning, the implications of technology for labor, capital punishment, the implications of environmental considerations for corporate expansion, the global implications of Third World needs and demands, the civil rights of homosexuals, the morality of suicide, and other highly disputed matters before the North American public.

The study of argument is, of course, very closely linked to such controversial issues. As the study progresses, you will find examples drawn from various sides of such disputes. They will serve, however, either to illustrate general points about argument or else to provide practice in recognizing and evaluating arguments critically. The focus in this text, then, is not on resolving these controversies, and you should not get up your hopes that it will.

The focal point of this text is rather on surveying the broad general features of argument. To repeat, it aims at helping you develop skills in
      (a) argument identification,
      (b) argument evaluation, and
      (c) argument preparation and presentation.
These skills are basic to critical reasoning. By developing these, you can learn how lines of thought and positions are put forward and defended in books, articles, texts, magazines, TV documentaries, etc. In addition, you can learn how to structure and communicate your point of view better in term papers, essays, oral presentations, etc.

What you should expect to gain from this text,

8

then, are skills in each of these three areas. If
such skills are developed, then this text will
have served its purpose. Once these skills have
been developed, however, they should in turn help
you clarify the issues at stake in the controversies in which you become embroiled and help you
participate in these disputes effectively. But
you're on your own there. This text won't tell
you what side you wish to take--only how to state,
defend, and put across whatever side you wish to
take.

(4) The study of argument is an especially important study in today's society. While this will
become much more apparent as you progress in the
study of argument, your attention is at this point
drawn to the following key areas of importance:

> (a) the study of argument is essential for
> informed thought and action.

Arguments occur when people try to find out what
is true or what ought to be done. Arguments therefore figure prominently in contexts of deliberation and decision-making--in fact, wherever rational discussion is taking place. By studying arguments, you are embarking on a course of study that
is basic to informed thought and action.

This study is particularly important for any society such as ours which stresses knowledgeable
participation in its affairs. It is equally
important for any individual who seeks to equip
himself with defences against sheer gullibility,
emotionalism, or irrationality in personal decision-making.

> (b) the study of argument should help in
> the following important areas:
>> to open up alternate courses of action,
>> to suggest different policies, or
>> to make apparent new avenues of thought.

By mastering the skills at which the study of
argument aims, you should become more aware of the
possibilities involved in any area of controversy.
By knowing more about argumentation, you may be
able to see different sides to an issue, or to

9

envisage different courses of action. If this
happens, the study of argument can serve to extend
the horizons of personal thought and action, thereby helping to overcome "one-dimensionality." In
other words, the study of argument can be an anti-
dote to a restrictive and narrow perspective on
the issues encountered in everyday life.

(5) The study of argument <u>requires close analytic
focus on your part</u>. That is, it requires close
inspection of just what is said or written when
people present arguments. This usually involves
careful attention to the interrelationships between the various sentences people utter or write.

The study of argument is, then, not an impressionistic one. It cannot be mastered by a quick "once-
over." Nor is it a speculative or intuitive study,
one that opens up vast vistas of reality. Rather
it requires close attention to details and to the
nitty-gritty of language. It also requires practice, and the exercises assigned in this text must
be done faithfully if the desired skills are to be
acquired. It is not a subject which can simply be
read about.

It is now time to begin this study.

2.   The Basic Structure of Arguments

assertions

As we saw in section 1, arguments are reasoned out
positions. As such, they contrast with what are
called "assertions" or "claims."
> An <u>assertion</u> (or <u>claim</u>) is simply a
> statement put forward as true.
The difference between an argument and an assertion
is considerable.

Let us suppose that a 23-year old woman has just
made the following statement:
> Men are responsible for my having had
> two abortions, several unhappy marriages,

> a series of unfulfilling affairs, and a
> generally messed-up life.

This person is not offering an argument at all.
She is simply making an _assertion_ that men are
responsible for some particular events in her life
(abortions, marriages, affairs) and the state of
her life in general (as "messed-up"). She has
made no connection between men and her having had
two abortions, several unhappy marriages, a series
of unfulfilling affairs, and a generally messed-up
life. That is, she offered no grounds for suppos-
ing that her plight has anything to do with men at
all.

Indeed, her miserable state may have occurred because she has a hormonal imbalance, or because she
has an irritating personality, or because she is a
born loser, or because the world is controlled by
an evil genius who has singled her out for special
attention, etc. There are a lot of possible reasons for these events in her life and why her life
is as it is. In some way or other they may even
all be the result of men. In terms of what she
has said, however, no connection has been drawn
between her state and the attitudes or activities
of men. Perhaps she could make this connection,
if pressed, but the point is, she hasn't.

In a similar way, someone may contend that:
> Homosexuals shouldn't be allowed to marry.

or
> Indians in North American society have no
> choice but to become assimilated to the
> ways of the white man.

or
> Women's liberation is solely the product of
> technological advances in the control of
> reproduction and the social need to have
> more bodies to tend the machines of techno-
> logical society.

or
> "Born again" Christians are simply deluding
> themselves if they think they are in any way
> different from others in society.

In each of these statements, something is asserted

11

to be the case. A claim is made. But notice
something that is tremendously important: in no
case is the claim defended. No reasons are given,
for example, why homosexuals shouldn't be allowed
to marry. No reasons are offered to back up the
claim that Indians have no choice but assimilation.
No support is offered for the point of view expressed on women's liberation. No indications are
given why regenerated Christians are deluding themselves.

In each case above, a claim is put forward without
supporting considerations. Such statements are
called "assertions" or "claims." It is characteristic of an assertion that it expresses a point of
view without offering supporting reasons. Assertions are often made in the course of conversations, discussions, and talk generally. They are
not arguments, however.

Assertions need not occur simply as single statements. In conversations or in writing, people
often put forward a whole series of assertions
about a particular topic. For instance, consider
the following discussion:
> Reproduction in the year 2000 will not take
> place in the way in which we're familiar with
> the process. It will not occur in the
> woman's uterus as the result of individual
> decisions by men and women. It will occur in
> specially designed labs as the result of
> governmental decisions. In the year 2000
> women will have achieved true equality with
> men: they, too, will not be able to have
> babies!
This selection simply expresses a view concerning
the manner in which reproduction will occur in
the year 2000. It is simply a series of assertions about this particular topic.

Another example of a series of assertions is this:
> As an organizer I start from where the world
> is, as it is, not as I would like it to be.
> That we accept the world as it is does not
> in any sense weaken our desire to change it

into what we believe it should be -- it is
necessary to begin where the world is if we
are going to change it to what we think it
should be. That means working in the system.
(Saul Alinsky, Rules for Radicals (New York:
    Random House Vintage Books, 1971), p. xix)
In this selection, Alinsky is simply expounding
his view of where the effective community organ-
izer begins. He is simply stating his point of
view, not arguing on behalf of it.

Another example of a series of assertions is found
in the following selection:
    In 1965, in an article in Horizon, I coined
    the term "future shock" to describe the
    shattering stress and disorientation that
    we induce in individuals by subjecting them
    to too much change in too short a time.
    Fascinated by this concept, I spent the next
    five years visiting scores of universities,
    research centers, laboratories, and govern-
    mental agencies, reading countless articles
    and scientific papers and interviewing
    literally hundreds of experts on different
    aspects of change, coping behavior, and the
    future ... I came away from this experience
    with two disturbing convictions.

    First, it became clear that future shock is
    no longer a distantly potential danger, but
    a real sickness from which increasingly large
    numbers already suffer ...

    Second, I gradually came to be appalled by
    how little is actually known about adaptivity,
    either by those who call for and create vast
    changes in our society, or by those who
    supposedly prepare us to cope with those
    dangers.
    (Alvin Toffler, Future Shock (New York:
        Random House Bantam Books, 1970), p. 2)
In this passage, Toffler is just telling us when
he first noticed "future shock", how he went about
doing research into this phenomenon, and two
convictions he arrived at as a result of his

research. The passage represents a series of assertions.

People often string together a series of assertions. This happens, for instance, in minutes of meetings (this happened ... that happened ...etc.), in gossip (he and she did ... his wife did ... etc.), in explaining something to someone (e.g. in lecturing, in writing, etc.), or when someone is told off (e.g. in telling a 13-year old daughter that she can't stay out until 1 a.m.)

Arguments are not assertions. Nor are they a series of assertions. What, then, are they?

arguments

An argument is offered when reasons are presented by the arguer in support of the position he is advocating. Consider, for example, what this person has to say:
> Abortion ought not to be allowed because aborting a fetus is in fact killing a human being and killing human beings ought not to be allowed by society.

This person has put forward an argument. That is, he has advocated a position, namely:
> abortion ought not to be allowed

and he has offered reasons (two of them) on behalf of his position:
> 1. aborting a fetus is in fact killing a human being.
> 2. killing human beings ought not to be allowed by society.

You may not like this argument. You may disagree, perhaps vehemently, with what he is saying. You may want the person to expand or defend what he is saying in much greater detail. But notice carefully:
> liking or disliking an argument,

or
> agreeing with or disagreeing with an argument,

are separate matters from

14

offering or failing to offer an argument. This person has offered an argument, although, again, it is a very skimpy one.

An argument is a point of view which is backed up by supporting considerations. In an argument we are told not only <u>what</u> it is the arguer is advocating but also <u>why</u> the arguer thinks it is so. This is what separates an argument from an assertion: in an assertion, the reasons are not given in support of a point of view. Arguments have the following general structure:

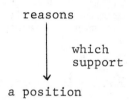

reasons

which
support

a position

To repeat, all arguments exhibit a "what-and-why" pattern, that is, a position ("the what") backed up by reasons ("the why").

In the study of argument, the position or point of view being defended by the arguer is called the <u>conclusion</u> of the argument. It is what all the considerations the arguer introduces into the discussion are designed to lead up to. The conclusion tells us <u>what</u> the arguer is advocating. On the other hand, the supporting reasons are called the <u>premises</u> of the argument. Using this standard <u>terminology</u>, the basic structure of an argument can be portrayed as follows:

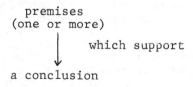

premises
(one or more)

which support

a conclusion

Some time ago, you will recall, an argument was characterized in a preliminary way as a reasoned

out position. That description served some initial
purposes. We are now at a point where a more refined description can be given:
>An _argument_ is a series of statements
>arranged in such a way that one statement
>is a conclusion and at least one statement
>is a premise which supports the conclusion.

A conclusion is said to be _supported by_ or to
follow from the premises. A premise is said to
support a conclusion. In an argument there is a
relationship of support between the sentences
spoken or written, one statement (the conclusion)
being supported by one or more other statements
(the premise or premises). An argument contains
one conclusion. It may, however, have more than
one premise.

3. Identifying the Basic Structure of Arguments

argument identification

Arguments must be clearly identified before they
can be critically considered. You should resist
the temptation to "jump the gun" and begin defending or attacking arguments until you have clearly
indicated their structure. Otherwise it will be
very unclear what you are defending or attacking.
Lumping together argument evaluation with argument identification only serves to produce con-
fusion. So, in this text, we will proceed one
task at a time. And the first task is argument
identification.

Argument identification requires picking out (a)
the conclusion, and (b) the premises of the argument. Let us begin, first of all, with two examples that were discussed in section 2 above. The
first example went as follows. A 23-year old woman claims that:
(a)   Men are responsible for my having had two
        abortions, several unhappy marriages, a
        series of unfulfilling affairs, and a
        generally messed up life.
As has already been indicated, this selection

16

simply makes an assertion which is unsupported. It
therefore contains no argument to be identified.

The second example, however, was this:
(b)   Abortion ought not to be allowed because
      aborting a fetus is in fact killing a human
      being, and killing human beings ought not
      to be allowed by society.
In this passage, an argument is presented. It
contains a conclusion, namely,
        abortions ought not be allowed.
Why ought abortion not to be allowed? The arguer
gives two reasons: (1) aborting a fetus is in fact
killing a human being, and (2) killing human beings
ought not to be allowed by society. Even though
these reasons are both spelled out in one sentence,
in identifying the structure of an argument, they
should be numbered and listed separately, as
follows:
        1. aborting a fetus is in fact killing a
           human being
        2. killing human beings ought not to be
           allowed by society.
These two reasons represent the premises of the
argument. By singling out the two premises and
the conclusion, the basic structure of the argument
has been identified.

standard format

In identifying the basic structure of arguments,
there is a standard format for displaying the
results neatly and concisely. The standard format
is this:
        (1) the premises are numbered and listed in
            the order in which they occur in the
            selection being examined.
        (2) once all the premises have been listed
            in order, a line is drawn beneath them.
        (3) the conclusion is placed beneath this
            line with a ".·." sign placed before it
            to indicate that it is a conclusion.

Using standard format, the argument we identified
in (b) above would appear as follows:

17

1. Aborting a fetus is in fact killing a human being.
2. Killing human beings ought not to be allowed by
   society.
_____

.˙. Abortion ought not to be allowed

In example (b) there were two premises to the argument. An argument may have any number of premises
all supporting the same conclusion. Because of
variations in the speaking or writing styles of
different arguers, <u>where</u> the conclusion occurs in
the selection under consideration may vary considerably. Sometimes, as in example (b) above, the
conclusion occurs at the beginning of the passage,
followed by supporting reasons. On other occasions, the premises are stated first, followed by
the conclusion at the end of the passage. Examples
of this will be given below. On some occasions,
too, the conclusion is repeated in slightly different words at various spots in the selection.

Because of this, in identifying the structure of
an argument, it is very important for you to sort
out <u>what supports what</u> in the passage under consideration. You will recall that an argument is a
series of <u>related</u> statements in which one statement
(the <u>conclusion</u>) is supported by others (the premises). In identifying the structure of an argument, it is the relationship between the various
statements that you have to unravel carefully.

locators

You will find that in many arguments the basic
structure is quite easy to make out. Often there
are important clue words that should indicate to
you the connections the arguer intends between the
statements he makes. You should make a point of
noting these clue words carefully, for they signal
basic structural features of the argument.

There are three main sorts of clue words or
phrases:
(1) words or phrases that help locate
    conclusions.

18

(2) words or phrases that help locate the general area in which premises are to be found.

(3) words or phrases that help locate particular premises.

We will discuss each of these in turn. In so doing we will also provide further examples of arguments whose basic structure is identified using standard format.

conclusion locators

The conclusion is what is being argued for in the selection. It is the basic position the arguer is defending, the main point he wishes to drive home.

There are a variety of words or phrases that often indicate that a conclusion is about to follow. Such clue words or phrases may be referred to as "conclusion locators." They include the following:

  thus...
  consequently...
  hence...
  as a result...
  so...
  therefore...
  we see, then, that...
  this points to the conclusion that...
  all this supports the view that...
  it follows from this that...
  one can conclude from all this that...
  ...shows that...

and so on. Such words and phrases often indicate that what follows them is a conclusion. In first reading over a passage, it is often good practice for you to make a point of underlining such words or phrases, thereby focusing your attention explicitly on one important clue as to the argument's structure. In this chapter key conclusion locators will be underlined as a help to you in these early stages of studying argument.

With these conclusion locators in mind, consider carefully the following example:

19

(c)   First of all, when taken regularly and in sen-
       sible doses, vitamin E helps eliminate chol-
       esterol from the blood system. Secondly, vit-
       amin E strengthens the heart muscles. Thirdly,
       vitamin E contributes to sexual stamina.
       <u>Therefore</u> vitamin E is beneficial to human
       health.
As you will quickly note, the 'therefore,' in the
last sentence helps locate the conclusion. It is
what follows the 'therefore' namely:
       vitamin E is beneficial to human health.
There are three reasons advanced in support of this
position, and the arguer has helpfully numbered
these. Using standard format for identifying the
basic structure, the argument would be displayed
as follows:
       1.   when taken regularly and in sensible doses,
            vitamin E helps eliminate cholesterol from the
            blood system.
       2.   vitamin E strengthens the heart muscles.
       3.   vitamin E contributes to sexual stamina.

       ∴ vitamin E is beneficial to human health.

Consider next this selection:
(d)   If I go to Jamaica for Christmas, the entire
       trip (air fare, accommodations, food, sight-
       seeing, gratuities, etc) will probably cost
       me close to $800. On the other hand, if I
       were to go to Florida, the whole holiday
       would only set me back about $500. Accord-
       ing to my budgetary calculations, I have
       only approximately $600 to spend on a Christ-
       mas holiday. I guess <u>it follows from this
       that</u> I will go to Florida for the Christmas
       break.
Again you will quickly note that the phrase "it
follows from this that..." helps locate the conclusion. It is what follows this phrase, namely,
       I will go to Florida for the Christmas
       break.
Several reasons lead up to this conclusion and
support it. The first sentence explores one option;
the second sentence, another; and the third sentence introduces yet another important consider-

ation. As set out, using standard format, the
structure of the argument appears as follows:

1. If I go to Jamaica for Christmas, the
   entire trip (air fare, accommodations,
   food, sight-seeing, gratuities, etc.)
   will probably cost me close to $800.
2. If I were to go to Florida, the whole
   holiday would only set me back about
   $500.
3. According to my budgetary calculations,
   I have only approximately $600 to spend
   on a Christmas holiday.

∴ I will go to Florida for the Christmas break.

general area premise locators

Just as conclusions are what is being <u>argued for</u>
in a passage, premises are what the <u>arguer is
arguing from</u>. Premises represent items of information brought forward by the arguer to defend <u>why</u>
his conclusion is so.

Many arguments contain key words and phrases that
help you to locate the general area of the passage
within which you are most likely to find the premises. Such expressions may be referred to as
"general area premise locators."

The function of general area premise locators is
to help you put your finger on the portion of the
passage in which premises are apt to be found.
General area premise locators include the conclusion locators. These words, after all, not only
indicate that the conclusion comes <u>after</u> them but
also that the premises are very likely to come
<u>before</u> them. The conclusion locators, then, help
point you in the right direction for finding the
premises; premises are apt to occur in that portion of the passage before the conclusion locator.

There are, however, other general area premise
locators. Some expressions typically serve to
indicate that the premises are generally to be

found after them. Such expressions include the
following:
    for...
    because...
    since...
    this is so for the following reasons...
    this can be seen from the following consider-
    ations...
    this is shown by the following consider-
    ations...
    this follows from...
And so on. Such expressions should alert the
reader that what follows these words are reasons
for what has already been said. They therefore
point the reader in the right direction for finding the premises of the argument. Again you should
make a practice of underlining such expressions, to
draw explicit attention to an important clue as to
the argument's structure.

In example (b) above, the word 'because' helped
draw attention to the reasons that support the conclusion the arguer had already stated. Consider
also this selection:
(e) Some scientists now believe that North America
    may be entering another ice age rather soon.
    This is so, they say, because studies of aver-
    age temperatures over the past 100 years have
    indicated a steady drop, particularly in the
    past couple of decades. Other studies have
    shown that ice ages come about with amazing
    rapidity, not millenia or even centuries, but
    just a few decades.
In this selection, the word 'because' is particularly important for understanding the structure of
what is said. It indicates that what comes after
it are the reasons for what has preceded it. In
other words, it helps locate the general area in
which the premises are to be found. They are to
be found after the 'because.' It should also be
noted that it helps locate the conclusion (what
comes before the 'because'). Using standard format,
the argument contained in this passage is displayed as follows:
        1. Studies of average temperatures over the past
           100 years have indicated a steady drop,

22

particularly in the past couple of decades.
2. Other studies have shown that ice ages come
about with amazing rapidity, not millenia or
<u>even centuries, but just a few decades.</u>

∴ Some scientists now believe that North America
may be entering another ice age rather soon.

specific premise locators

Not only are there words that indicate generally
where premises are to be found, there are also
words and expressions that help single out specific individual premises in an argument. These
expressions may be referred to as "specific premise locators." They include:
   (1) Devices arguers use for numbering prem-
      ises:
      e.g. first..., secondly..., thirdly...,
         etc.
      e.g. in the first place...in the second
         place...finally...
   (2) Devices arguers use to indicate the pro-
      gressive accumulation of different consid-
      erations that bear upon the same conclu-
      sion:
      e.g. for one thing...for another...
      e.g. ...furthermore...
      e.g. ...moreover...in addition...also...
      e.g. consider this...and this...and this...
   (3) Devices arguers use to contrast different
      considerations that bear upon the same
      conclusion:
      e.g. on the one hand...but on the other
         hand...
      e.g. ...however...
      e.g. ...but...
Again, on first looking over a passage critically
it is good practice for you to underline such expressions that help in picking out specific premises. The numbering device, for instance, was
very helpful back in example (c) in singling out
the separate premises of the argument.

Notice carefully the guides to argument structure that are contained in the following selection:

(f) <u>For one thing</u>, there are many archeological mysteries (e.g. the markings on the plains of Nazca visible only from the air, the giant statues on Easter Island, the Pyramids, etc.). Conventional archeology, <u>moreover</u>, is unable to come up with a convincing explanation for these mysteries. All these mysteries, <u>however</u>, can be explained by postulating visits to earth by beings from other planets some time in the earth's past. <u>Furthermore</u>, ancient religious mythologies and some ancient drawings have preserved the memory of such visits. <u>Therefore</u> it seems evident that the earth was visited at some time in the past by beings from other planets.

The 'therefore' indicates the conclusion of the argument. The other underlined words single out different considerations the arguer has assembled in support of his conclusion. Using standard format, the structure of the argument is displayed as follows:

1. There are many archeological mysteries (e.g. the markings on the plain of Nazca visible only from the air, the giant statues on Easter Island, the Pyramids, etc.)

2. Conventional archeology is unable to come up with a convincing explanation for these mysteries.

3. All these mysteries can be explained by postulating visits to earth by beings from other planets some time in the earth's past.

4. Ancient religious mythologies and some ancient drawings have preserved the memory of such visits.

∴ It seems evident that the earth was visited at some time in the past by beings from other planets.

Consider next this selection:

(g) Studies have shown that nearly 2/3 of University X's resident student body smoke pot daily. <u>In addition</u>, recent studies have indicated

that there is a strong correlation (better
than 60%) between smoking pot daily and lung
cancer. Hence it is likely that many of
University X's resident student body will
eventually develop lung cancer.
'Hence' indicates the conclusion of the argument.
The phrase, "in addition," indicates that one additional piece of information is being added to a
previously stated consideration. By paying attention to such important clue words, the structure
of the argument becomes quite visible. Using
standard format, it can be set out as follows:

1. Studies have shown that nearly 2/3 of
    University X's resident student body
    smoke pot daily.
2. Recent studies have indicated that there
    is a strong correlation (better than 60%)
    between smoking pot daily and lung cancer.

∴ It is likely that many of University X's
    resident student body will eventually develop
    lung cancer.

Examine next this terse argument put forward by
someone who thinks that evil and the existence of
God are incompatible:
(h) If God exists, there would be no evil in the
     world. But there is evil in the world.
        Consequently God does not exist.
'Consequently' here points out the conclusion of
the argument. There are two premises. The word
'but' helps to indicate to the reader that one
consideration is being contrasted with another.
Correctly displayed, the basic structure of the
argument would appear as follows:

1. If God exists, there would be no evil
    in the world.
2. There is evil in the world.

∴ God does not exist.

strategy

When reading over a passage in order to identify

the argument it contains, you should try to sort out what supports what. In doing this, the following strategy often proves helpful:

    (a) underline all available clue words.
    (b) locate the conclusion -- i.e. what the arguer is advocating.
    (c) locate the general area of the passage in which the premises are to be found.
    (d) single out specific premises -- i.e. those considerations that indicate why the conclusion advocated is so.

Basically this strategy suggests that you focus first on the what-is-advocated part of the argument (that is, on the conclusion). Then move to the why-it-is-so part (that is, the premises).

arguments with no clue words

The clue words we have been considering serve two main purposes: to signal the reader that an argument is present, and, to help the reader grasp what the argument is. In many arguments, however, the clue words are for the most part omitted, as being something that goes without saying. In such cases the strategy recommended above still applies: sort out what supports what, concentrating first of all on finding the conclusion. When clue words are absent, several tentative stabs may have to be made before you accurately grasp the structure of the argument.

Consider the following passage:

(i)   Breast-feeding is the preferred method for providing infant nutrition for at least the first few months of life....It contains factors that may be protective against infection during that vulnerable period, and is virtually mandatory where hygienic and sanitary conditions are inadequate. A breast-fed baby is less likely than a formula-fed baby to suffer allergy or infantile obesity.
    (Consumer Reports, March 1977, p. 157)

This passage contains three sentences, but no clue

words. Yet the sentences are related. The first
sentence makes a general claim about breast-feeding, that is, that it is the preferred method for
providing infant nutrition for at least the first
few months of life. This represents what the
arguer is advocating. It is the conclusion.

Why is breast-feeding the preferred method? The
next two sentences in the passage cite several
advantages. Note in passing that one of these
sentences states two reasons. These are the reasons (or premises) which support the conclusion
already stated. Using standard format, the argument is identified as follows:
  1. It (human milk) contains factors that may
     be protective against infection during that
     vulnerable period.
  2. It (human milk) is virtually mandatory where
     hygienic and sanitary conditions are inadequate.
  3. A breast-fed baby is less likely than a formula-
     fed baby to suffer allergy or infantile obesity.

  ∴. Breast-feeding is the preferred method for
     providing infant nutrition for at least the
     first few months of life.

Consider next this selection:
(j)   A contrary view sees technology as an almost
      unmitigated curse. Technology is said to
      rob people of their jobs, their privacy,
      their participation in democratic govern-
      ment, and, even, in the end, of their dig-
      nity as human beings. It is seen as
      autonomous and uncontrollable, as fostering
      materialistic values and as destructive of
      religion, as bringing about a technocratic
      society and bureaucratic state in which the
      individual is increasingly submerged, and
      as threatening, ultimately, to poison nature
      and blow up the world.
      (Emmanuel G. Mesthene, Technological Change
      (New York: New American Library, 1970),p.17)
The "contrary view" is that technology is an almost unmitigated curse. Why is this so? The next
two sentences present a whole host of reasons why

27

this is so. Using standard format, the argument is identified as follows:

1. Technology robs people of their jobs.
2. Technology robs people of their privacy.
3. Technology robs people of their participation in democratic government.
4. Technology robs people of their dignity as human beings.
5. Technology is seen as autonomous and uncontrollable.
6. Technology is seen as fostering materialistic values and as destructive of religion.
7. Technology is seen as bringing about a technocratic and bureaucratic society in which the individual is increasingly submerged.
8. Technology is seen as threatening, ultimately, to poison nature and blow up the world.

∴ Technology is an almost unmitigated curse.

Consider next this selection:

(k)   Married persons do live longer. This is a striking view, and in its defense sociologists, psychologists, and others have recently noted three main considerations:
● marriage tends to reduce the sort of stress and tension that wears down a person physically.
● marriage tends to reduce loneliness, social isolation, and the kind of emotional short-circuiting that occurs from simply "being alone."
● marriage helps to foster a healthy well-balanced, and well integrated sense of self-worth.

What is being argued for here is the claim that married persons do live longer.
It is the position being defended.

Why is this so? The arguer does not use the standard clue words, but he does provide indications of his own that help unravel the structure of what he says. Note the phrase "in its defense." This helps locate where the reasons are to be found. Note, too, the phrase "three main considerations," for this draws explicitly to our attention the number of reasons. Indeed he has used the '●' to single out these three reasons.

Using standard format, the argument would be identified as follows:

1. marriage tends to reduce the sort of stress and tension that wears down a person physically.
2. marriage tends to reduce loneliness, social isolation, and the kind of emotional short-circuiting that occurs from simply "being alone."
3. marriage helps to foster a healthy, well balanced, and well integrated sense of self-worth.

∴ married persons do live longer.

a final note

Some time ago, you will recall, an argument was defined as a series of statements arranged in such a way that one statement is a conclusion and at least one statement is a premise which supports that conclusion. Note here that the premise must support the conclusion in order to qualify as a premise.

Every now and then, however, you will come across the following sort of situation: an arguer puts forward reasons he thinks support the conclusion but you think don't. This poses a problem. A premise must support the conclusion in order to be a premise, and yet, in this instance, what is offered as a premise does not do so. What then: has the arguer made an argument or not?

The answer to this is not difficult to discern. The arguer has offered what he thinks is an argument. In so doing, however, he may perhaps have made a mistake. (How such mistakes can occur will be examined in Part Two of this text.) That is, while the arguer intends to offer an argument, he may fail to make a genuine argument.

At this point we need not condemn such failures, nor even detect them. Where there is good reason to suppose that a person is offering an argument, then this is the argument that should be identified. What the arguer intends is usually clear from the use of clue words, from the context, from how he has structured what he has to say, etc. If it seems clear that he is trying to put forward an argument, then this is what should be identified, even though we may not think the reasons are particularly good ones. As we progress in the study of argument, there will be ample opportunity to examine arguments critically and to consider whether what is offered as an argument really constitutes a genuine argument. At this point, give the arguer the benefit of the doubt and postpone argument evaluation for a while.

Recall Quiz

This recall quiz is designed to draw attention to important points raised in the text. After reading this chapter, try to answer the following questions.

(1)   What is an argument (preliminary account)?

(2)   Into what three main areas may the study of argument be divided? What does each area aim at teaching?

(3)   How do the descriptive and normative approaches to the study of argument differ? What approach is adopted in this text.

(4)   Does the study of argument advocate positions on particular controversial issues? If not, why not?

(5)   In what ways is the study of argument an important study?

(6)   Is the study of argument impressionistic? speculative? intuitive? or analytic?

(7) What is an assertion (or claim)?

(8) What is an argument (refined description)?

(9) How does an argument differ from an asser-
     tion?

(10) What does identifying the basic structure of
     an argument require?

(11) What is the standard format for displaying
     the basic structure of an argument?

(12) What do conclusion locators, general area
     premise locators, and specific premise loca-
     tors do? What are some examples of each
     type of locator?

(13) In identifying the basic structure of an
     argument, what strategy is suggested?

Exercise

Read the following passages carefully, noting
important key words where present. Using standard format, identify the structure of the argument contained in each of the selections below.

(1) Films such as "Taxi Driver," "Clockwork
     Orange," and "The Godfather Parts I and II"
     are obscene movies for the following reas-
     ons. First of all, such films revel in
     ultra-violence, glorifying violence for its
     own sake. Secondly, any film which glori-
     fies violence for its own sake is, in my
     estimation, an obscene film.

(2) Two out of three people interviewed pre-
     ferred Fresca to Pepsi. Therefore Fresca is
     the better drink.

(3) Look at all the evidence. For one thing,
     Oswald was a poor shot and could not have
     fired, reloaded, and fired the shots accur-
     ately within 6 seconds. Also, many witnes-
     ses claimed that they thought the shots came
     from the grassy knoll area and not from the
     Texas School Book Depository where Oswald
     was located. In addition, the angle of the

31

shot that hit President Kennedy differs from the angle of the shot that hit Governor Connally, although the Warren Commission maintains that this was the same bullet. The Zapruder film, moreover, shows in a spectacular way a shot of Kennedy in which his head moves violently backward, indicating a shot from in front of the motorcade. Oswald, therefore, could not have been the lone assassin of President Kennedy.

(4)   First of all, Oswald stated that he was standing in the doorway of the Texas School Book Depository when the motorcade was passing by. Secondly, several witnesses claim he was standing there. Thirdly, Altgens' photo of the motorcade shows a person standing at the entrance to the Texas School Book Depository bearing a strong resemblance to Oswald and what he was wearing that day (although some have conjectured that this was Bill Lovelady). It follows from this that Oswald could not have been an assassin of President Kennedy.

(5)   People are not free. I base my conclusion upon two main considerations. First of all, Skinner's research shows that a science of human behavior is possible. Secondly, if a science of human behavior is possible, then people are not free.

(6)   In the 1980's the flight of middle-class families to the suburbs will be arrested and reversed because the cost of gasoline will become prohibitive for most commuters and because the cost of cars and car maintenance will put ownership of cars well beyond the means of most wage earners.

(7)   Note, first of all, that abortion legitimizes the principle that the state has the right to terminate unwanted human life. Note, secondly, that this principle can easily be extended to apply to more than fetal life: for example, to the life of the aged, to the life of the mentally retarded,

to the life of criminals, to the life of burdensome welfare recipients, perhaps even to the life of political dissidents. Note, thirdly, that the state has no right to become involved in life-and-death decisions over its citizens. Consequently, abortion should be rejected by all people concerned with the preservation of human life.

(8) Hopelessly ill patients should be allowed to die with dignity. Moreover, allowing hopelessly ill patients to deteriorate while artificially sustaining life places a tremendous emotional burden on them and on their family and friends. Finally, prolonging human life needlessly creates an enormous expense for society to bear. Thus doctors should be allowed to terminate the life of hopelessly ill patients.

(9) Laws prohibiting the showing of obscene films ought to be abolished. For one thing, there is no applicable definition of 'obscene,' as courts have found out. Furthermore, there have been many studies which have demonstrated that obscenity releases tensions in a harmless manner. Moreover, people have a right to see obscene films if that's the sort of entertainment they desire.

(10) People who smoke cigarettes should be forced to pay for their own hospital and medical care because they know smoking is harmful to their health and because they have no right to expect society to pay for the consequences of their addiction.

(11) For one thing, it is impossible for a company such as the makers of Pop Toothpaste to show that their product makes for a better lifestyle (social popularity, sex appeal, etc.) than do the products of their competitors. For another thing, even if they could, it would be irrelevant to the intrinsic merit of the product. We can conclude from all this that companies such as the makers of Pop Toothpaste who claim

that their product makes for a better lifestyle should have their advertising claims
tested in court.

(12) I maintain that prisons should be abolished
and that persons convicted of crime should
be forced to work to make compensation to
society and all persons affected by their
misdeeds. I put forward this position for
a variety of reasons. First: prisons do not
rehabilitate. Secondly, prisons do not
punish. Thirdly, prisons make prisoners
resentful and more likely to commit further
crimes. Fourthly, prisons simply educate
criminals in more sophisticated means of
crime. Finally, persons who serve time in
prisons are ten times more likely to commit
a further crime than a person who has never
ever been in prison.

(13) (from a trial in divorce court, involving
a custody suit of a child)
lawyer: Exactly what is it you are claiming?
father: I claim that I should be granted
        full and complete custody of my 12
        year old son.
lawyer: On what do you base your claim?
father: On several grounds. For one thing,
        because of the nature of my work, I
        can give him more attention than can
        his mother. Moreover, a 12 year old
        boy needs a father more than a
        mother. Also, now that I've started
        living with Sylvia, I can provide
        him with a mother as well.

(14) It is very likely that there was once a
highly sophisticated civilization located
in the Atlantic, called Atlantis, which at
some time in the past suffered a tremendous
maritime disaster. All the evidence points
to this. There are great similarities in
cultural patterns in civilizations as far
removed as the Inca and Aztec empires in
south and central America and in Egypt.
There are similarities, moreover, in

34

language between Inca and Egyptian. There are also similarities in clothing. There are similarities in the type of boats used. And, finally, these similarities are inexplicable apart from some common origin.

(15) Church property ought to be taxed. After all, for the most part, such property is not used extensively, except on one day a week. Also, taxpayers should not be expected to have to subsidize people who want to go to church. Furthermore, taxation of church property would allow the churches an excellent opportunity to make a contribution to the general welfare of society.

(16) One the one hand, if you major in history, then chances are that you're not going to get a job when you graduate that makes use of the skills you've learned. If, on the other hand, you major in economics, then chances are quite good that you will get a job when you graduate that will make use of the skills you have learned. And, getting a job upon graduation that makes use of skills learned is important. Therefore, you should major in economics.

(17) Much of the aid sent to victims of natural disasters by various relief organizations has been useless. For one thing, local governments are often better able to cope with the crisis than a team of foreign "experts" who appear later to "study" the situation. For another, often the materials sent are inappropriate: wheat to rice-eating cultures, drugs to areas with no injection needles, temporary houses that take longer to erect than permanent ones, and so forth. Finally, what little is of use is often confiscated by greedy officials who turn a pretty profit.

(18) Poor people can't manage money properly... that's why give-away programs designed to uplift them invariably fail.

(19)   Married working mothers should get out of
       the labor force because they can make do
       with their husband's salary, young people
       need their jobs, and they're better off at
       home with their children.

(20)   Ernie: The Bible is contradictory.
       Bert: What?
       Ernie: Yup, you heard me. In Genesis 1 we
              see male and female created in one
              simultaneous act of creation whereas
              in Genesis 2 they are created separa-
              tely in two acts of creation. What's
              more, in Genesis 1 male and female
              are of equal importance whereas in
              Genesis 2 females are depicted as
              dependent upon males.
       Bert: Oh.

(21)   Ernie: You know, Bert, the rising divorce
              rate does not show that family life
              is becoming more unstable.
       Bert: That's a new twist, Ernie, but I'm
              not sure I see the basis for your
              saying that.
       Ernie: Well, for one thing, people today
              expect more out of marriage. Also,
              what with most women in the labor
              force, there are more pressures and
              strains placed on a marriage. Then,
              too, it is easier nowadays to get a
              divorce when things don't work out.
              There is, moreover, less stigma
              attached to being divorced now. In
              addition, with sensible access
              arrangements, the trauma for children
              can be minimized. Finally, most
              people who get divorced eventually
              remarry and stay remarried.
       Bert: Well that's quite convincing, Ernie.
              I guess most people should hurry up
              and get their first marriages out of
              the way!

(22)   (in the following selection, Bernard Gendron
       presents what he calls "the Utopian argu-

ment." What is "the Utopian argument"?)
What evidence do Utopians have for claiming
that technological growth will in the long
run bring about the virtual elimination
of every major social evil?...
It would be tedious and insufficiently
rewarding to examine every bit of Utopian
literature for evidence or arguments, or to
survey all the reasons Utopians seem to have
for being Utopians. Instead, I will present
and examine in some detail what I take to be
the best argument for the Utopian view...
This argument can be formulated as follows:
Premise 1: We are presently undergoing a
          post-industrial revolution in
          technology.
Premise 2: In the post-industrial age, tech-
          nological growth will be sustain-
          ed.
Premise 3: In the post-industrial age, con-
          tinued technological growth will
          lead to the elimination of econo-
          mic scarcity.
Premise 4: The elimination of economic
          scarcity will lead to the elimi-
          nation of every major social
          evil.
From now on I shall refer to this argument
simply as "the Utopian argument."
(Bernard Gendron, Technology and the Human
 Condition (New York: St. Martin's Press,
 1977), pp. 12,13)

(23) (In Plato's Crito, Socrates is depicted as
being in jail, waiting for his execution
to be carried out. A long-time friend of
Socrates', Crito, arrives and attempts to
persuade Socrates to escape. In so doing,
he says the following. (see below) What is
his argument on behalf of his conclusion:
∴ You, Socrates, ought to escape from
prison.)
...but listen to me even now and be saved.
If you die, it will not be a single mis-
fortune only for me. Not only will I be

37

deprived of a friend, the like of whom I
shall never find again, but many people who
do not know you or me very well will think
that I could have saved you if I were willing to spend money, but that I did not care
to do so...My money is available and is, I
think, sufficient...So, as I say, do not let
this fear make you hesitate to save yourself,
nor let what you said in court trouble you,
that you would not know what to do with
yourself if you left Athens, for you would
be welcomed in many places to which you
might go...Besides, Socrates, I do not think
that what you are doing is right, to give
up your life when you can save it, and to
hasten your fate as your enemies would
hasten it, and indeed have hastened it in
their wish to destroy you. Moreover, I
think you are betraying your sons by going
away and leaving them, when you could bring
them up and educate them...You seem to me
to choose the easiest path, whereas one
should choose the path a good and courageous
man would choose, particularly when one
claims throughout one's life to care for
virtue.
(Crito, 44b-45d, in G.M.A. Grube (trans.),
The Trial and Death of Socrates(Indianapolis:
Hackett, 1975), pp. 44-46)

CHAPTER TWO

A STANDARD FORMAT FOR IDENTIFYING THE STRUCTURE OF ARGUMENTS

In Chapter One we learned the basic structure of arguments; one or more premises and a conclusion. All the arguments identified so far have been of this rather simple sort: just premises and a conclusion, nothing more. Most arguments you will meet, however, are considerably more complex.

There are, of course, many reasons why arguments may be much more complicated than the ones we have met so far. Some arguments, for instance, may have their structure obscured by arguers who introduce a lot of irrelevant, repetitious, or distracting considerations. Such arguers make it difficult for us to grasp the exact point of the argument. Sometimes, too, the arguer may organize his thought poorly: he may become confused, or may just ramble on, or he may get sidetracked, etc., and fail to make a point clearly and cogently. In this case it is very difficult for us to know what the arguer is getting at.

But there is another reason for the complexity of arguments; there is much more to the structure of many arguments than simply premises and a conclusion. This is particularly important, for it concerns how arguers organize, dress up, and elaborate on the reasons they advance in defense of a position.

This chapter introduces you to these additional structural features of argument. They are features which make the detection of argument a bit more difficult, but also a lot more interesting.

1. The Structure of Complex Arguments

All arguments have, of course, premises (one or more) and a conclusion. As you know, these are the minimal structural features a collection of statements must have in order to be counted as an argument. In this section, three more structural features that <u>some</u> arguments have will be discussed.

This section will also introduce another matter. In Chapter One we adopted a standard format for displaying the structure of an argument: numbered premises set out vertically down the page, followed by a line, below which was placed a ".˙." sign and the conclusion. This standard format will be preserved, but <u>expanded</u>, in order to accommodate the additional structural features about to be introduced. The expanded format is intended to help you visualize the different roles statements play in an argument.

<u>support for individual premises</u>

Compare carefully the structural features of the argument contained in each of the following two passages:
(a) If God exists, then there would be no evil in the world. But there is evil in the world. Thus God does not exist.
(b) If God exists, then there would be no evil in the world. But there is evil in the world. Why just consider all the natural disasters such as floods and famines, social disasters like robberies and rapes, and all the insects like mosquitos that annoy people. Thus God does not exist.

Using standard format, the argument contained in (a) would be correctly identified as follows:
>   1. If God exists, then there would be no evil in the world.
>   2. There is evil in the world.
> _____

    .˙. God does not exist.
It is an argument of the simple variety: a couple of premises and a conclusion.

Consider (b), however. The argument it contains

has the same basic structure as the argument in
(a), that is, the same conclusion and the same two
premises. But there is an important difference:
in (b), premise 2 has been supported. That is,
the arguer in (b) cites natural disasters (such
as floods and famines), social disasters (such as
robberies and rapes), and insects (such as mosquitos) as evidence that there is evil in the world.

In other words, the arguer in (b) is supporting
his second premise. He is saying, in effect, that
if we take into account natural disasters, social
disasters, and insects, then there is good reason
to believe that there is evil in the world.
Support for an individual premise is another
structural feature some arguments have, and the
standard format must be expanded to incorporate
this important aspect of many arguments.

In the expanded standard format for identifying
arguments, you should imagine your worksheet divided into three spaces:
a left space   a center space   a right space
Each will be put to a different use. The
right space, referred to as "evaluation space," is
reserved for argument evaluation. This space will
be ignored for the time being. Part Two of this
book, which deals systematically with the whole
matter of evaluating arguments critically, will
make extensive use of this space. The space in
the center and on left are reserved for argument
identification, and the space is allocated as
follows:

The center space is called "the main argument
space," and in it will go, in usual standard format, the premises and conclusion of the main argument. With reference to (b) above, for example,
the main argument would be set out as follows:

(left space)   main argument space   evaluation space
    1. If God exists, then
      there would be no evil
      in the world.
    2. There is evil in the
      world.

∴ God does not exist.

The conclusion here is called "the conclusion of
the main argument." Similarly, the premises are
referred to as "the premises of the main argument."

That is not all there is to the argument contained
in (b), however. As you will recall, premise 2 is
supported. The space on the left of your worksheet is referred to as "support space," and it is
here that the supporting considerations are placed.
They are numbered, positioned to the left of the
premise they support, and an arrow is drawn from
them to the premise they support.

Correctly identified, using standard format, the
argument contained in selection (b) would be displayed as follows:

support space	main argument space	evaluation space
	1. If God exists, then there would be no evil in the world.	
1. Consider all the natural dis- asters such as floods and fam- ines, social disasters like robberies and rapes, and all the insects like mosquitos that annoy people.	→2. There is evil in the world.	

∴ God does not exist.

Notice carefully the relationship between what is
written in the support space and what is written
in the main space. The relation is one of support:
the arguer is contending that this consideration
(in support space) supports the point he is making
(in the premise of his main argument). It should
be evident, then, that in supporting an individual
premise, the arguer is presenting an argument.

42

Such arguments, where an arguer supports an individual premise, may conveniently be referred to as "a mini-argument."

The mini-argument in (b) has as its premise:
     Consider all the natural disasters such
     as floods and famines, social disasters
     like robberies and rapes, and all the
     insects like mosquitos that annoy people.
and its conclusion is:
     There is evil in the world.

There's an interesting feature of argument here that you should carefully observe. In relation to the main argument, premise 2 is a premise (since it supports the conclusion). In relation to the mini-argument, however, premise 2 is a conclusion (since it is itself supported by a premise). This serves to underscore a point mentioned in the last chapter: being a conclusion or being a premise depends upon what role or function the sentence plays in relation to other sentences in the passage. Getting the point of the passage depends upon sorting out these roles clearly.

To repeat: the premises of a mini-argument are placed in the support space of the extended format for identifying the structure of arguments. The premises of a mini-argument may conveniently be referred to as "mini-premises." Since mini-arguments are arguments in their own right, mini-premises are numbered separately for each main premise they support as their conclusion. Thus a mini-argument which supports main premise 2 is treated separately from a mini-argument which might support main premise 1 or main premise 3.

In (b) above, only one mini-premise was given by the arguer on behalf of one main premise in the main argument. In some arguments, however, several premises of the main argument are supported by mini-premises, as in the following:
(c)   I contend that God does not exist. Consider
       my reasons. On one hand, if God exists,
       then there would be no evil in the world.

> God, after all, is thought to be an
> omnipotent and just being, the very sort
> of being who would and could eradicate
> evil. But, on the other hand, there is
> evil in the world. Why just consider all
> the natural disasters such as floods and
> famines, social disasters like robberies
> and rapes, and all the insects like
> mosquitos that annoy people.

The structure of the main argument in (c) is easy
to discern: the conclusion is:
> God does not exist.

and the two main premises (indicated by "on the
one hand..." and "But, on the other hand...") are:
> 1. If God exists, then there would be
>   no evil in the world.
> 2. There is evil in the world.

The arguer supports his second premise, citing the
now familiar natural disasters, social disasters,
and insects. But the arguer also supports his
first premise. Why, if God exists, should there
be no evil in the world? Well, the arguer says,
after all (a locator that helps to indicate that
a reason is about to be given):
> God is thought to be an omnipotent and
> just being, the very sort of being who
> would and could eradicate evil.

This consideration supports premise 1 of the main
argument.

Just one final note before we reconstruct argument (c). Since we are not yet ready to make use
of "evaluation space," this heading will be temporarily omitted from our displays of reconstructed
arguments. In Part Two of this text, when we will
explicitly consider argument evaluation, this
space will be reintroduced and used extensively.

Back to argument (c). Correctly identified, it
would be displayed as follows:

support space	main argument space
1. God is thought to be an omnipotent and just being	1. If God exists, then there would be no evil

```
the very sort of being  ⎫                in the world.
who would and could     ⎬
eradicate evil.         ⎭

1. Consider all the natural ⎫
   disasters such as floods  ⎪
   and famines, social dis-  ⎪  ↗  2. There is evil
   asters like robberies and ⎬        in the world.
   rapes, and all the insects⎪
   like mosquitos that annoy ⎪
   people.                   ⎭
                                    _____

                                    ∴ God does not exist.
```

Similarly, in some arguments, the main premises
may be supported by several considerations.
(d) I maintain that an almighty and just God does
    not exist. First of all, it should be noted
    that if an almighty and just God exists, then
    there would be no evil in the world. Why
    this is so is evident from the following. A
    supreme being who tolerates evil is not just.
    Also, a supreme being who cannot eradicate
    evil is not almighty. Secondly, it should be
    noted that there is evil in the world, a
    feature of the world which is all too evident
    when one considers all the natural disasters
    such as floods and famines, social disasters
    like robberies and rapes, and all the insects
    like mosquitos that annoy people.

Again, the structure of the argument is pretty
transparent. There are two main premises, marked
by "first of all it should be noted that..." and
by "Secondly, it should be noted that..." which
support the main conclusion: "an almighty and just
God does not exist." The first main premise is
itself supported by two mini-premises.
   1. A supreme being who tolerates evil is not
      just.
   2. A supreme being who cannot eradicate evil
      is not almighty.

Using standard format, the argument contained in
(d) would be displayed as follows:

45

<u>support space</u>   <u>main argument space</u>

1. A supreme being who toler-
   ates evil is not just.   ⎫
2. A supreme being who cannot   ⎬ ⟋1. If an almighty and just
   eradicate evil is not   ⎭   God exists, then there
   almighty.   would be no evil in the
                                           world.

1. Consider all the natural   ⎫
   disasters such as floods   ⎪
   and famines, social dis-   ⎪
   asters like robberies   ⎬ ⟋2. There is evil in the
   and rapes, and insects   ⎪   world.
   like mosquitos that annoy   ⎪
   people.   ⎭

                                   _____

                                   .·. An almighty and just
                                       God does not exist.

In sum: one additional structural feature some
arguments may have is support for individual
premises.

unexpressed assumptions

Occasionally we may come across another feature
<u>some</u> arguments exhibit. Sometimes an argument
depends on, or assumes, a point the arguer has
failed to state explicitly. Usually there is no
maliciousness here, nor deceit: it is usually just
a point the arguer has neglected to mention because he simply overlooked it or else assumed it
was so obvious to everyone.

An <u>unexpressed assumption</u> is a position which the
arguer has taken for granted in the course of making his argument, which he has not explicitly
stated, and which plays an important role in
understanding the argument or in assessing its
worth. Unexpressed assumptions are simply that:
positions which the arguer has taken for granted
in the course of making his argument and which
enter into our understanding or assessment of it.
Such assumptions, when we encounter them, are
worth detecting and making explicit.

46

A few examples should make this feature of some arguments clear. Consider selection (b) again:

(b)   If God exists, then there would be no evil in the world. But there is evil in the world. Why just consider all the natural disasters such as floods and famines, social disasters like robberies and rapes, and all the insects like mosquitos that annoy people. Thus God does not exist.

(b) contains an unexpressed assumption. Note carefully the first premise. Here the arguer is clearly assuming that the existence of God is incompatible with the existence of evil. The existence of one rules out the existence of the other. Now, to be sure, the arguer hasn't exactly said this in his first premise, but, from the gist of premise 1, there is considerable textual warrant for us to suppose that he is assuming this. The assumption is a highly important one, for it represents a highly debatable view concerning the existence of God and God's relation to the existence of evil.

When an unexpressed assumption is encountered that seems to play an important role in an argument, it is helpful to have a means of displaying it in our reconstruction. The following convention is adopted. Unexpressed assumptions will be marked with wedge brackets ('<', '>'). The use of wedge brackets indicates that the arguer hasn't explicitly said this but that we who are identifying the argument have good reason to suppose that the arguer has made this assumption. The unexpressed assumption, clearly marked with < and > , is placed in the support space, adjacent to the premise of the argument which initially gave rise to the suspicion that the arguer may have made an unexpressed assumption in the course of arguing.

In accordance with the convention, the argument contained in (b) would be displayed as follows:

support space	main argument space
< the existence of God is incompatible with the exist-	1. If God exists, then there would be no evil

ence of evil.>   in the world.

1. Consider all the nat-
ural disasters such as
floods and famines, social
disasters like robberies
and rapes, and all the insects like mosquitos that
annoy people.

    → 2. There is evil in the
world.

———————————————

.˙. God does not exist.

Several precautions need to be made about displaying unexpressed assumptions. For one thing, as
has already been mentioned, the wedge symbols
(< and >) serve to indicate that we who are identifying the argument have read this unexpressed
assumption into the argument. Of course we can
do so legitimately only if we have good reason to
think the arguer has indeed made this assumption.
The use of < and > is not intended as a licence
to distort the arguer's reasoning.

For another thing, some limit needs to be placed
upon the unexpressed assumptions that are important in identifying the structure of an argument.
There may, for instance, be many remote assumptions, for example, that there is a world, that
this is the planet Earth, that you (the person
identifying the argument) are alive, that you
understand English, and so forth. Such remote
assumptions need not be displayed in setting
forth the structure of an argument. They are
assumptions that affect all arguments expressed
in English.

On the other hand, there may be relevant assumptions which do have an important bearing upon the
argument in question. The assumption detected in
(b) above, for instance, is one such assumption,
for the whole argument turns on whether or not
the arguer is correct in maintaining that the
existence of God is incompatible with the existence of evil. The assumption is relevant to
understanding the argument. Relevant assumptions

48

should be explicitly displayed in the standard format for argument identification.

Consider several other examples of arguments that contain unexpressed assumptions that play an important role in the argument.

(e)   Skinner's utopian society ought to be rejected for the following reasons. First of all,
the sort of society Skinner proposes in
Walden Two is a non-competitive, lifeless
society that lacks creativity and imagination. Secondly, the kind of society Skinner
proposes lacks the conditions that make for
festivity and fantasy, two significant and
particularly human traits. Then, too, the
type of society Skinner proposes would turn
people into robots.

The structure of the argument is easy to discern:
three main premises (marked by "first of all...,"
"secondly...," and "then, too,...") in support of
the conclusion: Skinner's utopian society ought
to be rejected. There is, however, an unexpressed assumption in connection with the third premise, namely that turning people into robots is
undesirable. The arguer hasn't exactly said
that, but in the context of what he has said about
Skinner's society, it would seem reasonable for us
to suppose that his third premise indicates an
undesirable trait.

Using standard format, the argument contained in
(e) would be reconstructed in the following
manner:

support space	main argument space
	1. The sort of society Skinner proposes in Walden Two is a non-competitive, lifeless society that lacks creativity and imag-ination.
	2. The kind of society Skinner proposes lacks the conditions that make fest-ivity and fantasy, two

significant and part-
icularly human traits.
3. The type of society
< turning people into   Skinner proposes
  robots is undesirable.> would turn people in-
                           to robots.
                           _____

                           ∴ Skinner's utopian
                             society ought to be
                             rejected.

Consider another example of an argument containing an unexpressed assumption.
(f) Indians in North America can either become
    assimilated and lose their identity or else
    remain separate and retain their own cultural
    traditions. They cannot, however, remain
    separate and retain their own cultural tradi-
    tions. After all, consider the pressures of
    advanced technological society, the inundation
    of television, the proximity of Indian settle-
    ments to major urban areas, the culture-laden
    values of North American schooling, etc.
    Thus Indians in North America will become
    assimilated and lose their identity.

In this selection, the first sentence states two
options facing Indians in North America, and it
is the first premise. The next sentence, which
rules out one of these options, is premise 2, and
it is supported by a mini-argument (which begins,
"after all,..."). The conclusion is indicated by
"thus...".

So far so good. The basic structure of the argument is clear enough. But note premise 1. It
contains an unexpressed assumption, namely, that
these two options are the only options. This is
an important, and debatable, assumption, for it
may very well be the case that there are other
possible options open for the Indian community in
North America (for example, to become part of
North American society and yet retain their own
cultural traditions). That, at least, is a possible option and one the arguer perhaps should

50

have taken into account. That the two options stated by the arguer are the only two options is an assumption that is relevant to the argument, and it should be explicitly displayed.

The argument contained in (f) would be set out as follows:

<u>support space</u>   <u>main argument space</u>
‹ these are the only   1. Indians in North America
   options ›   can either become assim-
                                   ilated and lose their
                                   identity or else remain
                                   separate and retain
                                   their own cultural trad-
1. Consider the pressures   itions.
of advanced technological
society, the inundation of   2. They cannot remain sepa-
television, the proximity   rate and retain their
of Indian settlements to   own cultural traditions.
major urban areas, the
culture-laden values of
North American schooling,   _____
etc.

                              .·. Indians in North America
                                   will become assimilated
                                   and lose their identity.

Other important unexpressed assumptions will be detected from time to time as the study of argument progresses. As we shall see, such unexpressed assumptions play an important role in argument evaluation in addition to argument identification, especially when the argument turns on the unexpressed assumption the arguer has made.

Unexpressed assumptions, then, are a second additional structural feature <u>some</u> arguments may have.

<u>auxiliary conclusions</u>

Some arguments may contain what might be called "an auxiliary conclusion." In some circumstances, in addition to making a main conclusion, the

51

arguer may go on either (a) to make a brief comment about the conclusion or else (b) to indicate
an immediate implication of the conclusion just
argued for. Such comments which may be present
in some arguments point generally to the significance the arguer attaches to the conclusion.

To the argument contained in selection (b), for
example, the arguer might have appended at the
end, after his conclusion, "God does not exist,"
a comment like "and that's too bad," or "and this
has important consequences for the future of
theology," or "this makes possible human freedom,"
and so on. Such comments indicate the import the
arguer attaches to the conclusion. They are
auxiliary conclusions.

In the extended standard format for identifying
arguments, an auxiliary conclusion, if present,
is placed in center space, immediately below the
main conclusion. So the following argument
(g) If God exists, then there would be no evil
     in the world. But there is evil in the
     world. Why just consider all the natural
     disasters such as floods and famines, social
     disasters like robberies and rapes, and all
     the insects like mosquitos that annoy people.
     Thus God does not exist. This has important
     consequences for the future of theology.
would be identified as follows:

support space	main argument space
⟨the existence of God is incompatible with the existence of evil⟩	1. If God exists, then there would be no evil in the world.
1. Consider all the natural disasters such as floods and famines, social disasters like robberies and rapes, and all the insects like mosquitos that annoy people.	2. There is evil in the world.
	∴ God does not exist.
	This has important consequ-ences for the future of

summary

Let's review what has been said so far in this
chapter. We've pointed out five basic structural
features arguments may have. These are:
    premises -- one or more
    a conclusion
    support for individual premises
    unexpressed assumptions
    auxiliary conclusions
And we have extended the basic format for identifying arguments to encompass three spaces: left,
center, and right spaces.

Structure and space have been coordinated as
follows:

---

center space - the main argument space, which
                contains
  1. premises of the main argument
  2. the conclusion of the main argument
  3. auxiliary conclusion (if any)

left space - support space, which contains
  4. premises of mini-arguments (if any)
  5. unexpressed assumptions (if any)

right space - evaluation space
    Critical comments we make upon the argu-
    ment in assessing its worth are placed in
    this space. We will ignore this space of
    the standard format until Part Two of this
    text.

It should be carefully noted that not all arguments contain support for individual premises,
unexpressed assumptions, or auxiliary conclusions.

The following chart helps visualize the relationship between the different parts of an argument
and the standard format.

argument identification		argument evaluation
support space	main argument space	evaluation space
unexpressed assumptions (if any)	premises of main argument	
premises of mini-arguments (if any)	_____	
	∴ conclusion of main argument	
	auxiliary conclusions (if any)	

2. Some Arguments Identified

some preliminaries

Before giving some more examples of this format
at work in identifying the structure of arguments,
there are a couple of preliminary matters you
should carefully note.

First of all, you should recall that what we are
identifying is the structure of the argument the
arguer has put forward. We are not yet at the
level of argument evaluation and so we have no
way of telling if the premises do a good or a
poor job of supporting the conclusion. In other
words, we're simply identifying as accurately
and as faithfully as possible the argument offered us by the arguer.

Secondly, by way of a reminder, because we're not
yet ready to engage in argument evaluation, we
shall temporarily ignore the right evaluation
space on our worksheets. This will also help us
save space. Don't forget, however, that there is

such a space.

Finally, there are a variety of equally acceptable
ways in which the information contained in the
mini-premises may be listed. In (b) above, the
mini-premise was written out as one sentence:
>   Consider all the natural disasters
>   such as floods and famines, social
>   disasters like robberies and rapes,
>   and all the insects like mosquitos
>   that annoy people.

It would have been perfectly legitimate to have
written it in an itemized fashion, as follows:
> Consider:
> (a) natural disasters (e.g. floods,
>   famines)
> (b) social disasters (e.g. robberies,
>   rapes)
> (c) insects (e.g. mosquitos)

or listed the information as three separate considerations, as follows:
> (1) natural disasters (floods,
>   famines)
> (2) social disasters (robberies,
>   rapes)
> (3) insects (mosquitos)

How this information is listed is purely stylistic: any of the above ways is acceptable, and it
is clear what it supports.

more on wedges

Wedges (the ＜ and ＞ symbols) were introduced in
section 1 in order to draw attention to the
unexpressed nature of assumptions which arguers
may on occasion make in the course of arguing.
Their use can be extended somewhat to indicate
other unexpressed features of an argument. That
is, on occasion, the arguer may omit saying something explicitly, believing that the person reading or hearing his argument would automatically
fill in what is obviously missing. Clearly this
again is not a licence to read into an argument
anything the reader wants to. Material placed

55

in wedges must be used cautiously, and with good
grounds. The following examples should help
illustrate this extended use of wedges.

Sometimes an arguer will not state the conclusion
explicitly, thinking it to be obvious from the
context. For example:
(h) All men are mortal. Socrates is a man. Ergo.
The conclusion is, of course, Socrates is mortal.
The arguer hasn't explicitly stated this, however,
probably because he considers it too obvious for
words. But since he has not explicitly stated it,
the conclusion will be placed in wedges, to draw
attention to its unexpressed nature.

Using standard format, the argument contained in
(h) would be depicted as follows:

support space	main argument space
	1. All men are mortal.
	2. Socrates is a man.

∴ < Socrates is mortal >

Another similar example:
(i) At Christmas time I have a choice: I can
    either go to the Club Med in Martinique, the
    Playboy Club in the Catskills, or else visit
    my aunt in Detroit. I can't afford Club Med.
    I don't like the Playboy Club in the Catskills.
    So I guess that indicates where I'll spend
    Christmas.
Although the arguer hasn't stated it explicitly,
the conclusion of his argument is: < I'll visit
my aunt in Detroit. > In displaying this argument,
the unexpressed conclusion will be placed in
wedges. Also notice the unexpressed assumption
in premise 1.

Using standard format, the argument contained in
(i) is set out as follows:

support space	main argument space
< These are the only three options >	1. At Christmas time I have a choice: I can either go to the Club Med in Martinique, the Playboy

        Club in the Catskills, or
        else visit my aunt in
        Detroit.
    2. I can't afford the Club
        Med.
    3. I don't like the Playboy
        Club in the Catskills.
        _____

    ∴ < I'll visit my aunt in
        Detroit at Christmas
        time >

Sometimes, too, an argument may contain an unexpressed auxiliary conclusion which the arguer may
hope we catch, even though he hasn't said it
explicitly. This often happens in the case where
the arguer is being ironical or sarcastic and
isn't seriously putting forward the position he
appears to be defending. It also happens when an
arguer is trying to show the absurd, silly, or
ridiculous consequences of another arguer's position, as in the following exchange:
(j) George: First of all, it should be noted
            that Jesus selected only men as
            apostles. Secondly, it should be
            noted the apostles formed the nucleus
            of the Christian ministry. Thirdly,
            if the church is to follow Jesus'
            example, then the priesthood must be
            male. The church, therefore, cannot
            ordain women to the priesthood.
     Bill: Hold on a sec, George. Look at what
            you're saying. You are saying, first
            of all, that what Jesus did is bind-
            ing on subsequent generations. Note,
            too, that Jesus selected Aramaic-
            speaking Jews of the first century
            A.D. as apostles. It would follow
            from this that the church cannot or-
            dain to the priesthood any one who
            is not an Aramaic-speaking Jew of the
            first century A.D.

George's argument is easy to identify. Using
standard format it can be reconstructed as follows:

main argument space
1. Jesus selected only men
   as apostles.
2. The apostles formed the
   nucleus of the Christian
   ministry.
3. If the church is to follow
   Jesus' example, then the
   priesthood must be male.

.˙.The church cannot ordain
    women to the priesthood.

Bill's argument is also easy to discern: two premises (indicated by "first of all,..." and "note,
too,...") and a conclusion. But note Bill's conclusion. Are we to think he is seriously advocating this obviously impossible position? Or are
we to gather, from the sheer impossibility of
what Bill is advocating, that he is trying to
show the absurd consequences to which George's
argument leads? Probably the latter is what Bill
intends. In other words, Bill's argument probably
contains an unexpressed auxiliary conclusion,
namely:
           < and this is absurd >
Being unexpressed, the auxiliary conclusion is
placed in wedges, indicating that it is something
we have read into the argument (although with
good reason).

We would display Bill's argument as follows:
support space   main argument space
1. You are saying that what
   Jesus did is binding on
   subsequent generations.
2. Jesus selected Aramaic-
   speaking Jews of the
   first century A.D. as
   apostles.

.˙.The church cannot ordain
   to the priesthood any
   one who is not an Aram-
   aic-speaking Jew of the

first century A.D.

< and this is absurd >

So: the use of wedges can be usefully extended to indicate unexpressed conclusions and unexpressed auxiliary conclusions.

strategy

The same advice on strategy in Chapter One still applies, but with the following proviso: it is generally helpful to sort out the main argument first, and then the mini-premises.

In reading over a selection containing an argument, the following steps are suggested:
   (1) Underline all locators.
   (2) Sort out the structure of the main argument.
   (3) Sort out the mini-arguments (if any).
   (4) Look for auxiliary conclusions (if any).
   (5) Look for unexpressed assumptions (if any).

some examples

Consider some further examples of argument identification using the expanded standard format.
(k)   It is clearly evident that marijuana should be legalized and tobacco banned. On the one hand, tobacco is detrimental to a person's health. Look at all the evidence. Study after study has indicated a connection between tobacco and cancer. Moreover, the Surgeon General himself has warned that tobacco is injurious to health. Marijuana, on the other hand, is not detrimental to health, producing only mild euphoria.

The structure of this argument should present no difficulties. The conclusion is stated at the outset: marijuana should be legalized and tobacco banned. And the two main premises are also clearly marked out by two locators: "on the one "hand...," and "on the other hand...". That takes care of the main argument. But what of the two sentences that come after "look at all the evidence?" These both support main premise 1. They are both mini-premises. The argument also contains two important assumptions, namely that what is detrimental to a person's health should be banned, and that what is not detrimental to a person's health should be legalized. In the context of this argument, these are highly important relevant assumptions. Unless they are made, the premises would have very little to do with the conclusion being advocated.

support space	main argument space
< what is detrimental to a person's health should be banned. >	1. Study after study has indicated a connection between tobacco and cancer. 2. The Surgeon General himself has warned that tobacco is injurious to health.	1. Tobacco is detrimental to a person's health.
< what is not detrimental to a person's health should be legalized. >		2. Marijuana is not detrimental to a person's health, producing only mild euphoria.
		∴ Marijuana should be legalized and tobacco banned.

Consider next this selection:

(1) In any discussion of abortion, it should be recognized by all parties at the outset that the fetus is human. There is no getting away from this: the fetus is an alive human child. Science, for instance, supports this position. The fertilized ovum is a new human life, with its own distinctive set of chromosomes and its own blueprint for development. Morality, too, supports this position. It's because the fetus is human that moral

60

problems arise. After all, if the fetus weren't human, we wouldn't care about it. The law, moreover, supports this position. The law states that abortions are permitted when continuation of pregnancy endangers the mother's life. Note the word 'mother': a mother is a mother of something, namely, a child. If the fetus weren't human, then the person carrying that fetus couldn't be a mother. So, since the law uses the word 'mother,' it clearly recognizes that the fetus is a human child. Science, morality and the law all back up the contention, then, that the fetus is human.

The conclusion of this argument is repeated three times, in the first, second, and last sentences. The conclusion is this: the fetus is human. Now ask, what supports this contention? The arguer has singled out three main considerations, and, in fact, readily draws our attention to them by saying:

> Science, for instance, supports this posi-
> tion. Morality, too, supports this position.
> The law, moreover, supports this position.

and by giving a helpful summary sentence towards the end of the argument:

> Science, morality, and the law all back up
> the contention, then, that...

These are the three main premises of the argument. (The summary sentence, of course, is not a premise, for it simply serves to wrap up the argument by repeating the three main points already mentioned).

Now the structure of the main argument has been picked out and the other sentences begin to fall into place. What follows each of the three main premises serves to support it. They are mini-premises. There are also some assumptions. In the first mini-argument it is assumed that by 'human' is meant biological humanity. It is an important assumption, for there are other under-standings of what it means to be human (e.g. being able to reason, think critically, function inde-pendently of the mother, etc.) and discussions of the abortion issue often turn on what definition of 'human' is being employed. Another assumption is made in the second mini-argument, namely, that morality concerns only humans. The presumption here is that if the fetus weren't human, then moral considerations wouldn't apply to it.

The argument contained in (1) would be displayed as follows:

<u>support space</u>   <u>main argument space</u>

⟨by 'human'   1. The fertilized
is meant   ovum is a new   1. Science supports the
biological   human life,   conclusion
humanity⟩   with...
             development.

⟨morality   1. It's because
concerns   the fetus is
only   human that   2. Morality supports the
humans⟩   moral prob-   conclusion
             lems arise.
        2. If the fetus
            weren't
            human, we...
            about it.

1. Law states that abortions
   are permitted when...life.
2. A mother is a mother of
   something...a child.
3. If the fetus weren't   3. The law supports the
   human, then...mother   conclusion
4. Since the law uses the
   word 'mother,' it...
   human child.

                           ∴ The fetus is human.

Consider, finally, this selection
(m)   DISTURBING NEWS
     Space authority, Dr. Charles Glatz, recently addressed the up-state UFO League of Investigators.
     Dr. Glatz claimed that UFOs are either figments of our imagination or else they

represent vessels containing life-forms
from other worlds.
He went on to say that UFOs are not figments
of our imagination. After all, he pointed
out, there have been over 25,000 sightings
of UFOs in North America over the past 25
years; people agree that UFOs are noiseless,
rapidly-moving discs of bluish light; and
these objects have been photographed and
filmed under rigorous conditions.
He concluded that UFOs represent vessels
containing life-forms from other worlds. And
he added that many people will find this conclusion highly disturbing.

The conclusion is readily apparent:
UFOs represent vessels containing life-forms
from other worlds.
And there is an auxiliary conclusion:
Many people will find this conclusion highly
disturbing.
The main premises are relatively clear:
   1. UFOs are either figments of our imagina-
      tion or else they represent vessels
      containing life-forms from other worlds.
   2. UFOs are not figments of our imagination.
The second premise is supported (notice the phrase,
"after all") by three main considerations. Also
notice that the first premise contains the unexpressed assumption, namely
   <these are the only options>
One additional option Dr. Glatz did not consider
was that they might be natural phenomena.

The argument contained in (m) would be displayed
as follows:

support space	main argument space
< these are the only options >	1. UFOs are either figments of our imagination or else they represent vessels containing life- forms from other worlds.

1. There have been over
   25,000 sightings of
   UFOs in North America
   over the past 25yrs.
2. People agree that UFOs
   are noiseless, rapidly-
   moving discs of bluish
   light.
3. These objects have been
   photographed and filmed
   under rigorous conditions.

2. UFOs are not figments
   of our imagination.

∴ UFO represent vessels
   containing life-forms
   from other worlds.

& many people will find
   this conclusion high-
   ly disturbing.

a final note

This chapter has introduced you to the main structural features of argument, given you a format for
reconstructing the argument, and provided you with
examples of this approach at work. Now it is time
for you to get into argument identification on
your own.

One final reminder. As this chapter points out,
some arguments have, in addition to premises and
conclusion, support for individual premises, unexpressed assumptions, and auxiliary conclusions.
It should be borne in mind, however, that not all
arguments have these features. Just because the
arguments displayed in this chapter exhibit these
features--they were chosen, after all, to illustrate them--this does not constitute a licence to
look for or read into arguments features which
simply aren't there. Not all arguments, for
instance, contain unexpressed assumptions that are
relevant to understanding the argument or to
assessing its worth. Don't go overboard here!

Recall Quiz

(1) In addition to premises and conclusion, what three additional structural features may some arguments have?

(2) In the expanded format suggested in this chapter, to what use is right space, center space, and left space put?

(3) Where are support for individual premises, unexpressed assumptions, auxiliary conclusions placed in the expanded format for displaying arguments suggested in this chapter?

(4) What is a "mini-argument"?

(5) What do wedges ($<$ and $>$) indicate?

(6) What strategy is suggested in identifying the basic structure of an argument?

Exercise #1
Using standard format, identify the argument contained in each of the following selections.
(note: 1. Remember suggested strategy for identifying arguments.
2. Remember that not all arguments contain support for individual premises, unexpressed assumptions, or auxiliary conclusions.)

(1) There is life after death. Many people who have "died" on the operating table have come back to life, telling of peace, amazing joy, and friends waiting to welcome them.

(2) California is a dangerous place in which to live. A large area of the state, after all, lies along the earthquake-prone San Andreas Fault. No one who values his life should therefore move to California.

(3) In the post-petroleum world, there are two main sources of energy: solar power and nuclear power. Nuclear power, however, has proven to be a dangerous way of providing power. Nuclear plants, after all, have been

plagued by a series of shut-downs, mechanical
failures, and by a variety of leakages of
radioactive material into the water and air
environment close to urban centers. It would
seem, then, that the wiser course of action
would be to explore the possibilities of solar
power.

(4) The Santa Claus myth is pretty well ensconced
in present day society. Yet for all that, the
Santa Claus story is a harmful cultural myth.
Just consider the following:
   - When children do find out the truth, as they
     inevitably do, they learn that parents lie.
   - It encourages children to fantasize and to
     avoid coping with the real world.
   - Its "spiritual message" is largely egocen-
     tric--what Santa Claus is going to get ME.
   - Because it teaches that good behavior is
     not good in and of itself but is something
     to be rewarded with material presents, it
     seriously retards the development of a
     responsible moral and social set of values.

(5) (in the following, what is the "crude syllogism" (or argument) on behalf of the Theory
of Vanishing Choice?)
...Put in its simplest form, this Theory of
Vanishing Choice rests on a crude syllogism.
Science and technology have fostered standard-
ization. Science and technology will advance,
making the future even more standardized than
the present. Ergo: Man will progressively lose
his freedom of choice.
(A. Toffler, Future Shock (New York: Bantam,
1971), p. 264)

(6) (in the following, what is Ernie's argument?)
Ernie: Toffler in Future Shock advocates
        what he calls "social futurism."
Bert: Really?
Ernie: Yup. No doubt about it.
Bert: Well, how does he back up that posi-
        tion?
Ernie: Well, first of all, he maintains that
        we are overwhelmed by changes. Then

	he points out that we are specifically overwhelmed by the acceleration of change itself: the rate of change has itself changed. Then he talks for pages and pages how these have had certain psychological and social eff-ects-transience, lack of permanence, apathy, and a sense of worthlessness for instance.
Bert:	No kidding!
Ernie:	No. Moreover, towards the end of the book he says that society today is faced with three prospects: massive adaptational breakdown, irrationality, or social futurism. He then says that the first two options are highly unde-sirable and can be avoided if people overcome their sense of lethargy. Finally he concludes that people ought to adopt the strategy of social futu-rism.
Bert:	Whew! I guess I don't have to read all 561 pages of Future Shock now.

(7) If substance X is hallucinogenic, then it'll turn the test solution floral green. The test solution, however, did not turn floral green. Thus substance X is not hallucinogenic.

(8) (in the following, what is Bruce's argument?)

Hal:	What's that you're reading, Bruce?
Bruce:	It's an article by a behavioural scien-tist named Milgram. It's entitled "Obedience"
Hal:	What's it about?
Bruce:	Well, the upshot of it is this: he claims that ordinary people obey people in authority, even to the ex-tent of inflicting a serious pain on other people.
Hal:	Really?
Bruce:	Yah.
Hal:	That's pretty far out. How does he support that view?
Bruce:	Well, first of all, he set up an experiment at Yale University in which

a person had to give an increasingly
severe electric shock to another
person when he made a mistake in
learning matched pairs of words.
However, and this is the interesting
part, the experiment was actually
rigged--there was no electric shock,
the learner was an accomplice, and
the person giving the shock didn't
know all this. Then, thirdly, when
the person administering what he
thought was a real shock to the
learner tried to stop, he was gently
ordered to continue by the scientist.
Finally, Milgram noted that over 50%
of the subjects tested were sufficiently willing to obey the authority
of the scientist to administer to
the learner what they thought was a
lethal electric shock.

Hal: Wow!

Bruce: Want to borrow the article? Milgram's
conclusion has really serious implications for political authority.

(9)   Nor is there anything smart about smoking.
a woman who smokes is far more likely than
her nonsmoking counterpart to suffer from a
host of disabling conditions, any of which
can interfere with her ability to perform at
home or on the job...Women who smoke have
more spontaneous abortions, stillbirths,
and premature babies than do nonsmokers, and
their children's later health may be affected.
(Jane E. Brody and Richard Engquist, "Women
and Smoking," Public Affairs Pamphlet No.
475 (New York: Public Affairs Committee,
Inc., 1972), p.2)

(10)   The Case for Suicide
It also appears that suicide no longer
repels us. The suicide rate is climbing,
especially among blacks and young people.
What's more, suicide has been appearing in
an increasingly favorable light in the

nation's press. When Paul Cameron surveyed
all articles on suicide indexed over the
past 50 years in the Readers' Guide to
Periodical Literature, he found that volun-
tary death, once portrayed as a brutal
waste, now generally appears in a neutral
light. Some recent articles even present
suicide as a good thing to do and are
written in a manner that might encourage
the reader to take his own life under certain circumstances. Last year, a majority
of Americans under 30 told Gallup pollsters
that incurable disease or continual pain
confer on a person the moral right to end
his life.
(Elizabeth Hall with Paul Cameron, "Our
Failing Reverence for Life," Psychology
Today, April 1976, p.108)

(11)   (in the following, what is the "standard
        fatalist argument"?)
        Fatalism does not deny that everything that
        happens has a cause. It only denies that
        human beings have the power to change the
        course of events...A standard fatalist
        argument during the 1940 bombing of London
        ran as follows:
            Either you are going to be killed by a
            bomb or you are not going to be. If you
            are, then any precautions you take will
            be ineffective. If you are not, all
            precautions you take are superfluous.
            Therefore it is pointless to take pre-
            cautions.
            (John Hospers, Introduction to Philo-
            sophical Analysis 2d ed. (Englewood
            Cliffs: Prentice-Hall, 1967), pp.322,
            323. The argument Hospers quotes is
            from Michael Dummett, "Bringing about
            the Past," Philosophical Review (1964))

(12)   A typical summation of the evils of
        marijuana use is contained in the following
        statement by Judge G. Joseph Tauro of the
        Massachusetts Superior Court,
            First, marijuana is universally recogni-

zed as a mind-altering drug which in
varying degrees and with unpredictable
effect produces a state of intoxication
sometimes referred to as "euphoric."
Second, in the United States marijuana
is customarily used for the explicit
purpose of inducing this state of intoxication.
Third, in varying degrees this state of
intoxication can cause a lessening of
psychomotor coordination and distortion
of the ability to perceive time, dist-
ance, and space....
Fourth, the habitual use of marijuana is
particularly prevalent among individuals
with marginal personalities exhibiting
feelings of inadequacy, anxiety, dis-
affiliation, alienation, and frustration
or suffering from neuroses, psychoses,
or other mental disorders....
Fifth, marijuana may have a disinhibit-
ing effect upon the user which tends to
aggravate his pre-existing mental state
or disposition. Thus its effects can
vary with individuals and can vary during different occasions of use by the
same individual.
Sixth, marijuana has no accepted medical
use in modern medicine....
Seventh, the use of marijuana is not part
of the dogma of any recognized Western
religion.
Eighth, marijuana has had a growing
attraction for the young and the adoles-
cent.
Last, but probably most significant, no
one can guarantee with any degree of
certainty that continued use of marijuana
will not eventually cause permanent
physical injury.
On the basis of these points, Judge Tauro
concluded that marijuana is a dangerous
drug,...and that the current penal laws
against the use or possession of marijuana
are therefore justified.

70

(Burton M. Leiser, Liberty, Justice, and Morals (New York: Macmillan, 1973), p. 135)

(13)   ... Virtually all large, complex organizations in the United States, for example, are best classified as bureaucracies, though the degree and forms of bureaucratization vary.

Its "ideal" form, however, is never realized for a variety of reasons. For one thing, it tries to do what must be (hopefully) forever impossible-- to eliminate all unwanted extraorganizational influences upon the behavior of members. Ideally, members should act only in the organization's interests. The problem is that even if the interest of the organization is unambiguous, men do not exist just for organizations. They track all kinds of mud from the rest of their lives with them into the organization, and they have all kinds of interests that are independent of the organization.

The ideal form also falls short of realization when rapid changes in some of the organization tasks are required. Bureaucracies are set up to deal with stable, routine tasks; that is the basis of organizational efficiency. Without stable tasks there cannot be a stable division of labor, the acquisition of skills and experience, planning and coordination, and so on. But when changes come along, organizations must alter their programs; when such changes are frequent and rapid, the form of organization becomes so temporary that the efficiences of bureaucracy cannot be realized....

Finally, bureaucracy in its ideal form falls short of its expectations because men are only indifferently intelligent, prescient, all-knowing, and energetic. All organizations must be designed for

71

the "average" person one is likely to
find in each position, not the super-
man....
(Charles Perrow, Complex Organizations
(Glenview, Ill.: Scott, Foresman & Co,
1972), p. 5)

Exercise #2 - Practice in Argument Preparation
                  and Presentation

format A - an in-class debate
    organization
    - the course director will divide the class
      into a number of small groups
    - each group will meet separately during
      class time to prepare a 2 to 3 minute argu-
      ment on behalf of the following conclusion:
          odd numbered groups: .'. ... * (affirm-
          ative)
          even numbered groups: .'. ... * (nega-
          tive)
    (* The conclusion, dealing with a topic of
    current controversial interest, will be
    assigned by the course director.)
    - maximum preparation time: _____ minutes.
    preparation
    - each group will select a leader quickly
      whose job it will be to coordinate discuss-
      ion in the group and to present the final
      argument the group composes together.
    - each member of the group is to help in pre-
      paring the argument.
    - in preparing your group's argument,
          a) brainstorm----list a whole variety of
              possible reasons that could support
              the conclusion
          b) select----settle on a number of impor-
              tant points (bearing in mind the time
              limit, what you think needs stressing
              what you think your opponents might
              say, what you think you can best
              defend, etc.)
          c) organize----make your important points

72

the main premises; back them up (mini-
premises). Add some stylistic flourishes to make them sound "real".
- be imaginative and creative as you think
about the assigned conclusion. Have fun
with the exercise.
- write out the argument in rough so that it
can be presented later on to the class.
If there's time, practice presenting it to
your group.
- during the preparation phase you may expect
the course director to visit your delibera-
tions simply to observe what is going on.

presentation
- at the end of the set preparation period,
the first odd numbered group will present
its argument, followed by the first even
numbered group, and so on, until all groups
have had their say.

discussion
- at the end of each affirmative and negative
round, or at the end of all the presentations, the course director will make comments on the content of style of each
presentation.
- he will then invite all participants to
consider how their own arguments and those
of the others might be improved.
- the group should also discuss the problems
involved in going from an argument on paper
to presenting an argument in speech.

format B - an essay

instructions
- prepare an essay that in a maximum of ___
words presents an argument on behalf of the
following conclusion:
surnames A to M: .'. ... * (affirmative)
surnames N to Z: .'. ... * (negative)
(* The conclusion, dealing with a topic of
current controversial interest, will be
assigned by the course director)
- follow standard essay style (complete
sentences, paragraphs, etc.), not the

standard format we have adopted for reconstructing the structure of arguments.
- in preparing your argument,
    a) brainstorm----list a whole variety of
       possible reasons that could support
       the conclusion
    b) select----settle on a number of impor-
       tant points (bearing in mind the
       space limitations, what you think
       needs stressing, what you think
       someone on the other side of the
       question might say, what you think
       you can best defend, etc.)
    c) organize----make your important points
       the main premises; back them up
       (mini-premises). Add some stylistic
       flourishes to make them sound "real".
- be imaginative and creative as you think
about the assigned conclusion. Have fun
with the topic.
- think, too, of how one goes about trans-
forming the bare structure of an argument
into an essay suitable for reading with
interest and enjoyment.

CHAPTER THREE

FURTHER PRACTICE IN ARGUMENT IDENTIFICATION

1. Searching for Structure

You are now equipped with a general theoretical
framework that can be brought to bear upon particular arguments. You know the major structural
features an argument may have, and you have a
format for displaying the interrelationships
between the various parts of an argument.

Before immediately turning to argument evaluation,
it is well worth your time and effort to consolidate this knowledge of argument structure and how
to recognize it. In fact you should aim at
"internalizing" it so that you become accustomed
to searching for and seeing structure in what you
read and what you hear. This process of consoli-
dating what you already know is particularly
important because many arguments we encounter in
everyday contexts are not as clear-cut as some of
the examples we have met so far in this text.

Searching for, and finding, the structure of many,
many arguments is, of course, often not very
difficult at all. In many cases, the structure
of an argument is clearly set out by the arguer:
the conclusion is readily identifiable, the premises are clearly singled out by various now-fami-
liar devices, and the premises are buttressed by
good, clear support. In such cases, the clear
structure of the argument facilitates good communication between the arguer and his audience. We
may not agree with the arguer, but at least the
arguer has done his part to ensure that his point
of view is put across well.

On the other hand, the structure of some argu-

75

ments may be muddy and hard for us to make out.
The arguer, for example, may not have stated his
conclusion clearly. Or he may not have taken the
trouble to single out his main premises for us in
a helpful manner. Or he may not have organized
his supporting considerations lucidly. And so
forth. When this happens, the arguer places a
much greater strain upon us, making it difficult
for us to grasp correctly the structure of what
he is saying. He runs the risk of our not being
able to distinguish clearly between what he is
advocating and why he is advocating that position.

Where the structure of an argument is obscure,
there is nothing we can do but to sort out the
argument as best we can. We can note where the
argument is clear, where it is troublesome, and
perhaps also why it is muddy. Also, where the
structure of an argument is unclear, we can expect
reasonable people to arrive at different results
concerning what they think the structure is. This
should be no cause for alarm, distress, or frustration. It is simply to recognize that in the context of communication, using the medium of language, some arguers fail to organize their thought
clearly. When this happens, our inability to
arrive at one and only one clearly agreed-upon
reconstruction is the fault of the arguer and the
way in which he has put together what he has to
say. We shall meet some arguments of this sort in
this chapter.

There are a number of reasons why the structure of
an argument may be obscure:

(1) Absence of premise and conclusion locators
The absence of such key words obscures the inten-
tions of the arguer, leaving us to infer from the
context what role each sentence plays. Sometimes
the context is helpful and we can guess reasonably
accurately what the arguer probably intended. On
other occasions, we may not be able to judge from
context and our guesses will differ widely.

(2) Distractions introduced by the arguer

In addition to making an argument, the arguer may also be interested in such matters as the following:

- using language to antagonize, annoy or amuse his audience
- using language in such a way so as to elicit sympathy for the position he is advocating
- following up side issues that crop up in the course of the argument, postponing coming to the main point
- introducing "red herrings" (that is, extraneous and irrelevant considerations) into the argument
- engaging in name-calling or similar abuse of other arguers
- making gestures, using intonation, or making facial movements, etc, in oral arguments
- qualifying, modifying, or retracting points already made.

And so on. Such matters may deflect our attention away from the structure of what is being said.

(3) Sloppy argument preparation or presentation.

The argument may be a complete mess so far as its construction is concerned -- jumbled, incoherent, possibly inconsistent information put together in a botched manner. Or the argument may be put across by the arguer in such a way that what is being said cannot clearly be made out. In either case, a poorly prepared or poorly presented argument severely diminishes the chances that we can detect its structure with any degree of clarity.

In all these instances it is difficult to find the structure of the argument simply because it hasn't been made clear by the arguer. In such circumstances it would be foolish for us to expect precision, as if there were one and only one correct interpretation of every argument. Because of the complexities of language and communication, and because of the circumstances in which arguers sometimes argue, there are many arguments whose structure (either in part or in whole) is open to considerable interpretation and dispute. When this happens, we must simply muddle through as best we can.

2. Some Potential Troublespots

what to do about space limitations

The worksheet on which we identify the structure of the argument (and, don't forget, later on evaluate it) will begin to become quite crowded unless we adopt certain standard conventions for condensing information. These include:
- use of dots (...) between the first and last parts of a sentence
- use of abbreviations for words
- use of paraphrase, on occasion, so long as the original meaning is preserved.

And, by ignoring temporarily evaluation space on the right side of the format, we can save further space for the time being.

what to do about repeated information

Arguers will sometimes repeat points in the course of presenting an argument in order to drive home to us points they want to emphasize. A main premise, for instance, may be repeated several times. This occurs particularly in oral arguments where speakers tell us at the outset what main points they plan to raise, then proceed to develop these main points one by one, and then summarize them at the end so as to refresh our memory of just what was said in the course of the present-ation. Similarly, the conclusion of an argument may be repeated. It may be stated, for instance, at the beginning of an argument, and then repeated at the end.

Obviously repeated information need not be dupli-cated in our format for identifying the structure of an argument. Consider the following argument:
(a) Objection 1. It seems that the will of God is changeable. For the Lord says (Gen.vi.7):

<u>It repenteth me that I have made man.</u> But
whoever repents of what he has done, has a
changeable will. Therefore God has a changeable will.
(St. Thomas Aquinas, <u>Summa Theologica</u>, q.19,
  art.7)

The first sentence here states a position: the will
of God is changeable. The next two sentences give
reasons (note the 'for' and the 'but') for this
position. They are the main premises of the argument. The sentence beginning 'therefore' simply
repeats in a slightly different way the conclusion
stated at the outset.

<u>support space</u>	<u>main argument space</u>
	1. The Lord says (Gen.vi.7): "It repenteth me that I have made man."
	2. Whoever repents of what he has done has a change-able will.

∴ God has a changeable will

Consider next this selection, again from Aquinas:
(b) <u>Objection 1.</u> It seems that in Holy Scripture
    a word cannot have several senses, historical
    or literal, allegorical, tropological or
    moral, and anagogical. For many different
    senses in one text produce confusion and
    deception and destroy all force of argument.
    Hence no argument, but only fallacies, can
    be deduced from a multiplicity of proposi-
    tions. But Holy Scripture ought to be able
    to state the truth without any fallacy.
    Therefore in it there cannot be several
    senses to a word.

Again the conclusion is repeated, although the
first sentence represents a much fuller statement
of the conclusion than does the last. It indicates
explicitly the different sorts of senses (that is,
meanings) scripture can have. In reconstructing
the argument, either conclusion can be stated, although the fuller one is probably preferable.

In the rest of the argument there are some helpful locators. Notice 'hence.' This indicates that what comes after it follows from what has preceded it. We have here a mini-argument, the mini-premise being:

> Many different senses in one text produce confusion and deception and destroy all force of argument.

and the conclusion of the mini-argument being:

> No argument, but only fallacies, can be deduced from a multiplicity of propositions.

This, of course, is premise 1 of the main argument. The sentence beginning "But..." represents main premise 2.

The argument in (b) would be displayed as follows:

support space	main argument space
1. Many different senses in one text produce confusion and deception and destroy all force of argument.	1. No argument, but only fallacies, can be deduced from a multiplicity of propositions.
	2. Holy Scripture ought to be able to state the truth without any fallacy.
	∴ In Holy Scripture a word cannot have several senses, historical or literal, allegorical, tropological or moral, and anagogical.

what to do about background information

In presenting an argument, many arguers set out what they have to say within the context of how they become interested in the controversy, what prompted them to speak or write, who the participants are, what considerations are needed to place the argument in perspective, etc. Such information represents background information. Such information is useful in understanding the argument and in appreciating its significance. While background information is important, it's not part of the argument. It does not, therefore, enter into our identification of the structure of the argument.

<u>what to do about examples</u>

Examples in arguments can be somewhat tricky, depending on what <u>purpose</u> the examples serve in the argument. For the most part, examples tend either
>to <u>support</u> a point being made (indicating <u>why</u> it is so)
or else
>tu <u>illustrate</u> a point being made (indicating for example, <u>how</u> or <u>to what extent</u> it is so).

Consider the following example:
>Temperatures in the Northern Hemisphere have fallen by an average of $1°F$ over the past 30 years, as the following examples show: in November 1948 the average temperature in Chicago was $58°$ while in November 1978 it was $57°$. New York City shows a similar decline.

The data for average temperatures for Chicago and New York City provide some evidence for the more general statement that temperatures in the Northern Hemisphere have fallen by an average of $1°F$ over the past 30 years. That is, the examples cited <u>support</u> (at least to some extent) the main point. Where examples support a point, they are placed in support space as a mini-premise.

Consider another example:
>Many authors have contended recently that what is needed is more extensive governmental control over the policies and practices of private industry. Mesthene, Toffler and other social futurists, for example, have all advocated this.

The examples here serve to tell us <u>who</u> some of these many authors are. They do not indicate <u>why</u> they contend that what is needed is more extensive governmental control over the policies and

practices of private industry.   In other words,
the examples here <u>illustrate</u> or <u>clarify</u> the point
being made.   It is as if the person had said:
"Many authors (e.g. Mesthene, Toffler, and other
social futurists) have contended recently that..."
Where examples illustrate, or extend, or clarify
the point being made, they should be included as
part of that point.

In many cases, however, the precise purpose of
examples is not entirely clear from the context.
In such ambiguous circumstances, those who construe the examples as answering the question
"why?" will place this information in left space
of the format as providing support to some point;
those who interpret the examples as answering
such questions as "what?" or "who?" or "how?" will
incorporate such information as part of the point
which they illustrate or amplify.

<u>what to do about information after a colon;
semi-colon</u>

In general, the information that comes after a
colon (:) simply extends the point made in the
part of the sentence before the colon occurs.   So
the whole sentence should be treated as one point.
For example, the information contained in the
following sentence should be treated as one point:
> Indians in North American society have
> three options: to become assimilated, to
> remain separate, or to retain cultural
> identity with integration into mainstream
> North American life.

Semi-colons (;) are another story.   Usually semi-
colons separate out different pieces of information.   In such cases, then, what semi-colons
separate are usually different reasons.   The argument contained in the following selection, for
instance, would contain three premises (each
separated by a semi-colon):
(c)   I am the best qualified person for the
      position as Marketing Manager because I am
      the most experienced in the manufacture,

82

distribution, and marketing of gizmos; I
have a superb track record, having proved
myself in sales at Gizmo Corporation; and
I am both able and willing to travel as
necessary to the various branch plants.
Accordingly, the argument contained in (c) would
be displayed as follows:

support space   main argument space

1. I am the most experienced
   in the manufacture, distribution, and marketing of
   gizmos.
2. I have a superb track record, having proved myself
   in sales at Gizmo Corporation.
3. I am both able and willing
   to travel as necessary to
   the various branch plants.

∴ I am the best qualified
   person for the position as
   Marketing Manager.

what to do about sentences which list considerations

Some sentences contain a list of considerations
which support a point. We are already familiar
with such sentences: e.g. argument (b) in Chapter
Two contained a sentence which went as follows:
> Why just consider all the natural disasters
> such as floods and famines, social disasters
> like robberies and rapes, and all the insects
> like mosquitos that annoy people.

It was pointed out in Chapter Two that there are
several ways in which the information contained in
the sentence may be entered in the standard format:
> (1) as one premise
> (2) as one premise, with the specific consid-
>   erations itemized
> (3) as three separate premises.

Either method is equally acceptable, being purely
a matter of style. It should be clear, however,
that should you choose method (1) or (2), while

another person chooses method (3), the numbering of your premises will differ. This should not prove disconcerting, for you both will have the same information supporting the same main point.

3. Some Arguments Identified

In this section, a variety of different arguments will be identified, using standard format. They come from sources typical of college or university level reading. These examples are of a more complex nature than the ones we have met so far in this text, but they are amenable to the same sort of treatment.

In order to get maximum benefit from this section, you should not just read these pages over once lightly. You should work through this section, selection by selection. To develop your apprenticeship as a budding argument detector, you should read over carefully each of the following selections several times. Then, on a separate sheet of paper, do your best to identify the argument it contains, using standard format. In doing this, remember basic strategy - underline clue words (where present), and sort out the main argument first, then the mini-premises. Finally compare your work with the identification and discussion given in the text.

Consider, first of all, this selection:
(d) Many a reader will raise the question whether findings won by the observation of individuals can be applied to the psychological understanding of groups. Our answer to this question is an emphatic affirmation. Any group consists of individuals and nothing but individuals, and psychological mechanisms which we find operating in a group can therefore only be mechanisms that operate in individuals. In studying individual psychology as a basis for the understanding of social psychology, we do something which

84

might be compared with studying an object
under the microscope. This enables us to
discover the very details of psychological
mechanisms which we find operating on a large
scale in the social process. If our analysis
of socio-psychological phenomena is not based
on the detailed study of human behavior, it
lacks empirical character and, therefore,
validity.
(Erich Fromm, Escape from Freedom (New York:
Avon Books, 1965), p. 158)

This selection begins with a question the reader
of Escape from Freedom is apt to have raised by
page 158: can findings won by the observation of
individuals be applied to the psychological understanding of groups? Fromm, we learn, has a
definite position on this matter. He says, "our
answer to this question is an emphatic affirmation." In other words, Fromm is maintaining:
    Findings won by the observation of individ-
    uals can be applied to the psychological
    understanding of groups.
This represents the conclusion of his argument.
Fromm then offers several reasons which support
this position.

Notice carefully Fromm's next sentence:
    Any group consists of individuals and
    nothing but individuals, and psychological
    mechanisms which we find operating in a
    group can therefore only be mechanisms
    that operate in individuals.
Observe the word 'therefore' in this sentence.
There are two points raised in this sentence: (i)
that any group consists of individuals and nothing
but individuals, and (ii) that psychological
mechanisms which we find operating in a group can
only be mechanisms that operate in individuals.
The word 'therefore' indicates that point (ii)
follows from point (i). We have here a mini-argument, (i) being support for (ii) which is the
first main premise.

The three final sentences in (d) each make

85

separate points in support of the conclusion. One
sentence makes an analogy (looking at individual
psychology to understand social psychology is like
studying an object under a microscope). Another
sentence indicates what this process enables the
observer to find. The concluding sentence points
out the importance of basing social psychology on
a detailed study of human behavior. These three
sentences represent three additional premises of
the main argument.

support space

main argument space

1. Any group consists of individuals and nothing but individuals.

1. Psych. mechanisms which operate in a group can only be mechanisms that operate in individuals.

2. In studying indiv. psych. as a basis for understanding social psych., we do something which might be compared with studying an object under the microscope.

3. Studying indiv. psych. enables us to discover the very details of psych. mechanisms which we find operating on a large scale in the social process.

4. If our analysis of socio-psychological phenomena is not based on the detailed study of human behavior, it lacks empirical character and therefore validity.

∴ Findings won by the observation of individuals can be applied to the psychological understanding of groups.

Consider next this argument:
(e)   It should be abundantly clear that New
      Testament Christianity rejects the immortality
      of the soul.

86

For one thing, the various writings in the
New Testament (e.g. 1 Corinthians 15:13,
Romans 8:23, and many other passages) speak
only of "resurrection of the dead" or
"resurrection of the body," not "immortality
of the soul."

For another thing, the notion of the dead
being resurrected is a very different notion
from the soul's being immortal, as can be
readily discerned from the following considerations. First of all, if the soul were
immortal, then it could never die, and the
person would continue on forever. Yet, for
New Testament Christianity, continuation of
life is a conditional matter, conditional,
that is, upon having entered the New Life
made possible by Jesus Christ. Secondly,
it is important to notice that the New
Testament never divides the nature of man into two distinct types of substances, e.g.
soul and body. From the New Testament perspective (building upon its Judaic founda-
tions), man is a complex unity of willing,
thinking, feeling, and doing, and, as such,
either stands apart from or is united with
God as a whole person. Thirdly, notice the
New Testament attitude towards death.
Socrates, in the Greek tradition, believing
in the immortality of the soul, confronts
death calmly, almost as a friend. Jesus,
on the other hand, confronts death as an
enemy to be struggled with and finally to
be defeated.
(A longer, more sophisticated version of
this argument is to be found in Oscar
Cullmann, Immortality of the Soul or
Resurrection of the Dead? (London: Epworth
Press, 1958), reprinted in Terence Penelhum
(ed.), Immortality (Belmont, California:
Wadsworth, 1973), pages 53-85)

In (e), the conclusion is stated first. It is:
    New Testament Christianity rejects the
    immortality of the soul.

Why should this be abundantly clear? The arguer
gives two main reasons (which are the two main
premises):
   1. The various writings in the New Testament
      (e.g. 1 Corinthians 15:13, Romans 8:23,
      and many other passages) speak only of
      "resurrection of the dead" or "resurrec-
      tion of the body" not "immortality of the
      soul."
   2. The notion of the dead being resurrected
      is a very different notion from the soul's
      being immortal.
Note that in premise 1 the examples serve to indicate which writings in the New Testament make the
point in question. They are thus included as part
of the point itself.

Notice, too, that the second main premise is itself supported by three considerations. To save
space on our format, these can be paraphrased as
follows:
   1. Immortality of the soul means that the
      soul never dies; yet in the N.T. continua-
      tion of life is conditional.
   2. The N.T. does not divide man into two
      substances (soul, body) but views man as
      a complex unity of willing, thinking,
      feeling and doing.
   3. Compare Socrates' view (immortality of
      soul) with Jesus' attitude towards death.

The argument contained in selection (e) would be
displayed as follows:
   <u>support space</u>   <u>main argument space</u>
                              1. Various writings in the
                                 N.T. (e.g. 1 Cor. 15:13,
                                 Romans 8:23, etc.) speak
                                 only of "res. of the dead"
                                 or "res. of the body,"
                                 not "imm. of the soul."
1. Imm. of soul means   2. The notion of the dead
soul never dies; yet in   being resurrected is a
the N.T. continuation of   very different notion
life is conditional.   from the soul's being
                               immortal.

2. The N.T. does not divide
man into two substances but
views man as a complex unity
of willing, thinking, feeling, & doing.
3. Compare Socrates' (imm.
of soul) view with Jesus'
attitude towards death.

.'. New Testament Chris-
    tianity rejects the
    immortality of the
    soul.

Letters to the editor often contain arguments,
although these are not always organized as clearly
as they might. Consider the following letter to
the editor of Playboy:
(f)   Double Your Fun
    L. Solomon states in the October 1974 Playboy
    Forum that bisexuality is just a vogue and
    that people experiment with it "at real risk
    to their psychological stability." Not so.
    Bisexuality is not a transitory fashion; it
    has always been a characteristic of human
    nature, as innumerable behavioral scientists
    have pointed out. What's new is that our
    society is beginning to admit that it is
    possible to have--and to express-sexual feel-
    ings for members of both sexes. This change
    has occurred suddenly, but I think it will
    be with us for a long time to come.

    By living as a bisexual, you have twice as
    many people to love and you learn twice as
    much about sex. It is the only way to become
    a sexually complete person. I suggest that
    anyone who has ever been attracted to a per-
    son of his or her own sex should try doing
    something about it at least once.
                    (Name withheld by request)
                    East Boston,Massachusetts.
    (Playboy, January 1975, p.54)

The anonymous author of this letter to Playboy is

89

responding to a point of view that L. Solomon had expressed in a previous issue of this magazine. This represents background information, placing the letter in context, and does not form part of the anonymous author's argument.

The anonymous author's argument begins with his statement, "Not so." Note that this "not so" negates two points raised by L. Solomon. It negates (i) that bisexuality is just a vogue, and it negates (ii) that people experiment with it at real risk to their psychological stability. The anonymous author of the letter to the editor of Playboy is thus maintaining:
1. Bisexuality is not just a vogue.
2. Experimentation with bisexuality does not involve risk to psychological stability.

As becomes evident later on, these two claims are used to support a more general point. These two claims represent the two main premises in his argument.

Both of these main premises are supported. Main premise 1 (Bisexuality is not just a vogue) is supported by the following considerations:
1. Bisexuality is not a transitory fashion; it has always been a characteristic of human nature, as innumerable behavioral scientists have pointed out.
2. What's new is that our society is beginning to admit that it is possible to have --and to express--sexual feelings for members of both sexes.
3. This change has occurred suddenly, but it will be with us for a long time to come.

These, then, are mini-premises in support of premise 1 of the main argument.

Next the anonymous author of the letter goes on to discuss the merits of bisexuality. He makes the following points (which may be listed in one sentence or separated as follows):

90

1. By living as a bisexual, you have twice
   as many people to love.
2. By living as a bisexual, you learn twice
   as much about sex.
3. It is the only way to become a sexually
   complete person.

These points relate to main premise 2. That is,
they support the claim that experimentation with
bisexuality does not involve risk to psychological
stability. These, then, are mini-premises in
support of main premise 2.

The letter concludes with a suggestion:
  Anyone who has ever been attracted to a person
  of his or her own sex should try doing something about it at least once.
This suggestion is made by the arguer on the basis
of the two main premises already stated. It is
the conclusion of his argument.

Argument (f) would be displayed as follows:

support space	main argument space
1. Bisexuality is not a trans fashion; it has always been a char. of human nature, as innumerable behavioral scientists have pointed out. 2. What's new is that our soc. is beginning to admit it's possible to have--and to express--sexual feelings for members of both sexes. 3. This change has occurred suddenly, but it will be with us for a long time to come.	1. Bisexuality is not just a vogue.
1. By living as a bisexual, you have twice as many people to love. 2. By living as a bisexual, you learn twice as much about sex. 3. It is the only way to become a sexually complete person.	2. Experimentation with bisexuality does not involve risk to psychological stability.

91

.˙. Anyone who has ever been attracted to a person of his or her own sex should try doing something about it at least once.

As has already been mentioned, some arguments, otherwise clear, contain troublespots. One such argument is the following presented by Rudolf Bultmann at the beginning of a famous essay:
(g) The cosmology of the New Testament is essentially mythical in character. The world is viewed as a three-storied structure, with the earth in the center, the heaven above, and the underworld beneath. Heaven is the abode of God and of the celestial beings--the angels. The underworld is hell, the place of torment. Even the earth is more than the scene of natural, everyday events, of the trivial round and common task. It is the scene of the supernatural activity of God and his angels on the one hand, and of Satan and his demons on the other. These supernatural forces intervene in the course of nature and in all that men think and do. Miracles are by no means rare. Man is not in control of his own life. Evil spirits may take possession of him. Satan may inspire him with evil thoughts. Alternatively, God may inspire his thought and guide his purposes.
(R. Bultmann, "New Testament and Mythology," in Kerygma and Myth (New York: Harper and Row, 1961), p. 1)

There should be no difficulty in identifying the conclusion of Bultmann's argument. It is the first sentence:
    The cosmology of the N.T. is essentially mythical in character.
Nor should there be any difficulty in seeing that the rest of the paragraph supports this conclusion, either directly or indirectly. The difficulty lies in determining what constitutes the premises

92

of the main argument and what constitutes supporting premises for these in turn.

Why is the cosmology of the New Testament essentially mythical in character? Well, the first
reason is obvious. Bultmann states:
    The world is viewed as a three-storied
    structure, with the earth in the center,
    the heaven above, and the underworld beneath.
So far so good. This is premise 1. Note the next
three sentences dealing with heaven, hell, and
earth. These expand the discussion, indicating
how these are conceived of in New Testament terms.
They are probably best represented as three additional main premises. (Note here that these
three sentences do not indicate why the world is
viewed as three-storied; so they are not mini-
premises in support of main premise 1.)

But note the sentence about earth being more than
the scene of natural, everyday events. Why is it
thought of in this way? Bultmann gives some
reasons (these would be mini-premises on behalf
of this main premise). They include:
    1. It is the scene of the supernatural
       activity of God and his angels on the
       one hand, and of Satan and his demons
       on the other.
    2. These supernatural forces intervene in
       the course of nature and in all that men
       think and do.
    3. Miracles are by no means rare.

But note the next sentence:
    Man is not in control of his own life.
Is this an additional mini-premise supporting the
contention that earth is more than the scene of
natural, everyday events? Or is it a separate main
premise in its own right? Has Bultmann ceased
talking about the New Testament conception of
earth and moved to talking about the New Testament
conception of man? Is it a separate topic?

The context doesn't help us here, and we are faced
with a choice: either to place the sentence "Man

is not in control of his own life" in support
space (supporting the main premise about earth
being more than the scene of natural, everyday
events) or else placing it in main argument space
as an additional main premise. In terms of what
Bultmann has written, there is no way of resolving
this ambiguity. Either way of reconstructing it
would be equally plausible.

Notice that whatever way you choose to reconstruct
the argument, the sentence
    Man is not in control of his own life
is supported in turn by three considerations:
    1. Evil spirits may take possession of him.
    2. Satan may inspire him with evil thoughts.
    3. Alternatively, God may inspire his thought
       and guide his purposes.

So: bearing in mind this fairly localized ambiguity in the argument, either of the following
reconstructions would be correct:

(I) <u>support space</u>   <u>main argument space</u>

1.Evil
spirts
...him.
2.Satan
may in-
spire
...evil
3.God
may in-
spire
...pur-
poses

1.It is the scene
  of the supernat...
  on the other.
2.These supernat
  forces...men
  think and do.
3.Miracles are by
  no means rare

→4.Man is not in
   control of his
   own life.

1.The world is viewed
  as a 3-storied struc-
  ture, with earth in
  the center, heaven
  above, and under-
  world beneath.
2.Heaven is the abode
  of God and of the
  celestial beings--
  the angels.
3.The underworld is
  hell, the place of
  torment.
4.Even the earth is
  more than the scene
  of natural, every-
  day events, of the
  trivial round and
  common task.

∴ The cosmology of the N.T. is essentially mythical in character.

(II) <u>support space</u>

<u>main argument space</u>

1. The world is viewed as a three-storied structure, with the earth in the center, the heaven above, and the underworld beneath.
2. Heaven is the above...the angels.

1. It is the scene of the supernat...on the other.
2. These supernat. forces...men think and do.
3. Miracles are...rare.

3. The underworld...torment.
4. Even the earth...common task.

1. Evil spirits...him.
2. Satan may...thoughts.
3. God may...purposes.

5. Man is not in control of his own life.

∴ The cosmology of the N.T. is essentially mythical in character.

At issue between interpretation (I) and (II) is whether or not the sentence "Man is not in control of his own life" constitutes a distinct separate premise of the main argument or whether it is a mini-premise in support of some other point. From the context, it is impossible for us to tell which Bultmann intended. Perhaps a slight preference could be accorded the first interpretation, on the grounds that the conclusion explicitly mentions 'cosmology' and cosmology usually has to do with cosmic entities like heaven, hell and earth rather than terrestrial entities like man. However, not much of substance hangs on which reconstruction we put forward.

A somewhat more muddled argument is found in the

following selection:
(h) Flextime (Flexible Working Hours) often makes workers more productive because being treated as responsible adults gives them greater commitment to their jobs. As a result it decreases absenteeism, sick leave, tardiness and overtime, and generally produces significant increases in productivity for the work group as a whole. For example, in trial periods in three different departments the U.S. Social Security Administration measured productivity increases averaging about 20 percent. Many companies that have tried flextime have recorded increases of at least five to 10 percent, and none has reported a decline. (Barry Stein et al., "Flextime," in Psychology Today, June, 1976, p. 43)

The general point of the selection appears to be:
    Flextime often makes workers more productive.
And a reason is given (note the "because"):
    Being treated as responsible adults gives
    them greater commitment to their jobs.
An assumption here seems to be that Flextime treats people as responsible adults. But note the sentence: "As a result, it...." As a result of what? And what does "it" refer to? To Flextime? To being treated as responsible adults? To greater job commitment? It's hard to tell from the context. At any rate, "it" (whatever it is) decreases absenteeism, sick leave, tardiness, and overtime, and generally produces significant increases in productivity for the work group as a whole. This probably represents an expanded version of the conclusion, spelling out in greater detail the sort of productivity being considered.

Then a sentence occurs beginning with "for example" --an example of what? Productivity, it would appear. And it, and the following sentence, would appear to provide support (rather than illustration) for the claim that Flextime increases productivity. Thus what is said in this sentence, and in the concluding one, would both be premises.

There's a considerable amount of judgment and interpretation in this analysis, but it's the best that can be done in the light of what is written in the selection. Bearing in mind its tentative nature, the argument is perhaps reconstructed as follows:

support space	main argument space
< Flextime treats people as responsible adults >	1. Being treated as responsible adults gives them greater commitment to their jobs.
	2. In trial periods in three different departments the U.S. Social Security Administration measured productivity increases averaging about 20 percent.
	3. Many companies that have tried flextime have recorded increases of at least five to 10 percent, and none has reported a decline.

∴. Flextime often makes workers more productive.

(or ∴. Flextime decreases absenteeism, sick leave, tardiness and overtime, and generally produces significant increases in productivity for the work group as a whole.)

Many arguments make reference to studies or scientific experiments in the course of developing a conclusion. Consider, for example, this selection.

(i) The medical community has long debated the effects of tobacco smoke on non-smokers. Now recent studies have bolstered the contention of many physicians that, apart from the clear health hazard to smokers, tobacco smoke has harmful effects on non-smokers as well. In

97

fact, in 1972 the U.S. Surgeon-General devoted
fully a quarter of his 226-page report, "The
Health Consequences of Smoking," to the
effects of smoke on non-smokers. Other
people's smoking, says the report, is retard-
ing fetal growth and increasing the incidence
of premature birth; is exacerbating respiratory allergies in children and adults; and
is causing acute irritation and taxing hearts
and lungs of non-smokers by filling the air in
smoky rooms with carbon monoxide, the deadly
poison found in automobile exhaust.
(Reader's Digest, July 1974, pp.102, 104)

The conclusion is:
Apart from the clear health hazard to smokers,
tobacco smoke has harmful effects on non-
smokers as well.
This conclusion is bolstered by recent studies,
says the selection, although only one such study
is in fact cited, namely, that conducted by the
U.S. Surgeon General in 1972. That report cites
specific scientific findings. These may be usefully itemized as follows:
Other people's smoking:
a) retards fetal growth;
b) increases incidence of premature birth;
c) exacerbates respiratory allergies in children and adults;
d) causes acute irritation and taxes the hearts
and lungs of non-smokers by filling the
air with carbon monoxide.
This information constitutes the premise which
supports the conclusion. On what is this finding
based? On the U.S. Surgeon General's 1972 report
entitled "The Health Consequences of Smoking."
Because this report contains the information which
supports the first premise, it is positioned in
the support space of the format.

support space	main argument space
1. U.S. Surgeon General's 1972 report entitled "The Health Consequences of Smoking"	1. Other people's smoking: a) retards fetal growth; b) increases incidence of premature birth;

c) exacerbates respiratory
   allergies in children
   and adults;
d) causes acute irritation
   ...with carbon monoxide.

∴ Apart from the clear
  health hazard to smok-
  ers, tobacco smoke has
  harmful effects on non-
  smokers as well.

In this selection, the general over-all point, the
conclusion, is supported by the findings of many
scientific studies which are summarized in the U.S.
Surgeon-General's 1972 Report. The details of
these studies are not entered into here; only the
findings of the studies are mentioned in premise
1. The name of the Report is helpfully included,
however, since it provides the source of the information contained in premise 1. Anyone wanting to
check out the veracity of the information could
conceivably obtain the Report and read the relevant
portions.

In reading arguments that refer to studies or
experiments, you should carefully note the following kinds of information that such arguments usually contain. Unravelling these will greatly help
you discern the structure of the argument.
   (1) the number of studies
Note carefully how many different studies or experiments are referred to in the course of the argument. Often these are identified by the name of
the researcher. Then trace through in each study or
experiment the following:
   (2) the details of the study or experiment
Note carefully what details of the study or experiment are given in the argument: e.g., the number
of subjects tested, the method of testing, when
and where the study was carried out, the length of
the study, etc.
   (3) the finding of the study or experiment
Note carefully what the study or experiment indicates or shows--its basic "finding:"

99

(4) the general over-all point
Note, where applicable, the general over-all point
the arguer makes on the basis of the findings.

In general, (4) is based on (3) which, in turn, is
based on (2). Seen in reverse, the flow of support
is from the experiment or study (2), to the finding
(3), to the general over-all point which one or
more studies may indicate (4). This can be depicted
visually. Suppose, for instance, an arguer appeals
to one study in the course of supporting a general
over-all point. The structure of this sort of argument could be sketched schematically as follows:

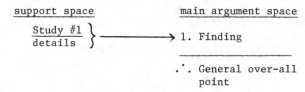

Or suppose an arguer appeals to three separate
studies, all of which support the same general
over-all point. Schematically this sort of argument can be sketched as follows:

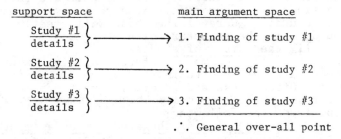

The schematic sketches clearly show the flow of
support from the details of the studies to their
findings to the general over-all point. With
these schemas in mind, carefully consider the
structure of the arguments contained in the next
two selections:
(j) The No Smoking section of an airplane is like-

ly to contain as much tobacco smoke as the smoking section does, according to a recent study conducted by John Walker of the Energy Resources Co. of Cambridge, Massachusetts. Walker found that the ventilation system spreads smoky air democratically throughout the plane.

During a Boeing 707 flight from Boston to Los Angeles, Walker measured the number of particles in both sections of the cabin at various intervals. One hour into the flight, his detector found 18,000 tobacco particulates per cubic centimeter in the nonsmoking area and 50,000 in the smoking section of the aircraft. But after another hour, the particulate level in the nonsmoking section actually "surpassed the smokers' section," reports Walker.

The particulate count ranged from a high of 150,000 just before the plane took off to a low of 14,000 in midflight, when most passengers were asleep.
(<u>Science Digest Special</u>, Spring 1980, p. 99)

The <u>general over-all</u> point is stated at the outset:
> the no smoking section of an airplane is likely to contain as much tobacco smoke as the smoking section does.

This, of course, is the conclusion of the argument. It is based on one study -- John Walker's. His <u>finding</u> is stated explicitly (note the helpful phrase "Walker found...".):
> the ventilation system spreads smoky air democratically throughout the plane.

This is the main premise. This, in turn, is supported by the various <u>details</u> of the study (the Boeing 707 flight; the number of tobacco particulates in smoking and non smoking sections of the plane 1 hour and 2 hours into the flight; the high and low particle count).

We are now in a position to display the argument contained in selection (j).

support space	main argument space

John Walker's study
1. On a Boston to Los Angeles
Boeing 707 flight, tobacco
particles in both cabin sections were measured.
- 1 hr into flight:
  18,000 particulates/cc
  (nonsmoking)
  50,000 particulates/cc
  (smoking)
- 2 hrs into flight:
  particulate level in
  nonsmoking section
  surpassed smoking
  section.
- ranged from high of 150,000
  (just before take-off) to
  low of 14,000 (in midflight
  when most asleep)

1. The ventilation sys-
   tem spreads smoky
   air democratically
   throughout the plane.

.˙. The nonsmoking sec-
tion of an airplane
is likely to contain
as much tobacco smoke
as the smoking sec-
tion does.

Consider next this selection:
(k) By human standards the number of signals
    employed by each species of animal is sever-
    ely limited. One of the most curious facts
    revealed by recent field studies is that even
    the most highly social vertebrates rarely
    have more than 30 or 35 separate displays in
    their entire repertory. Data compiled by
    Martin H. Moynihan of the Smithsonian Insti-
    tution indicate that among most vertebrates
    the number of displays varies by a factor of
    only three of four from species to species.
    The number ranges from a minimum of 10 in
    certain fishes to a maximum of 37 in the
    rhesus monkey, one of the primates closest
    to man in the complexity of their social
    organization....

102

In the extent of their signal diversity the
vertebrates are closely approached by social
insects, particularly honeybees and ants.
Analyses by Charles G. Butler at the Rotham-
sted Experimental Station in England, by me
at Harvard University and by others have
brought the number of individual known signal
categories within single species of these
insects to between 10 and 20....
(Edward O. Wilson,"Animal Communication,"
in Communication (San Francisco: Freeman &
Co., 1972), p. 32)

Again we have an argument which refers to various
studies and so it is important to sort out the
number of studies, the details, the findings, and
the general over-all point.

Let's begin with the last item. The general over-
all point (or conclusion) is the first sentence:
    By human standards the number of signals
    employed by each species of animal is
    severely limited.
This conclusion is supported by two main sorts of
studies: studies on the vertebrates by Moynihan
(paragraph one), and studies on insects such as
the honeybees and ants by Butler, Wilson and
others (paragraph two). Having come this far, the
details and findings of each study need now to be
unravelled.

Consider Moynihan's data. The details here are
unfortunately sketchy--recent field studies. The
data support (note the helpful word "indicate")
the finding that
    among most vertebrates the number of displays
    varies by a factor of only 3 or 4 from
    species to species (from a min. of 10 in fish
    to a max. of 37 in rhesus monkeys).
Interestingly enough, this finding supports in
turn a yet more general finding
    even the most highly social vertebrates rare-
    ly have more than 30 or 35 separate displays
    in their entire repertory
This is main premise 1, for it, in turn supports

103

<u>the general over-all point</u> (the conclusion).

We now have the flow of support traced for the
first study and we find that it involves a slightly more complicated arrangement than the initial
schema indicated. This need not throw us off,
since what supports what is clearly indicated.
In our format, the "yet more general finding"
appears as premise 1 in the main argument space;
the finding which supports it is placed in support
space, and the details which support it are mentioned even further to the left in support space.

A similar development occurs in the second study
in paragraph two. No details are given of the
studies by Butler, Wilson and others on insects
such as honeybees and ants. What is indicated,
however, is their finding, namely:
     the number of individual known signal
     categories within single species of
     these insects is between 10 and 20.
This finding in turn supports a yet more general
finding:
     in the extent of their signal diversity
     the vertebrates are closely approached
     by social insects, particularly honeybees
     and ants.
This in turn supports the general over-all point,
the conclusion. It is the second main premise.

The argument contained in selection (k) can now
be identified as follows:

support space		main argument space
Moynihan's study recent field studies	1. Among most verte- brates the...(10 in fish to a max. of 37 in rhesus monkeys)	1. Even the most highly social vertebrates rarely have more than 30 or 35 separate displays in their entire repertory.
Butler, Wilson & others studies on honey-bees, ants	1. The number of ... between 10 and 20	2. In the extent of their signal diver- sity the vertebrates are closely approach- ed by social insects,

particularly honey-
bees and ants.

∴ By human standards
the number of sig-
nals employed by
each species of
animal is severely
limited.

some final comments

Hopefully you will have patiently and carefully
worked through these selections and compared your
results with the discussion in the text. This
will have provided you with valuable practice in
the skills involved in argument identification.
It's been something of an apprenticeship training
program.

Now it's time to consolidate what you have learned and Exercise #1 below provides yet more opportunities to practice. In identifying the arguments
contained in these selections, remember
     (1) the basic strategy in identifying the
        structure of all arguments, and
     (2) the major elements involved in arguments
        which feature studies or scientific
        experiments.
You're on your own!

Recall Quiz

(1) What are some of the reasons why the structure
of an argument may be obscure?

(2) Should we always expect that each and every
argument will have one and only one correct
identification? If not, why not?

(3) What suggestions were made for handling the
following: space limitations on the worksheet?
repeated information? background information?
examples? information after a colon? informa-

105

tion after a semi-colon? sentences which list
considerations?

(4) In reading arguments that refer to studies or
experiments, about what structural details
should we become clear in identifying the
argument?

Exercise #1

Using standard format, identify the argument contained in each of the following selections:

(1) The diet works because it specifically mobili-
zes fat, stimulates the release of ketones and
fat mobilizers, thereby, suppressing hunger;
causes a disproportionately greater loss of
fat; helps eliminate excess water; stabilizes
blood sugar; lowers insulin levels and corti-
sol levels; and delivers a metabolic advantage.
(Robert C.Atkins, Shirley Linde, Dr. Atkins'
Super-Energy Diet (New York: Bantam, 1977),
p. 130)

(2) There are several ways of settling labor-
management disputes: striking to force demands
or else third-party binding arbitration.
Striking to gain one's demands is an out-dated
and unhelpful method of resolving disputes.
For one thing, it holds up innocent people as
hostages. Furthermore, workers rarely recoup
their losses after a strike. And, what's
more it creates a climate of hostility and
paranoia in the work environment. Consequently labor-management feuds should be settled
by binding third-party arbitration.

(3) Samuel Butler's The Authoress of the Odyssey
was first published in 1897 and is still
available in a modern edition. Butler argues
on behalf of two main theses: first, that the
Iliad and the Odyssey were composed by two
different authors approximately two hundred
years apart, the Odyssey being the later of
the poems; second, that the Odyssey was
written by a young woman living on

Sicily.

It is this notion that the Odyssey is the work of a woman which concerns the present issue. In order to make his case. Butler first tries to remove initial doubts on the part of the reader by showing that there were women poets at the time the epic was composed. He then goes on to examine closely internal evidence which the poem itself provides that could lead one to suppose that it was the work of a woman. The poet, for example, has made numerous errors which Butler tells us no man would make, such as describing a boat as having a rudder fore and aft. Much of the story is built around feminine interests of home and family life. In contrast to the foolish foibles of mankind, womankind in the Odyssey is portrayed as something to be taken very seriously. Men are consistently placed in the position of needing the support and wise counsel of women.

(Dennis Dutton, "Plausibility and Aesthetic Interpretation," Canadian Jr. of Philosophy 7 (1977), pp.336,337)

(4) Many reasons have been advanced by those who favor the retention of legislation forbidding homosexual behavior....
1. Homosexual activity is offensive. It is a source of disgust to those who find themselves in a position where they must witness public displays of behavior that offend ordinary moral, religious, and even aesthetic feelings. Public lavatories, parks, and theaters become the gathering places of homosexuals who are looking for sexual contacts....
2. Homosexual activity is unnatural.
3. Homosexual activity is dangerous. Its practice by some people encourages others to do the same, and, if everyone or even if large numbers of persons were to become homosexuals, there would be no future for the human race. Furthermore, homosexuality may

lead, as Lord Devlin pointed out, to a
general moral breakdown and to the destruc-
tion of vital social institutions.
4. Homosexuals tend to molest children....the
effect of liberalized legislation would be
to bring the homosexuals out into the open,
to increase their numbers, and to encourage
them to prey upon the young boys whom they
find most attractive.
5. When homosexuals do seduce youngsters,
they often initiate them irreversibly into
their way of life.
6. Homosexuality is a promiscuous way of
life. Few homosexual relations are more
than one-night stands, and fewer still have
any semblance of permanence. Aside from the
blatant immorality of such a life, it encourages the spread of venereal disease, and it
leads to loneliness, misery, and unhappiness
for those who become entangled in it....
7. Those who become entangled in the homosexual life are afflicted by serious psychological problems--by feelings of guilt, by
insecurity, and by constant fear of disgrace
and ruin.
8. Homosexuals are unreliable and are poor
risks. They should not be given sensitive
jobs, either in government or in industry....
  (Burton M. Leiser, Liberty, Justice, and
  Morals (New York: Macmillan, 1973), pp.36,
  37).

(5)   To sum up, my argument has been that having
      a right to life presupposes that one is
      capable of desiring to continue existing as
      a subject of experiences and other mental
      states. This in turn presupposes both that
      one has the concept of such a continuing
      entity and that one believes that one is
      oneself such an entity. So an entity that
      lacks such a consciousness of itself as a
      continuing subject of mental states does
      not have a right to life.
        (Michael Tooley, "Abortion and Infanticide,"
        in Marshall Cohen et al (eds.), The Rights

and Wrongs of Abortion (Princeton: Princeton Univ. Press, 1974), p. 64)

(6) There is nothing in the historical record to
      show that censorship of religious or politi-
      cal ideas has had any lasting effect. Christ-
      ianity flourished despite the efforts of the
      Roman Emperors to suppress it. Heresies and
      new religions developed and flourished in
      the Christian era at the height of religious
      suppression. The theories of democracy did
      not die out even though kings opposed them.
      And the efforts in recent times to suppress
      the Communist ideology and to keep it from
      people has not had a measurable or determin-
      able success.
           (Eugene McCarthy, untitled article in
           Censorship: For and Against, introduced
           by Harold H. Hart (New York: Hart, 1971),
           p. 117)

(7) In spite of these menacing developments
      (nuclear weapons, overpopulation, biological
      and psycho-pharmacological engineering,
      cybernation, changes in the environment) we
      remain unable to forecast the social consequ-
      ences of technology. This is partly because
      of the limited vision of both the non-
      scientists and the scientists. The first
      group does not have sufficient knowledge of
      technology to sense the potentialities of
      new developments and therefore cannot predict
      their social impact, and they are too pre-
      occupied with conventional assessments of
      political issues and impacts. The second
      group is aware of the technological possibil-
      ities but is not sufficiently sensitive to
      their social implications. Some of the
      scientists care only about the success of
      their favorite projects. Some apply to these
      problems a personal pseudo-sociology made
      useless by its arrogance or naivete. And
      still others dodge responsibility by arguing
      that technology itself is neither good nor
      bad, that its virtues are determined by its
      uses.

Another reason why the social repercussions of science are difficult to forecast is that we have too little understanding of the social processes. This limitation has been fostered by the disinclination of the natural scientist and the government operator to stimulate work in the social sciences. The bureaucrat feels threatened by the possibility that formalized knowledge will replace "experience" and "political knowhow." Furthermore, the social sciences might demonstrate that the products of technology, or even science itself, need social control.
  (D.N. Michael, "Science, Scientists, and Politics," in Willis H. Truitt, T.W. Graham Solomons (eds.), Science, Technology and Freedom (Boston: Houghton Mifflin, 1974), p. 180)

(8) An expert on ancient religious practices, Manly P. Hall, hypothesizes in his book, The Secret Teachings of All Ages, that the Pyramid was built by survivors of Atlantis, the lost continent. Some suggest that the leading scientists of the Atlantean civilization became aware of an impending disaster and, in order to salvage the treasures and knowledge of their age, emigrated out of the destructive reach of the cataclysm to other lands. One of these lands, theorizes Hall, was Egypt, where the Atlanteans established centers of learning, built, like their native temples, in pyramidal shapes. In these learning centers they hid their secrets, embodied in symbolic language, to be uncovered and understood only by those who were worthy of acquiring and using this sacred knowledge.

In this chapter titled, "The Initiation of the Pyramid," Hall notes that it is highly unlikely that the Egyptians erected the Pyramid because the interior walls are void of inscriptions, paintings, and other symbolism usually associated with elaborate royal decorations.

(Max Toth and Greg Nielsen, <u>Pyramid Power</u>
(New York: Destiny, 1976), p. 100)

(9) <u>The Centralization of Control</u>
Television is dominated by a relative handful
of the largest corporate powers in the
world....

In 1960 the trade publication <u>Advertising Age</u>
commented, "Network television, particularly,
is largely the creature of the 100 largest
companies in the country."

Though there are more than 400,000 corporations in America, the 100 largest advertisers
in the country accounted for 83 percent of
all network television advertising during
that year. The top twenty-five of these
accounted for 65 percent of the 83 percent.
Since that time, the ratio has scarcely
altered.

Public television also fits that mold. During 1975 more than 40 percent of all public-
television programming was paid for by these
same 100 companies: mainly oil, chemical,
and drug companies.
    (Jerry Mander, "Arguments for the Elimina-
    tion of Television," <u>Penthouse</u> (March 1978),
    p. 131)

(10) <u>Those Second Thoughts are Usually Best</u>

<u>True</u> or <u>false</u>? Changing an answer on a
multiple-choice test is usually a mistake,
because most people's initial impulse is
correct.
<u>False</u>.
Contrary to what teachers have told us for
years, changing your answer not only increases your chances of doing better, but, in addition, the more answers you change, the
higher your score is likely to be. Psychol-
ogist Gerald R. Stoffer and two associates
from Pacific Lutheran University gave nine
standard academic multiple-choice exams to 76
college students, and two technical multiple-
choice exams to 107 Air Force enlistees.

111

For each test, there were considerably more wrong-to-right changes than right-to-wrong changes.

More than two-thirds of both groups improved their scores by changing answers. When the researchers compared scores based on initial answers with those based on final answers, however, they found that students at the top of the class remained there whether their changes were taken into consideration or not. Further, the researchers discovered that in both groups of test-takers, those with the highest scores changed the fewest answers.

Their advice: if you know the subject well, sticking to your first impulse won't hurt you. If you are shaky, you might profit by making some changes.
    (Psychology Today (March 1978), p. 114)

(11) The effect of imposed stereotypes has been clearly demonstrated by experiments in the United States. In one, (Philip Goldberg, "Are Women Prejudiced Against Women?" Trans-Action, University of Washington, April 1968, pp. 28-30) a number of university women were selected to read six articles. Some concerned "masculine" subjects such as city planning, others treated neutral subjects such as the history of art, and still others were about such "feminine" interests as dietetics. In some booklets, three articles were signed with male and three with female names. In others, the male and female "authorship" was reversed. The women were asked to read and appraise each article, without having their attention called to the authors' names. In all cases, articles under male signatures received higher ratings. It was concluded, in the study, that the respondents' choices had been influenced by belief in the intellectual superiority of men.
    (Report of the Royal Commission of the Status of Women in Canada (Ottawa, 1970)

112

p. 13)

(12) A recent five year study at a major electro-
nics company indicates that getting fired may
have a lot to do with overreaching.
Among 2,000 technical, sales, and managerial
employees who were followed during their
first five years with the company, the 173
people who eventually were fired started out
with much higher expectations of advancement
than either the 200 people who left volun-
tarily or the people who remained. On a
questionnaire given during their first week
on the job, more than half the people who
were fired within the first two years ranked
themselves among the top 5 percent of typical
people in their job category. Only 38 percent of those who stayed with the company
ranked themselves that highly.
(Psychology Today, March 1980, pp.25)

Exercise #2 - Further Practice in Argument Prepara-
tion and Presentation

format A - an in-class debate

Same format as in Ex.#2 in Ch. 2 (see p.72),
except that after each round of presenting
arguments, each group will huddle for a
couple of minutes to prepare and present a 1
minute response.

In preparing your argument, it is important
to anticipate as best you can the sorts of
considerations your opponents are likely to
advance.

format B - an essay

Same format as in Ex.#2 in Ch. 2 (see p.73),

Exercise #3 - Finding Arguments

Collect 2 arguments from a newspaper, magazine,
book, etc. Then identify the argument each selection contains, using standard format.

CHAPTER FOUR

THE ARENA OF CONTROVERSY

1. The Wider Context of Argument

the human context

So far in this text we have focused entirely on
argument structure and on argument identification.
Just to summarize what we have done up to this
point: we've learned the basic structural features
of an argument, and we have gained some practice
in learning how to identify arguments accurately.

This is a good beginning. Argument identification
must take place before argument evaluation. We
need to know what the argument is before we can
consider how good it is. Before we leave argument
identification and pass on to argument evaluation,
there is another side to this aspect of the study
of argument that needs to be recognized.

You may have noticed that we've been looking at
arguments in isolation from the contexts in which
they occur as arguments. In other words, so far
we've just been inspecting the arguments themselves, observing their structural features, and
forgetting about the human context in which they
occur.

The wider context of argument is provided by the
whole arena of controversy in which arguments are
found. Arguments are typically made and discussed
in inter-personal situations, as people thrash
out different points of view within the formats
provided by society and culture generally. In
studying argument, we need to be aware of some
of the important considerations and issues that

115

arise when examining arguments in relation to the broader personal, social and cultural contexts within which argumentation takes place.

This chapter focuses on four important relationships arguments have to various features of the wider context in which they occur. It will raise some issues which these interrelationships pose, and examine some of them briefly. And it will also provide an opportunity for you, the student of argument, to enter into the arena of controversy and to gain experience in preparing and presenting an argument.

four interrelationships

Before we probe these four interrelationships, you should note the following general points about argument. They are obvious, perhaps, but they need to be recognized nonetheless.

(1) Arguments rarely occur alone. The reason for this is that arguments are found in contentious contexts, as people try to sort out what to do or what is true about some particular issue. Usually, when one person presents an argument, someone else jumps in with an argument in reply. In following a controversy or in working our way through an issue, what we normally come across is not an argument but rather an exchange of arguments, that is, a whole collection of arguments that relate to the matter under discussion.

In any exchange of arguments there is usually considerable disagreement. It is important to note where the disagreement occurs. It might be over the conclusion; or it might be over a particular premise; and so on. It is also important to note how the controversy develops, who responds to what point, what points get dropped, what new considerations are introduced, etc. This requires looking at arguments in relation to other arguments, noticing how they stack up against each other and where they differ.

(2) Arguments are made by arguers
This obvious point needs to be noticed. Up until
now no mention has been made in this text of the
persons involved in arguing. People, after all,
are the key participants. In any controversy
they are the ones who disagree, who make and
exchange arguments.

Arguers, of course, have their own concerns,
various vested interests, and different objectives in arguing. What role do arguers play in
argumentation? How do their concerns, interests
and objectives affect the course of a controversy?
And how do these affect its outcome? Questions
of this sort arise when arguments are considered
in relation to the arguers themselves.

(3) Arguments are examined by us, the
students of argument.
Arguers aren't the only persons involved in
argumentation. We should not forget ourselves,
we "argument analysts" (as we may conveniently
refer to ourselves). We inspect controversies
and the arguments they contain as arguers battle
to and fro. In so doing, in identifying and
evaluating arguments, we do not enter into the
arena of controversy itself. Rather we stand
back from the fray, adopting a god-like stance,
and calmly survey what takes place before us.
We try to sort out who is saying what, and we
judge it critically.

We, too, of course, have our own concerns, our
various vested interests, and our objectives in
examining controversies. What role do these
play in our attempt to identify arguments accurately and to judge them critically and fairly?
How do they affect our perception of the argument's structure and our estimation of its worth
as an argument? Questions of this sort arise
when arguments are considered in relation to
argument analysts who identify and evaluate
arguments critically.

(4) Arguments occur within the frameworks
of society generally.

Arguments play an important role in society.
Indeed society creates formats for rational
discussion of issues (e.g. meetings, legislatures,
courts, etc.), and provides opportunities where
contentious points of view can be discussed and
criticized (e.g. on radio, TV, in newspapers,
in classrooms, etc.). Societies differ in terms
of these formats. In a society such as ours,
however, one that attempts to encourage individual participation in political decision-making,
rational argument is supported by political
objectives and by political rights, such as the
right to free speech and the right of free
association.

But what role ought argument to play in our
society? And what role does it in fact play?
How does the systematic and rational presentation
of evidence relate to attempts to persuade, to
prod, to pressure, or to manipulate people into
accepting a position? Indeed what is the whole
role of reason in society? Such far-reaching
issues as these are raised when arguments are
considered in relation to society generally.

In sum, these four comments point to four important relationships arguments have when the wider
context of argument is considered. To recapitu-
late, these four relationships are as follows:

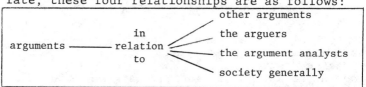

We'll discuss these relationships one-by-one,
noting in greater detail what issues each of them
raises. Some of these issues will be discussed
in the text: others are best left for general
discussion in class.

2. Arguments in relation to other Arguments

brief exchanges

Consider the following brief exchange of arguments:

(a) Ernie: Old people have the right to die with dignity. When faced with certain death due to terminal illness, the aged should be allowed to make "a living will" requesting the doctors not to use extraordinary means to prolong their life. The medical profession, moreover, accustomed to extending the quantity of life, should change its focus to encompass the quality of life. That's why I think the law should be changed to allow euthanasia on demand for terminally-ill old people.

Bert: I disagree. After all, many old people aren't in a position to make a living will: they're either afraid of dying and want to pretend everything is O.K. or else they're too sick to make a rational request. Also, if the medical profession changes its focus, then doctors will soon take it upon themselves to judge the quality of life in other cases, e.g. the depressed, the maimed, the unemployed, etc. as well as the terminally ill.

In examining arguments in relation to other arguments, what we're essentially doing is comparing the arguments with one another. In a simple exchange, whereby one speaker presents one argument and another speaker another argument, this sort of comparison can best be accomplished by doing the following:

(1) identify the argument of each arguer.
(2) state how the second argument relates to the first argument. (This will tell us where the disagreement lies.)
(3) state how the first arguer could reply

to the second arguer. (This will tell us
<u>how</u> the exchange is apt to continue.)

Following this outline, let us first of all identify the argument of each speaker. In setting out
Bert's argument, note that he begins with "I disagree." With what is Bert disagreeing? It should
be evident that he's disagreeing with the conclusion of Ernie's argument. Bert is maintaining,
in other words, that the law should not be changed
to allow euthanasia on demand for terminally-ill
old people. Because he hasn't said this explicitly, these words will be placed in wedges.

Ernie's argument
support space

main argument space
1. Old people have the right to
   die with dignity.
2. When faced with certain
   death due to terminal illness, the aged should be
   allowed to make a "living
   will" requesting the doctors
   not to use extraordinary
   means to prolong their life.
3. The medical profession,
   accustomed to extending the
   quantity of life, should
   change its focus to encompass the quality of life.

∴. This law should be changed
   to allow euthanasia on
   demand for terminally-ill
   old people.

Bert's argument
support space

main argument space
1. Many old people aren't in
   a position to make a living
   will: they're either afraid
   of dying and want to pretend
   everything is O.K. or else
   they're too sick to make a
   rational request.
2. If the medical profession

changes its focus, then doctors will soon take it upon themselves to judge the quality of life in other cases, e.g. the depressed, the maimed, the unemployed, etc., as well as the terminally-ill.

∴ < The law should not be changed to allow euthanasia on demand for terminally-ill old people. >

Next consider how Bert's argument relates to Ernie's. This can be simply stated as follows:
(1) The conclusion of Bert's argument disagrees with the conclusion of Ernie's argument.
(2) Bert's argument ignores premise 1 of Ernie's argument.
(3) Premise 1 of Bert's argument attacks premise 2 of Ernie's argument.
(4) Premise 2 of Bert's argument attacks premise 3 of Ernie's argument.

Consider then the possible ways in which Ernie could reply to Bert:
(1) Ernie could capitulate -- that is, he could agree with Bert.
(2) Ernie could elaborate on his premise 1 which Bert ignores.
(3) Ernie could attack premise 1 of Bert's argument (or else modify his own premise 2 so as to accommodate the point expressed in Bert's premise 1).
(4) Ernie could attack premise 2 of Bert's argument (for example, by showing that these horrible consequences would not follow).

This completes our comparison of the two arguments.

We know wherein the disagreement lies. And we have some inkling of how the exchange could continue. How it actually will go, of course, is another matter, and depends on what Ernie wants to show and how long he is prepared to argue. Note that comparisons depend upon accurate argument identification.

Consider another simple exchange between two speakers.

(b) Mary: The heart of the abortion issue is the question: what is a person? In my judgment, and in the opinion of many others today, a human organism is a person only (a) when it is capable of interacting actively with other people and the world, and (b) when it is capable of rational thought. A fetus isn't a person. Why? Because a fetus can't interact actively with other people and the world, and it isn't capable of rational thought. Therefore aborting a fetus isn't the same thing as killing a person.

Judy: I agree, first of all, with your definition of 'person'. There is, however, another issue that must be carefully considered: when does a human organism become a person? A fetus doesn't become a person just by being born. Infants and young children, after all, aren't persons, since they are incapable of engaging in rational thought, although they can, to some extent, interact actively with other people and the world. Thus the killing of infants and young children isn't the same thing as killing a person. And it, too, ought to be permitted.

Let us first of all identify the argument of each participant in this exchange.

Mary's argument
support space

1. A fetus can't interact actively with other people and the world.
2. A fetus isn't capable of rational thought.

main argument space

1. The heart of the abortion issue is the question: what is a person?
2. In my judgment, and in the opinion of many others today, a human organism is person only (a) when it is capable of interacting actively with other people and the world, and (b) when it is capable of rational thought.
3. A fetus isn't a person

∴ Aborting a fetus isn't the same thing as killing a person.

Judy's argument
support space

1. They are incapable of rational thought.
2. They can, to some extent, interact actively with other people and the world.

1. Infants and young children aren't persons.

main argument space

1. I agree with your definition of 'person'
2. There is another issue that must be carefully considered: when does a human organism become a person?

3. A fetus doesn't become a person just by being born.

∴ The killing of infants and young children isn't the same thing as killing a person

& it, too, ought to be permitted.

123

How do the two arguments compare?
  (1) The conclusion of Mary's argument speaks
       of abortion, whereas the conclusion of
       Judy's argument speaks of infanticide
       (that is, the killing of infants and
       young children). Both agree that these
       acts do not involve the killing of a
       person. Judy is advocating infanticide
       (as well as abortion).
  (2) Premise 1 of Judy's argument agrees
       with premise 2 of Mary's argument. That
       is, they both agree on the definition of
       'person'.
  (3) Premise 2 of Judy's argument raises
       another issue than the one stated in
       premise 1 of Mary's argument.
  (4) Premise 3 of Judy's argument extends the
       line of thought expressed in premise 3
       of Mary's argument, pointing out that a
       fetus doesn't become a person just by
       being born.
  (5) Both arguers make use of the agreed-upon
       definition of 'person'. In Mary's case,
       this definition is used to support the
       view that a fetus isn't a person; in
       Judy's case, that infants and young
       children aren't.

What are some of the possible ways in which Mary
could respond to Judy?
  (1) Mary could agree with Judy's conclusion.
       That is, she could acknowledge that
       Judy's extension of her own argument to
       cover the cases of infants and young
       children is correct.
  (2) If Mary wants to maintain, however, that
       prior to birth fetuses aren't persons,
       whereas after they are--in effect uphold-
       ing her own conclusion while denying
       Judy's conclusion--she would then have
       to show how the agreed-upon definition
       of 'person' doesn't apply to infants and

young children in such a way as to rule
out their being persons.

Again, by considering the exchange of arguments
in this fashion, we gain an understanding of how
the arguments interrelate and how the discussion
could continue. Let us take a look, however, at
a much longer exchange of argument.

longer exchanges

Consider carefully the following contentious
exchange on the subject of freedom between Castle
and Frazier in B.F. Skinner's novel Walden Two.
Note what each is saying to the other at each
stage of the discussion. Frazier speaks first.
(c) "I deny that freedom exists at all. I must
     deny it--or my program would be absurd. You
     can't have a science about a subject matter
     which hops capriciously about. Perhaps we
     can never prove that man isn't free....But
     the increasing success of a science of
     behavior makes it more and more plausible."

"On the contrary, a simple personal experience makes it untenable," said Castle. "The
experience of freedom. I know that I'm
free....And what's more--you do, too....When
you deny your own freedom for the sake of
playing with a science of behavior, you're
acting in plain bad faith....At least you'll
grant that you feel free."

"The 'feeling of freedom' should deceive no
one," said Frazier. "Give me a concrete
case."

(Castle) picked up a book of matches. "I'm
free to hold or drop these matches."

"You will, of course, do one or the other,"
said Frazier....The determining forces may
be subtle but they are inexorable. I suggest
that as an orderly person you will probably
hold-ah! you drop them! Well, you see, that's
all part of your behavior with respect to me.

You couldn't resist the temptation to prove
me wrong....You had no choice."

"That's entirely too glib," said Castle.
"It's easy to argue lawfulness after the fact.
But let's see you predict what I will do in
advance. Then I'll agree there's law."
   (B.F. Skinner, Walden Two (New York:
   Macmillan, 1948), pp. 257,258)

In this selection both Frazier and Castle present
a series of arguments in the course of talking
about freedom. Frazier's position is clearly
stated in his opening speech. He contends that
freedom does not exist at all, and he supports
his claim with several reasons. These can be
paraphrased as follows: (1) that he has to deny
freedom, or else his program (in Walden Two)
would be absurd, (2) that there can't be a science
about a subject matter which hops capriciously
about, and (3) that the increasing success of a
science of behavior makes the view that man is
not free more and more plausible. Using standard
format, Frazier's position can be reconstructed
as follows: For ease of reference, let's call
this "Frazier's first argument" (F1).

(F1)   support space   main argument space

1. Freedom must be denied
   or else the Walden Two
   program would be absurd.
2. There can't be a science
   about a subject matter
   which hops capriciously
   about.
3. The increasing success of
   a science of behavior
   makes the view that man
   is not free more and more
   plausible.

∴ Freedom does not exist
  at all.

Castle, however, rejects Frazier's conclusion
(see his speech which begins "On the contrary..."
which serves to indicate that he is about to put

126

forth a position which denies what Frazier is
maintaining). He contends that freedom does
exist, and he offers some reasons to back up
this conclusion. These can be paraphrased as
follows. First of all, he appeals to "a simple
personal experience:" the experience of freedom
assures him that he is free. Moreover, he accuses
Frazier of plain bad faith: he, too, knows that
he is free, and when he denies his freedom for
the sake of playing with a science of behavior,
he's acting in plain bad faith. Castle continues
that at least Frazier will grant that he feels
free. And he gives a concrete case, when asked
to by Frazier: Castle contends that he is free
either to hold or to drop a book of matches.

Using standard format, Castle's argument can be
reconstructed as follows. For ease of reference,
let's call this "Castle's first argument" (C1).

(C1)   support space   main argument space
                                1. The experience of freedom
                                   assures me that I'm free.
                                2. You also know you're free,
                                   and when you deny your own
                                   freedom for the sake of
                                   playing with a science
                                   of behavior, you're acting
                                   in plain bad faith.
                                3. At least you'll grant that
                                   you feel free.
                                4. I'm free either to hold
                                   or to drop a book of
                                   matches.
                                   _____

                            .˙. ‹Freedom does exist.›

The debate between Frazier and Castle has now
become contentious, Frazier claiming that freedom
does not exist, while Castle affirming that it
does. Frazier decides to attack the example of
freedom that Castle has used; and, in so doing,
advances his second argument (F2) which may be
reconstructed as follows:

(F2)   support space   main argument space
                                1. The determining forces may

127

              be subtle but they are
              inexorable.

2. You couldn't resist the
      temptation to prove me
      wrong. (That's all part
      of your behavior with
      respect to me)
      ———————————————————————

∴. You had no choice (in
      dropping the book of
      matches).

Castle rejects this analysis--"That's entirely
too glib," he says. He challenges Frazer: "...
let's see you predict what I will do in advance.
Then I'll agree there's law." (Of course, by 'law'
here, both Castle and Frazier mean scientific law,
not governmental regulations). As we know from
the context, Frazier has been unable to predict
what Castle would do with the book of matches.
The upshot of Castle's line of reasoning is that
his behavior in dropping the matches does not
obey scientific law.

As reconstructed, mentioning some points evident
from the context, Castle's argument would appear
as follows:

(C2) <u>support space</u>   <u>main argument space</u>

1. If you could predict in
      advance what I will do,
      then I'll agree there's
      law.

2. < You couldn't predict
      what I would do with the
      book of matches.>
      (Castle doesn't actually
      say this--there is no
      need to, since the con-
      text makes it clear that
      Frazier had been unable
      to predict what Castle
      would do with the book of
      matches
      ———————————————————————

∴. < My behavior wasn't
      controlled by law. >

The discussion, of course, doesn't end here.
Frazier goes on, for instance, to claim that he
has been misunderstood. He never claimed he
could predict behavior and he in fact denies that
human behavior is predictable--"there are often
too many factors to be taken into account." This
represents the beginning stages of his next argument (it would be F3.) And so the discussion
goes on in Walden Two, as Castle and Frazier argue
back and forth for quite a few pages, trying to
clarify the issues, support contentions, and
persuade the other to adopt a different point of
view.

In longer exchanges, comparing arguments proceeds
in much the same fashion as in shorter exchanges:
    (1) identify the arguments of each speaker.
    (2) state the relationship between each argu-
        ment and the one directly preceeding it,
        and
    (3) state the possibilities open to each
        speaker in continuing the discussion.
We have already done (1) and so we now turn to
the second task.

Let us consider how the arguments of Castle and
Frazier relate to one another in Walden Two.
After Frazier had presented his first argument,
Castle had several options: he could have attacked
any one or other of the premises in Frazier's
argument, or he could attack Frazier's conclusion.
He chose the latter, to attack the conclusion
Frazier had put forth. In so doing, in his first
argument, Castle appeals to experience in premise
1, assumes that Frazier would likewise have had
experiences of this sort in premise 2, and contends that Frazier would at least admit to the
feeling of being free in premise 3. He then gives
an example of being free either to do or not to do
something in premise 4. In this way he supports
a very different conclusion than the one Frazier
had put forth.

After Castle had offered his first argument,
Frazier, in responding to him, also had several

options: he could have attacked any one or other of Castle's four premises, or else he could have attacked his conclusion. Notice carefully what he does not do. He does not, for instance, attack Castle's first premise (the experience of freedom premise), nor does he attack his third premise (the feeling free premise). Rather he attacks the example Castle had given in his fourth premise, and he tries to show that it does not support what Castle thinks it supports. That is, he tries to turn the example around to suit his own line of reasoning, namely, that there is no freedom. And so he presents his second argument, contending that there are determining factors in accordance with which Castle's behavior operates.

Castle rejects Frazier's analysis of his example, as set out in premise 2 of F2. Analysis of the event after it has occured is what is much too glib. Castle contends that predictability is what counts and this Frazier has been unable to do. In setting forth his second argument, Castle is beginning to explore what must be involved in his opponent's position. Is predictability involved? His line of reasoning, if more fully articulated, would go as follows: If human behavior operates in accordance with scientific law, then surely it must be predictable. It wasn't (at least Frazier couldn't do it with respect to the example of dropping the book of matches). So, therefore, human behavior doesn't operate in accordance with scientific law.

Frazier doesn't accept this conclusion, however. As the argument continues, he attacks premise 1 of C2: he denies that human behavior is predictable. And this is the thrust of his next argument. This leaves open, of course, just what is involved in Frazier's position that human behavior is not free. As the discussion proceeds, what would need to be clarified is just what is involved in Frazier's claim. If by the claim that human behavior is not free and operates in accordance with scientific law is not meant that human behavior is predictable, then just what is meant?

We can sum up this discussion as follows:

the arguments	how the arguments relate

F1

1. Freedom must be denied or else the Walden Two program would be absurd.
2. There can't be a science about a subject matter which hops capriciously about.
3. The increasing success of a science of behavior makes the view that man is not free more and more plausible.

The conclusion of F1 sets forth Frazier's position.

∴ Freedom does not exist at all.

C1

1. The experience of freedom assures me that I'm free.
2. You also know you're free, and when you deny your own freedom for the sake of playing with a science of behavior, you're acting in plain bad faith.
3. At least you'll grant that you feel free.
4. I'm free either to hold or to drop a book of matches.

The conclusion of C1 attacks the conclusion of F1 (thus Frazier and Castle are on a collision course). C1 ignores the premises of F1, introducing new considerations.

∴ ⟨ Freedom does exist. ⟩

F2

1. The determining forces may be subtle but they are inexorable.
2. You couldn't resist the temptation to prove me wrong. (That's all part of your behavior with respect to me).

The conclusion of F2 attacks premise 4 of C1, ignoring the other premises of C1.

∴ You had no choice (in dropping the book of matches).

C2

1. If you could predict in advance what I will do, then

131

I'll agree there's law.
2. < You couldn't predict
what I would do with the
book of matches. >

The conclusion of C2
attacks premise 2 of F2
(analysis of the event
after it has occurred
is much too glib;
predictability is what
counts.)

∴ < My behavior wasn't
controlled by law. >

F3

1. There are too many factors
to be taken into account (when
predicting behavior).

.
.
.

The conclusion of F3
attacks premise 1 of C2
(denies that predictab-
ility is at all invol-
ved).

∴ Behavior is not always
predictable.

Let us turn now to the third task, that of stating
the possibilities open to each speaker in contin-
uing the discussion. In the exchange between
Frazier and Castle in Walden Two there are several
important features to notice. For one thing, the
focus of the debate has shifted somewhat, away
from the conclusion of F1 towards the correctness
or incorrectness of Frazier's analysis of the
example Castle introduced in C1. The debate is
becoming more focused on what the example of
dropping the book of matches does or does not show.

Furthermore, notice that one point that Castle
introduced in C1 has been lost sight of in the
debate, namely, his insistence that the personal
experience of freedom assures him that he is free.
Notice, too, that at every step in the discussion,
there are a variety of ways in which the argument
could have been developed by the participants.
If instead of being drawn into a discussion of
dropping the book of matches Castle had reverted
to his argument from personal experience and the
experience of feeling free, the argument could

132

perhaps have taken quite a different turn.
Perhaps, as the discussion continues, the speakers will return to points that have been lost
by the wayside.

There is, however, another matter to consider
when considering the possibilities open to each
speaker. The arguments of each individual
speaker themselves constitute a chain or line of
reasoning. Frazier is engaged in one line of
reasoning; Castle in another. It is therefore
important to consider not only how the arguments
of each speaker relate to the arguments of
other speakers; it is important to examine how
the arguments of one speaker relate to other
arguments he has put forward. Focus on this
aspect of argument development will provide us
with a clear picture of the case the speaker is
putting forward.

A case is a line of reasoning, composed of two
or more arguments, put forward by a speaker to
support a more general position. For example,
a person arguing either for or against abortion
on demand may introduce one argument from personal experience, another argument from morality,
another one from legal decision, etc. By joining
together a series of arguments, the person is
constructing a case. Similarly, in Walden Two,
Frazier is building a case (arguments F1, F2, and
F3) as is Castle (arguments C1 and C2).

In examining this aspect of the exchange, we
should consider such questions as the following:
what is the arguer's case (that is, what is the
more general point the individual arguments are
designed to support)? Are the arguments consistent? Do the arguments advance the case? Do
the arguments serve to make the general point of
the case clearer (e.g. by making more explicit
what the arguer is or is not maintaining; by
introducing qualifications; etc.)?

In the Walden Two example, the case Frazier is
constructing involves the general claim that all

133

human behavior is controlled by scientific law. The arguments advanced are consistent with this position. F1 denies that freedom exists. F2 rejects Castle's example. And F3 begins to clarify his claim somewhat, for it rejects predictability as part of what he is maintaining. The case, however, is still a long way from completion. Frazier still has to make much clearer than he has exactly what he is defending. If predictability is not involved, then what does the claim that all human behavior is controlled by scientific law amount to? In addition, Frazier will need to make explicit, at some point, whether he is contending that all human behavior is totally controlled by scientific law or whether it is only partially controlled by scientific law.

In a similar way, Castle's case defending freedom, is only just beginning. C1 rejects Frazier's position, and C2 queries the element of predictability. At some point Castle will have to make clear how freedom of action relates to a science of human behavior which at least seems to indicate that manv (if not all) actions operate in accordance with patterns describable by science. Moreover, at some point, Castle should pick up on his point that the experience of freedom assures him that he is free. Castle will need to give examples of experiencing freedom.

In sum, the various sorts of ways in which the discussion can continue are as follows:
> (1) Either speaker could develop points that have been overlooked in the discussion to date (e.g. Castle's point in premise 1 of C1).
> (2) Each speaker could develop points necessary for clarifying and defending the case each is trying to make.
> (3) One speaker could capitulate, agreeing with the other.

3. Arguments in relation to the Arguers

Since arguments are exchanged by arguers, it is

sometimes helpful for us to take into account
the personal objectives and aspirations of each
of the participants in the controversy. In
looking at an exchange of arguments between arguers, questions such as the following become important for consideration:
- what do arguers hope to accomplish by
  arguing?
- what are they arguing for?
- what success do they have in communicating
  their arguments to each other?
- how willing are they to have their own
  positions modified in the light of cogent
  counter-considerations other arguers present?
- how open are the arguers to new ways of
  looking at the issue under debate?
- to what extent is their own initial position modified in the course of argument?
- what is the outcome of the discussion (e.g.
  agreement, continued disagreement, etc.)?
- what issues have been resolved in the
  discussion? what issues remain to be resolved.

Another question is this:
- to what extent do the arguers perceive
  the point of view of other arguers as
  arguments?
This last question is particularly important, for
the answer to it provides a clue to answering some
of the previous questions listed above. To perceive an argument as an argument involves recognition not just of a conclusion but also of premises.
It requires being aware that not only has a position been put forward, but also that it has been
backed up with reasons. In some situations,
especially emotionally charged ones, the following
may occur: the arguer may actually present an
argument whose structure other arguers in the
controversy may fail to recognize. Their
attention, for example, may be rivetted on a
conclusion they particularly detest. When this
occurs, even though the arguer has put forward
an argument, his argument is not perceived as an

argument by other participants in the discussion.

This sometimes happens, for instance, in current discussions of the pros and cons of abortion or the civil rights of the gay minority. In some discussions of these topics, arguers are so strongly committed one way or another that they are unable to see that their opponents are indeed offering arguments. They simply hear a conclusion with which they violently disagree, and not the reasons offered by their opponent on behalf of this stance. An Abortion-on-Demand proponent, for instance, on hearing a presentation by a Right-to-Lifer, or vice versa, may just take in the general stance of the opponent (hearing, that is, just his general conclusion) and then lunge in with a savage counter-attack that totally ignores the reasons (premises) his opponent has advanced for consideration. Such a discussion is unlikely to be profitable.

Such instances are not just confined to the discussion of abortion. Similar cases can be found in some religious or political discussions where the participants assume that their stance, and only their stance, is the correct one and that all other stances are to be dismissed. A discussion of this nature, where the reasons offered by an opposing arguer are disregarded, simply involves the issuing of edicts on a take-it-or-leave-it basis. Such a discussion precludes the possibility that a rational exploration of the issue will be undertaken by the participants. A discussion of this sort, moreover, is unlikely to resolve issues, reach agreement, have initial positions modified, exhibit openness, or involve any genuine exchange between the arguers, because the arguers are more concerned to batter each other than to argue with each other. In such situations, one arguer says one thing, another says "not so," sometimes backing this up with name-calling. Where arguers fail to perceive opposing positions as arguments (that is, where they only perceive conclusions and not reasons, even though reasons are given by the opposing

136

party), their own initial position is unlikely to be modified in the course of the discussion by cogent counter-considerations (since these are simply blocked out).

One important clue that a profitable discussion is in the offing is the extent to which an arguer perceives the argument put forward by an opposing arguer as an argument. In such instances, the arguer perceives not only his opponent's conclusion, but also his opponent's reasons. While he may vehemently detest the conclusion advanced by his opponent, that he is able to perceive his opponent's argument as an argument indicates that he is at least listening to what his opponent has to say. If in addition to listening carefully he picks up on the reasons his opponent brings forward, and critically examines them in the course of replying to his opponent, a profitable discussion is likely to ensue.

With respect to the exchange between Frazier and Castle in Walden Two, the two arguers are trying to sort out the nature of human behavior: is it totally determined, or are at least some acts free? At the outset, the arguers are poles apart, Frazier upholding determinism, Castle denying it. Each is attempting to persuade the other of the truth of his position. While they disagree with each other's conclusion, it is important to note that each listens to the other's argument. There is, in this case, a rational exploration of the very complex issues that underlie this whole matter. Both Frazier and Castle examine the reasons each other cites on behalf of the other's position. Since the discussion is just in its infancy, it is too early to predict what the eventual outcome of the Frazier-Castle exchange will be.

4. Arguments in relation to the Argument Analysts

Just as arguments are put forward by arguers,

they are also inspected and judged by argument analysts. The role of the argument analyst in the correct identification and careful evaluation of the argument is particularly important.

The argument analyst stands at least initially outside of the controversy under examination. He may be a person who like the reader of this text is interested in learning more about the structure and processes of reasoning. Or he may be a person interested in following the various lines of reasoning that are being advanced as a discussion unfolds. Or he may be an observer of a controversy who is trying to become clear about the various positions being put forth before becoming personally involved in the discussion. In these instances, the argument analyst is engaged in a process which calls for attentive and accurate identification of the various arguments that make up the discussion on the one hand and on the other hand for careful evaluation of their merits as arguments.

The process of accurate argument identification and careful argument evaluation in which the argument analyst is engaged involves more than simply knowing that arguments have a structure and that they can be evaluated in terms of specific criteria. The process requires training in listening attentively to the structure of the argument as it is put forward by the person making the argument. Our task as argument analysts is one of reconstruction: reconstruction of the argument that is being offered by the speaker or writer (and subsequent evaluation of it). The values, beliefs, interests and commitments of the argument analyst ought not to intrude upon the matter under discussion. Such traits should not interfere with our perception of the argument as an argument nor our assessment of it as an argument.

As argument analysts we ought to be able to identify the various arguments in a controversy accurately. In terms of the Castle-Frazier exchange in the <u>Walden Two</u> passage cited earlier in this chapter, for instance, we ought to be able to pick out the respective arguments of each speaker, regardless of our own personal stance on the question of whether human actions are free or determined. Similarly, in listening to other contentious issues such as abortion, capital punishment, the role of multi-national corporations, welfare schemes, the merits of capitalism and similar ethical and political topics, we ought to be able to identify carefully the structure of the argument as it is offered by the arguer.

This is especially difficult in instances where the arguer is putting forward a position with which we disagree or find repugnant or offensive. As has already been pointed out, in such cases, the tendency may be for us to gloss over the reasons the arguer has advanced on behalf of his conclusion. When this occurs, assuming that the arguer has in fact offered an argument, we have failed to perceive the argument offered as an argument. Accurate reconstruction of an argument, particularly one we dislike, requires considerable training. We should not dismiss the possibility that an argument can be presented for positions with which we disagree. In fact even good arguments may be made for positions we fail to favor. We have been given ample opportunity to practice focusing on the structure of arguments. In each case, the task has been to bracket our own personal convictions, beliefs, values and interests, and to reconstruct, as accurately and as faithfully as possible, the argument that has been put forward by the speaker or writer.

Similarly, in evaluating arguments, we, as argument analysts, should examine the argument in terms of its merits as an argument. We should resist the temptation to combat a position with which we disagree with a simple "t'isn't so." Such a response focuses simply on the disagreed-

with conclusion, and not on the reasons the arguer has advanced on behalf of his position.

5. Arguments in relation to Society generally

Societies differ in the extent to which they
foster rational discussion of issues and provide
forums for the systematic exchange of arguments
on behalf of opposing views. Why this is so is
a complex story and need not be entered into here.
It has to do, in part, with the extent to which
a society, or some institutions within society,
absolutize a truth--that is, make the claim that
this particular position, and only this particular position, is completely or absolutely true.
Such a view serves to rule out rational discourse
on topics covered by the absolutized truth. Such
claims abound in the world's political, social
and religious ideologies.

In all societies, of course, the rational discussion of issues is affected by such forces as:
personality conflicts; pressure groups on government; the interplay between business, labor,
consumer and governmental sectors; and, very
generally, the realities of party politics in any
institution. These certainly affect the oppor-
unities for rational discussion, the extent to
which arguments will be listened to, and the sort
of acceptance they will receive in decision-making bodies.

Bearing in mind both ideological and pressure
group factors, there are some very important
questions concerning the role of rational discussion and argumentation in society generally. Such
general questions include the following:
  - when do people argue?
  - why do people argue?
  - how are arguments generally resolved?
  - how, in general, do the values, commit-
    ments, and beliefs of individual arguers
    affect their ability to hear and under-

140

stand the arguments of other arguers?

The question, <u>when</u> do people argue? can have many different answers. One answer is: in many different contexts. People, for example, argue in legal contexts, when lawyers give reasons for claims such as the following.
-so and so-is/is not-guilty
-so and so-ought/ought not-to be convicted
and so on. Similarly, people argue in political contexts, when they, or politicians or legisla-tors, give reasons for claims such as the follow-ing:
-such and such a policy-is/is not-the best way to combat inflation.
-such and such a piece of legislation-should/should not-be enacted as law.
-such and such a law-should/should not-be changed.
etc. People also argue about matters involving ethical considerations, for instance, in giving reasons for claims such as the following:
-extra-marital sex-is/is not-right so long as both partners know and approve.
-hospitals-ought/ought not-to allow abortion on demand.
-governments-have/have not-the right to lie to their citizens for the sake of national security.
-society-should/should not-control the number of children parents can have.
and so on. People argue about business:
-should I invest in company X, company Y or company Z?
-do I make more money in the long run by renting a house and by saving or by buying a house?
etc. About scientific results and their signifi-cance for people:
-what effect does vitamin C have on the common cold?
-what effect would rapid entry into another Ice Age have on world politics?
-is aggression innate in people or is it culturally acquired?

> -do the potential hazards of nuclear
> power plants outweigh their advantages
> in an energy-hungry world?

etc. There are a great many different contexts
in which people argue: about religious beliefs
and practices, about historical incidents and
their significance, about the interpretation of
texts and documents, about personal matters, etc.

One answer, then, to the question when do people
argue? is that people argue in many different
contexts about many different matters. This
answer, however, can be simplified. People
basically argue when there is an issue they wish
to decide by rational means. The issue may be
a theoretical one: what is true about some particular matter. Or the issue may be a practical
one: what should be done in some particular
situation. In either case, people argue in order
to reach a decision rationally.

This answer indicates one basic reason why people
argue: to resolve pressing matters rationally.
The rational resolution of issues involves the
scrutiny of arguments on various sides of an
issue and their careful consideration. The
production and evaluation of arguments is the
main ingredient in the process of rational
decision-making.

As an exchange between arguers, however, rational
decision-making is only one way in which issues
can be resolved. There are other ways of reaching decisions. Fighting, violence, and intimidation of various sorts are also means of settling issues and disputes. Similarly, issues and
disputes can be settled by whim, fancy, irrational arbitrariness, gut feel, and the like, without consideration of evidence. Such means are
often effective and decisive. Argument represents an alternative to these methods.

No one, obviously, can be compelled to be rational, any more than one can be compelled to take

an interest in issues of social and personal concern. No one, that is, can be forced to enter into the complex and rather demanding process of listening to, producing, defending, modifying, challenging, and evaluating arguments in order to arrive eventually at a carefully thought-out decision. If we wish to be rational, however, then this is the sort of process in which we must engage.

Broadly speaking, when people argue, they are trying to accomplish two main objectives:
    (1) to present a good argument, and
    (2) to persuade the reader or hearer to
        accept a specific point of view.
There may, of course, be other objectives in specific instances, e.g. to amuse, to entertain, to annoy, etc., by means of argument. But, broadly speaking, these are the two main objectives of argument.

Each objective involves different considerations. The first has to do with the intrinsic evidential worth of the argument. Evidential worth has to do with the structure of the argument: does it have a clear conclusion? is the conclusion well supported? and so on. The second objective has to do with the persuasive worth of the argument. In general, this has to do with the argument's appeal and interest. Does it make the thought "come alive"? Is it clearly stated? Is it presented in such a fashion that other people will grasp it accurately, be convinced by it, and accept it? Is it interesting?

In devising an argument, both evidential and persuasive considerations ought to be taken into account by the arguer. By taking into account evidential considerations, the arguer will provide a basis upon which rational decision-making can proceed. By taking into consideration persuasive characteristics, the arguer demonstrates a sensitivity to the intended recipient of his argumentative efforts and an awareness of the processes involved in the communication

143

of arguments. The following principles concerning evidential and persuasive worth are recommended:

(1) Arguments ought to have good intrinsic
    evidential worth.
(2) Arguments ought to have good persuasive
    worth.
(3) Arguments ought not to be such that they
    exhibit good persuasive worth to the
    elimination of good evidential worth.

Recommendation (3) contends that arguments ought
not to be devoid of evidential worth, however
important persuasive worth may be. As will be
seen in a subsequent chapter, recommendation (3)
is particularly important. Some arguments
contain only persuasive worth, and these are
seriously defective.

Occasionally the following recommendation has
been argued for:

(4) Readers or hearers of an argument ought
    to be persuaded solely by the argument's
    intrinsic evidential worth.

Recommendation (4) is not advanced in this text.
It over-emphasizes the importance of evidential
worth to the detriment of the communicational
and personal factors that affect the worth of an
argument. A good argument contains both evidential and persuasive worth.

How, then, do we judge good evidential worth and
good persuasive worth? This brings us to the
subject matter of Part Two of this text: argument
evaluation.

Recall Quiz

(1) To what does "the wider context of argument"
    refer?

(2) When considering arguments in their wider
    context, what four interrelationships ought
    we to take into account?

(3) What sorts of things should we consider when
    comparing arguments with one another (a) in

brief exchanges, and (b) in longer exchanges?

(4) What is a "case"?

(5) What sorts of questions are raised in considering arguments in relation to the arguers involved in the controversy?

(6) In considering arguments in relation to the argument analyst who is surveying the controversy, what ought the argument analyst be able to do?

(7) In considering arguments in relation to society generally, what sorts of questions are raised?

(8) To what does "the evidential worth of an argument" refer? "Persuasive worth"?

(9) What basic principles concerning evidential and persuasive worth are recommended in this text?

Exercise #1

For each of the following brief exchanges,
a) using standard format, identify the argument of each arguer,
b) state how the second argument relates to the first argument, and
c) state how the first arguer could reply to the second arguer.

(1) Jim: Religion is destructive of human values. Look, for example, at all the wars religion has spawned throughout history and today in Northern Ireland, the Near East, and many other places. Religion divides people into compartments, even in the school systems in some countries where people learn how and why they are different. Religion breeds intolerance and a lack of understanding and sympathy for people of other persuasions.

   Joe: I disagree with you. Sure, religion has contributed to wars. But this

145

only looks at half the evidence:
religion has contributed to understanding and human betterment. After
all, the development of hospitals,
orphanages, schools, old folks homes,
and the like were largely started and
paid for by religious groups.

(2) Ellen: By using available scientific knowledge concerning human behavior,
people in Walden Two can be condition-
ed into a better way of life. The
school system, moreover, can be
designed so as to eliminate from
society such negative emotions as
competitiveness, ambition and envy
which prevent a truly cooperative
society from emerging. Experts in
planning, too, will govern the community rather than ambitious lawyers or
vote-getters as in our society.
Therefore I think Walden Two would
create a better sort of society than
the one we currently have.

   Susan: I don't think so. After all, condi-
tioning simply results in robots. And
"negative emotions" (as you call them)
such as competitiveness and ambition
can't be eliminated from human nature
simply by manipulating the environment
because such traits are innate in
people and because what's innate cannot be modified by environmental
modification.

(3) Mark: There are two ways of dealing with
criminals: either rehabilitate them or
punish them. I think, however, that
rehabilitating them is no longer a
viable option. First of all, the cost
of rehabilitation has skyrocketed,
involving astronomical administrative
costs, costs for increased numbers of
prison and social workers, review
board costs, prison guard retraining

programs, etc. Secondly, rehabilitation is ineffective: it does not deter
crime. Thirdly, there are conflicting
methods of rehabilitation: on-site
versus off-site methods, individual
versus group methods, artificial
versus natural environment methods,
and so on and so forth. Fourthly, it
seems to many, and with some justification, that prisoners are getting
too good a lifestyle for what they
have done. I suggest, therefore,
that we simply revert to the other
option: punish them.

Phil: I agree with you that rehabilitation
is no longer a viable goal. I disagree, however, with you that there
are only two options: there is a
third possibility--restitution.
Restitution would have several advantages: it would, first of all, satisfy
our demands for fairness; secondly,
it would reduce costs of imprisonment;
and, thirdly, it would give the offen-
der work that has value in the eyes
of society, thereby contributing to
his sense of self-worth and dignity.
I therefore suggest that we explore
ways of changing the prison system so
as to allow criminals to make full
and fair restitution to their victims.

(4) Ruth: I've thought about the matter a lot
and I've come to the conclusion that
God exists. My reasoning goes as
follows. First of all, you will admit,
Shirley, as will others, that the
universe exhibits design. O.K. so far?
Here's my next step. If the universe
exhibits design, then it must have a
designer. After all, you don't get
design without a designer. Thirdly,
if the universe has a designer, then
that designer must be God. There is,
after all, no other possible candidate

147

for the job of universe-designer.
Hence God exists. I think, Shirley,
that that's a pretty strong argument.

Shirley: Hold on a sec. I think I should have
stopped you a minute ago, Ruth. I
think the very first step in your
argument is biassed. Why? Well,
note that you use the word 'design'
and this implies <u>conscious</u> planning,
thereby tilting the whole argument
unfairly towards your conclusion.
Note, too, that if you had used the
word 'order' in your first premise,
you would not have been led up the
divine garden path, for, after all,
that there is order in the universe
does not presuppose an orderer.

(5) Erica: The earth must have been visited in
ancient times by cosmonauts from
outer space. And these cosmonauts
are the gods of ancient mythology.

Rose: What evidence do you have of that?

Erica: Well, several things. For one thing,
there are many unexplained mysteries
from ancient times: the Pyramids,
the Plain of Nasca, the statues on
Easter Island, Stonehenge, and so on.
All these mysteries, moreover, involve
major architectural feats: gigantic
buildings or massive excavations. In
addition, there are also maps showing
the major continents and the <u>land</u> mass
of Antarctica. Also, notice that
primitive artists always depict the
gods as coming from chariots in the
sky and that they appear to have
space helmets on. For these reasons,
then, I think my point is well taken.
What do you say?

Rose: I agree with all your reasons. However, I think your conclusion ought
to be this: therefore, ancient man
was much more advanced than we now
give him credit.

(6) (In the following selection, identify first
    of all what Judith Jarvis Thomson calls "the
    most common argument" and then her argument
    against this initial argument.)

Most opposition to abortion relies on the
premise that the fetus is a human being, a
person, from the moment of conception. The
premise is argued for, but, as I think, not
well. Take, for example, the most common
argument. We are asked to notice that the
development of a human being from conception
through birth into childhood is continuous,
then it is said that to draw a line to choose
a point in this development and say "before
this point the thing is not a person, after
this point it is a person" is to make an
arbitrary choice, a choice for which in the
nature of things no good reason can be given.
It is concluded that the fetus is, or anyway
that we had better say it is, a person from
the moment of conception. But this conclusion
does not follow. Similar things might be
said about the development of an acorn into
an oak tree, and it does not follow that
acorns are oak trees, or that we had better
say they are. Arguments of this form are
sometimes called "slippery slope arguments"-
the phrase is perhaps self-explanatory-and
it is dismaying that opponents of abortion
rely on them so heavily and uncritically.
(Judith Jarvis Thomson, "A Defense of
  Abortion," Philosophy and Public Affairs 1
  (1971), as reprinted in Marshall Cohen et al.,
  The Rights and Wrongs of Abortion (Princeton
  University Press, 1974), p. 3)

Exercise #2

This exercise is intended to provide experience
in identifying article-length arguments. Using
standard format, identify the argument contained
in the following articles assigned by the course
instructor.

(1) B.F. Skinner, "Freedom and the Control of
    Men," The American Scholar 25 (1955-56),
    reprinted in the Bobbs-Merrill Reprint Series
    in the Social Sciences (#PS 263).
    > task: identify Skinner's argument in
    > this article on behalf of the claim that
    > "the so-called 'democratic philosophy'
    > of human behavior to which it also gave
    > rise is increasingly in conflict with
    > the application of the methods of science
    > to human affairs."

(2) Stanley Milgram, "Behavioral Study of Obedi-
    ence," The Journal of Abnormal and Social
    Psychology 67 (1963) and reprinted in the
    Bobbs-Merrill Reprint Series in the Social
    Sciences (#P 521)
    > task: identify Milgram's argument in this
    > article on behalf of the claim that many
    > people (more than would be expected)
    > willingly obey authority they consider
    > legitimate.

(3) D.L. Rosenhan, "On Being Sane in Insane
    Places," Science 179 (Jan. 19, 1973), pp. 250-
    258.
    > task: First of all, identify Rosenhan's
    > argument that there is no clinical basis
    > for diagnosing patients as sane or
    > insane; then identify his argument that
    > the hospital environment depersonalizes,
    > alienates, renders powerless, etc. the
    > patient.

(4) Plato, Crito (any recent translation)
    > tasks: (1) Using paraphrase and the
    > standard format, briefly identify the
    > premises of the main argument Socrates
    > uses in reply to Crito, in which he
    > rejects escaping from prison; (2) consi-
    > der how Socrates' argument relates to
    > Crito's argument urging him to escape
    > (see the gist of this argument on pp. 3 ,
    > 38 of this text); and (3) consider how
    > Crito might respond to Socrates.

(1)   In this exercise, the course director will
      instruct you to follow either format A or
      format B.

      format
      A. Read over the following situation and
         then do task A (see below)
      B. The course director will divide the class
         into an even number of smaller groups.
         Each group will meet together in class
         to do the following exercise. Each group,
         moreover, will quickly select a leader
         who will help coordinate discussion and
         report the results to the class as a
         whole. Each group should read the follow-
         ing situation very carefully and then
         begin task B (see below).

situation

The situation under consideration is between
father and mother.

Father separated from mother about two and a
half years ago in order to take up residence with
a younger woman. That relationship has flourish-
ed and reconciliation between mother and father
is now impossible. Divorce is inevitable, Father
has also left behind two children, a boy who is
now 11 and a girl who is now 6. The boy in
particular is attached to his father. Father
sees both children on a regular basis and enjoys
a good relationship with them. He wants to
continue being their father.

Both parents work and have comparable, reasonably
good, middle class incomes. Both are satisfied
with their work. The children live with their
mother and she must care for them on a day-to-day
basis, coping with the daily trials and tribula-
tions in their young lives. The mother deeply
resents her husband's actions and the intrusion
of the younger woman.

The younger woman also sees the two children and

has developed an important relationship with
them. Although she wants a family of her own,
she would not at all mind being their mother
should their father be granted custody. She,
too, works and enjoys a reasonably good income.

As you can well imagine, the separation has been
bitter and complicated. There is no need here
to recite all the sordid details. Suffice it
to say that so far the mother and father have
been unable to come to any agreement on any of
the following matters: custody of the children,
visiting rights, property division, level of
child support, etc.

Both father and mother are now in divorce court,
with their respective lawyers, before a judge.
The judge will decide the issues in question,
taking into account not only fault but also the
general welfare of the children.

task

A. Prepare and write up, in standard essay style,
   (length to be determined by the course direct-
   or), an argument that defends the following
   conclusion:
   ∴ The father should be granted custody of
      both children (surnames:A-M)
   ∴ The mother should be granted custody of
      both children (surnames:N-Z)
   Your aim is to prepare a good clear argument,
   one that will enable the judge to decide
   rationally in your favor. In preparing your
   argument, you are, of course, free to make up
   details within the framework of the general
   situation outlined above.

B. Odd-numbered groups are the father; even-
   numbered groups are the mother. Each group
   is to prepare an argument of about 3-4 minutes
   duration in support of the following conclusion:
   ∴ I should be granted custody of both
      children.
   Your aim is to prepare and present a good
   clear argument, one that will enable the

judge to decide rationally in your favor.
In preparing your argument, you are, of
course, free to make up details within the
framework of the general situation outlined
above.

The course director will set a suitable
limit for preparing your argument. Once
the argument has been prepared, your leader
will present it verbally on your behalf,
as your group confronts one of the opposing
groups.

(2) <u>format</u>

A. As is (1) above.
B. As in (1) above.

situation

Rosa, a 27 year old married mother of two boys
(aged 5 and 3 years old), has been arrested for
prostitution. The charges against her are clear:
a detective from the morality squad was contacted
by her agent, Rosa received money from the detective, and she undressed in his presence.

Rosa is a bit perplexed by all this. She is a
call-girl--she readily admits this, with perhaps
a touch of pride--working to make ends meet.
She is a prostitute by career choice. She has a
B.A. from a local college where she majored in
economics and political science. She is well
read, and enjoys travel and gourmet food. Upon
graduation, she found the job market unattractive
and ill-suited to someone who wished to combine
career with motherhood.

Her husband is also a college graduate (in psychology) and has a good position with an advertising
agency. She works as a call-girl with her husband's knowledge and consent. Rosa prefers to
look after her children during the day, being
opposed to the impersonal, disease-ridden atmos-
phere of most day care centers. She prefers to
work in the evening, when her husband (Bob) can

be home to look after the children.

Rosa does most of the housework, including the grocery shopping, and does most of the cooking, except on those rare occasions when Bob surprises her with a Sunday brunch. Both Rosa and Bob say they have a good marriage, and are happy.

Rosa works through an agent, confining her activities from 8 p.m. to 1 a.m., 5 days a week, 3 weeks per month. Her earnings vary somewhat, but on a typical week she grosses $1200 per week, gives $480 (i.e. 40%) to her agent, and takes home $720 tax-free dollars per week. She receives regular medical treatment, covered by medical insurance. Her agent is well paid to select only middle and upper class patrons who will avoid physical abuse. She has developed a regular clientele who now form about 75% of her business. She has been doing this for about 2 and 1/2 years now.

Rosa feels that her career choice has been a good one. It doesn't take her out of the home all that much. It gives her time with her children. It gives her a social life with Bob. It brings in good money, allowing them a much better lifestyle than would be otherwise be possible. And in a tight economy, it's attractive work.

Nonetheless, Rosa is in court, faced with a prostitution charge.

task

A. Prepare and write up, in standard essay style (length to be determined by the instructor), an argument that defends the following conclusion:
.˙. Rosa ought to be convicted of prositution (surnames: N-Z)
.˙. Rosa ought not be convicted of prostitution (surnames: A-M)
Your aim is to prepare a good clear argument. In preparing your argument, you are, of

154

course, free to make up details within the
framework of the general situation outlined
above.

B. Odd-numbered groups are the prosecuting
    lawyer who is maintaining:
    ∴. Rosa ought to be convicted of prostitu-
        tion.
    Even-numbered groups are Rosa's lawyer, who
    is defending the view that
    ∴. Rosa ought not to be convicted of
        prostitution.
    Each group is to prepare an argument of
    about 3-4 minutes duration in support of the
    assigned conclusion. Your aim is to pre-
    pare and present a good clear argument, one
    that will enable the judge to decide ration-
    ally in your favor. In preparing your argu-
    ment, you are, of course, free to make up
    details within the framework of the general
    situation outlined above.

    The instructor will set a suitable limit for
    preparing your argument. Once the argument
    has been prepared, your leader will present
    it verbally on your behalf, as your group
    confronts one of the opposing groups.

    If time permits, your instructor may request
    that each group make a brief 1-minute
    counter-argument to the argument they have
    just heard from an opposing group.

PART TWO

ON EVALUATING ARGUMENTS

CHAPTER FIVE

ARGUMENT EVALUATION: SOME PRELIMINARY STEPS

1.   Some Preliminaries

The perfect argument is like the perfect crime:
hard to plan and even harder to carry out successfully. Most arguments we meet have flaws of one
sort or another, and it is important for us to be
able to spot these defects. By doing so, we will
be providing ourselves with defenses against
being taken in by poor, faulty reasoning. In
addition, by knowing when a position is sufficiently supported -- and when it isn't -- we'll be
able to place our beliefs and actions on a
rational footing.

We come, then, to the task of argument evaluation
-- our critical inspection of the argument presented to us. This is the subject matter of the
rest of this book. The various chapters in this
part of the text systematically unfold the different kinds of considerations we should take into
account when judging the worth of an argument.

These different considerations will be presented
as a series of "steps," each one focusing on
some major feature of an argument. We will
proceed in a piecemeal fashion, examining one
step at a time. Only by the end of this part of
the book, when all the steps have been made clear,
will we be able to piece them all together and
have a complete picture of the range and scope
of argument evaluation.

In evaluating arguments, we will make extensive
use of the right space of the standard format, the
space, you will recall, we have reserved for our
critical comments on the argument's worth. As we
proceed through the various steps in argument
evaluation, the appropriate kind of comments that
should be placed in this space of the standard
format will be discussed.

the point of argument evaluation

Many arguments contain flaws, blemishes, or imperfections of one sort or another that mar their worth as arguments. Such arguments may be said to be "defective" in one respect or another. Speaking of flawed arguments as "defective" is important here, for the word 'defective' has some useful overtones that help clarify the main objectives of argument evaluation.

One important overtone is that the word suggests that there are <u>reasons</u> for the defectiveness. Consider, for example, some consumer item, say a new tape recorder, a new suit, or a new car. If it should turn out to be defective, it is not enough simply for us to say "it's defective" when taking it back to the store or dealer for satisfaction. We have to be able to say where and how it fails to measure up to par. We will have to point out specific parts of the item and give reasons why we consider it to be defective.

The same is true of arguments. It's not good enough simply to say "it's defective." We have to be able to locate <u>where</u> it is defective and say <u>why</u> we consider <u>it to be</u> defective, by giving reasons and by singling out specific parts of the argument that contain these flaws. This highlights two main objectives of argument evaluation:
  (1) to be able to point out <u>where</u> arguments are defective
  (2) to be able to indicate <u>why</u> arguments are defective
But this isn't all there is to argument evaluation.

There is another useful overtone associated with the notion of defectiveness. Defectiveness is something that can be <u>overcome</u>. The defective consumer item, for instance, can be sent back to the factory for repair before being returned to the consumer. Similarly, too, the defective argument can be sent back for further work before again being considered by the argument analyst. In many cases, what is defective about an argument

can be remedied, with the result that a better
argument is produced. This draws attention to
a third purpose of argument evaluation:
   (3) to be able to indicate <u>ways of improving</u>
       defective arguments.

This positive side to argument evaluation should
not be forgotten as we plunge deeper into the
pathology of reasoning in this and subsequent
chapters. From time to time ways of improving
defective arguments will be indicated. This
points to two other purposes of argument evalua-
tion--knowing defectiveness so that we may avoid
such flaws in arguments we make, and knowing
defectiveness so we may spot these in other
people's arguments and have a basis on which to
respond to them:
   (4) to be able to avoid defectiveness in
       preparing and presenting one's own
       argument.
   (5) to be able to respond effectively to
       arguments (by focusing on their defects
       and by challenging them).

<u>kinds of defectiveness</u>

In identifying the structure of arguments, it
has been our policy right from the outset to
reconstruct the argument offered by the arguer as
faithfully and as accurately as possible. That
is, we have concentrated on identifying the structure of what might be termed "the offered argument." An <u>offered argument</u> is simply the argument
actually put forward by the arguer.

Offered arguments fall into one or other of three
main categories when we critically analyse them:
   (1) the offered argument may be a genuine
       argument, free of defects.
In this case, the offered argument satisfies the
requirements of a <u>genuine argument</u>, having, that
is, premises that actually do support the conclusion. And, being free of defects, it would

satisfy all the steps of argument evaluation. It would be a good argument. Such an argument would be a joy to behold!

Such arguments, however, are rare. The next case is more likely:
>(2) the offered argument may be a genuine argument whose worth as an argument is somewhat impaired.

In this case, the offered argument is again a genuine argument (having premises that actually do support the conclusion). It is an argument, however, that is defective, exhibiting the kind of defectiveness that reduces the worth of an argument (just as an impaired driver is still a driver, although his driving performance is lessened).

There are, of course, many factors that may reduce an argument's worth as an argument. These will be discussed in due course. These defects may be relatively minor, or relatively serious, and arguments which contain some flaws may range in worth from (roughly speaking) pretty poor to pretty good.

In situation (2) the argument is still an argument, but flawed. The third situation, however, represents quite a different state of affairs:
>(3) the offered argument may fail entirely to be a genuine argument.

In this case the arguer has made a very serious blunder indeed. He has put forward as an argument what is in fact not a genuine argument at all. He has advanced something that only looks like an argument; in actuality, what he has offered as "reasons" fail to support what he has offered as a "conclusion."

An offered argument which fails to be a genuine argument may conveniently be referred to as a bogus "argument" (or purported "argument," or sham "argument"). A bogus argument is no argument at all; it only purports to be one. It is not even a poor argument; it is totally counterfeit.

Offered arguments which are in reality only bogus
arguments lack evidential worth and ought therefore not to be acceptable. There are many factors
which may disqualify what a person offers as an
argument from being the real thing, and these will
be discussed subsequently.

Notice carefully that the kind of defect mentioned in situation (3) differs markedly from that in
situation (2). In (2) the defectiveness simply
<u>reduces</u> the worth of an argument as an argument.
It is still an argument. It just isn't as good
as it could be. In (3), however, the kind of
defectiveness that is involved <u>rules out</u> what is
offered as an argument from being a genuine one.
It destroys its worth as an argument.

To sum up:

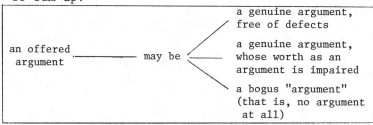

an offered argument	may be	a genuine argument, free of defects
		a genuine argument, whose worth as an argument is impaired
		a bogus "argument" (that is, no argument at all)

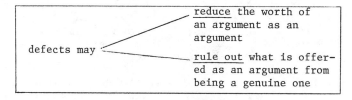

| defects may | <u>reduce</u> the worth of an argument as an argument |
| | <u>rule out</u> what is offer-ed as an argument from being a genuine one |

<u>evaluating arguments</u>

As has already been said, we approach argument
evaluation in a series of 10 steps, focusing on
one step at a time. Each step concentrates on one
particular aspect of argument. This is intended
to provide training in learning to look systematically at different facets of an argument. Usually

163

the untrained mind simply lunges at some despised conclusion and says "not so" or else simply dismisses the arguer as a "jerk" (or worse!). There's much more to the disciplined evaluation of arguments.

As we go through these steps, a couple of things should be borne in mind. For one thing, complete evaluation of an argument won't be possible until we have mastered all 10 steps. That will take quite a while. Until then we'll focus simply on one step at a time, learning how to apply it. Only by the last chapter will we be in a position to do a complete masterful appraisal of arguments.

It should also be noted that we evaluate both main arguments and also mini-arguments. Mini-arguments, after all, are arguments in their own right and they deserve decent consideration. How this is done will be seen shortly. For another thing, you should not expect all arguments to exhibit all defects. Some arguments simply manifest one major defect conspicuously; others, several defects, even quite a few. In addition, as we shall see, even when an argument has several defects, some may loom as much more serious than others. Arguments are much like people or cars in this respect: a person who succumbs to lung cancer may also have had hearing and eyesight problems, a liver ailment, hardening of the arteries, arthritis, etc., and a car which conks out because of a dead battery may also have a rusty fender and poor brakes.

One final note. Argument evaluation shouldn't be performed just in a mechanical fashion. It should be fun and should provoke thought and creative classroom discussion. Consider: what defects are the most serious? How could this argument be remedied? And so forth. In this way the purposes of argument evaluation will be served.

It's time now to consider the various steps in argument evaluation. In this chapter we will examine 4 very basic ones.

2. Step #1

Step #1
Look at the premises in the argument and
draw attention to those that need support
or more support.

Step #1 directs our attention to the premises of
the argument. Inspect them carefully. Look at
what support they are given. Look both at the
premises of the main argument and those of the
mini-arguments. Some premises may require
support; others, more support than is given by
the arguer.

In a good argument, premises are supported, some
more than others. This is inherent in the very
nature of a premise. A premise, after all, is
used to support a conclusion. To do this, they
must be deployed by the arguer in such a fashion
as to gain our acceptance of them,so that we are
led, nodding assent from one to another, until
we are finally confronted by the conclusion. To
achieve this goal, premises need to be backed
up by considerations that defend the point of
view they express. How much back-up is needed in
any one particular argument depends in part on
the particular context in which the arguer is
arguing, on his purpose in arguing, on his persis-
tence, on his degree of commitment to the point
of view he is advocating, etc.

In looking at premises in terms of the support
they receive from back-up considerations, it
would be foolish to expect that each and every
premise in the argument and in the mini-arguments
will be supported. That could simply lead to an
"infinite regress"--to the never-ending job of
shoring up each and every premise, mini-premise,
"mini-mini-premise" that we add and so on. That
would be impossible, as well as absurd and unreasonable. It is not unreasonable, however, to

demand that at the very least the important
premises be well supported.

In looking over a group of premises in an argument, some will probably stand out as more important than others--the conclusion will depend more
on them than on others. A rough guide here is
that an important premise is one whose absence
from the argument would seriously throw into
question the worth or even the sense of the argument. It is essential that these premises be
supported, and supported well. It is also desirable that the other premises be supported as well,
at least well enough so as not to interrupt "the
flow of acceptance" as we move thoughtfully from
one premise to another.

Let's consider Step #1 in relation to some arguments. Consider this argument for instance:
(a) (In Shakespeare's Hamlet) Hamlet suffers from
    an Oedipus complex. Thus he could not possi-
    bly have a serious relationship with Ophelia
    or avenge his father's death.
Such an argument will persuade no one--it's like
the "bare bones" sort of argument we first met
back in chapter 1. To get this argument off the
ground, support is needed for premise 1. For
example, what is an "Oedipus complex"? What
evidence is there in the play that Hamlet suffers
from it? How does it affect his relationships
with people (such as Ophelia, his mother, his
step-father, etc.)? And so forth. Unless matters
such as these are presented and discussed, premise
1 could not possibly gain our acceptance. In
other words, it needs support.

We would indicate this by making the comment
"support needed" in evaluation space adjacent to
the premise and by drawing a line from the
comment to the premise in question. Our work
in identifying and evaluating this argument would
be displayed as follows:

support space	main argument space	evaluation space
	1. Hamlet suffers from an Oedipus complex.	← support needed

.˙. He could not possibly
have a serious relationship
with Ophelia or avenge his
father's death.

Consider next this selection:
(b) The parables of Jesus are important and mind-
provoking stories, but their real nature has
usually been overlooked. Many people have
simply construed them as explanations in
which Jesus, hard pressed to explain his view
of the Kingdom of God, tells a story.

My view is quite different, and it goes as
follows. The parables of Jesus are really
pieces of poetry (not explanations). Poetry,
moreover, is by its very nature open-ended,
allowing different readers to gain quite
different insights and interpretations.
(...supported by 18 mini-premises, omitted
here for lack of space...) Thus the parables
of Jesus also allow different readers to
gain quite different insights and interpretations.

The first paragraph in (b) is simply background--
it provides the context in which the arguer is
arguing. But notice what he does in this argument: he sets forth two main premises, but
supports only the second. No support at all is
given to premise 1. This is foolish reasoning,
since premise 1 is at least as important as
premise 2 in establishing the conclusion. Indeed,
since the context indicates that this arguer is
arguing against a different view of the parables
of Jesus (one that sees them as explanations),
premise 1 is absolutely crucial. In brief, it
needs support. So in evaluating this argument, we
would comment as follows:

support space	main argument space	evaluation space
	1. The parables of Jesus are really pieces of poetry (not explanations)	⟵ support needed

167

```
1. ...  ⎞         2. Poetry is by its very
2. ...  ⎟              nature open-ended,
   ⋮    ⎬─────→        allowing different
18. ... ⎠              readers to gain quite
                       different insights and
                       interpretations.
                       ────────────────────

                    ∴ The parables of Jesus
                       also allow different
                       readers to gain quite
                       different insights and
                       interpretations.
```

Consider next this argument:
(c) There are four qualities an entity must have
    in order to be considered alive: assimilation,
    growth, reproduction, and movement. Some
    computers have these four characteristics:
    such computers can assimilate information,
    can cause knowledge to grow, can reproduce
    themselves, and, if suitably programmed, can
    move about physically. Thus some computers
    are alive.

The argument contains two main premises and a
conclusion. Its first premise is unsupported, and
yet it is an important one in relation to the
conclusion. Who defines 'life' in this fashion?
Are there only these four qualities (or are there
others)? Must an organism exhibit all four
qualities (or perhaps just three or two of these
traits)? And so on. The premise also needs to be
supported. The same thing is true of the second
premise. It, too, is important and it is unsupported. What computers for instance, can do all
this? In evaluating this argument in terms of
Step #1, our work would appear as follows:

support space   main argument space   evaluation space

              1. There are 4 qualities ←─support needed
                 an entity must have in
                 order to be considered
                 alive: assimilation,
                 growth, reproduction,
                 and movement.

168
```
```

2. Some computers have ←—— support needed
   these 4 character-
   istics: such compu-
   ters can assimilate
   information, can
   cause knowledge to
   grow, can reproduce
   themselves, and, if
   suitably programmed,
   can move about
   _____physically._____

∴ Some computers are
   alive

Sometimes the problem is not that no support has
been given important premises but that they have
been insufficiently supported. In this case they
need more support. Consider, for instance, the
following portion of an argument.
(d) ....Thirdly, religion fosters a sense of
     brotherhood and a tolerance of other people.
     After all, look at the work of Mother Teresa
     in Calcutta. Fourthly,....(rest of the
     argument omitted)
In this excerpt from an argument, we have main
premise 3 and one mini-premise which supports
premise 3. Note, however, that premise 3 has not
been supported to any great extent. A lot of
questions quickly come to mind: is the work of
Mother Teresa typical of religion in action?
What about religious feuds and wars over the
centuries? And so forth. Clearly this premise
needs "more support." (Indeed, as the mini-premise stands, it is hardly informative. What is
Mother Teresa's work in Calcutta? How does it
relate to brotherhood and tolerance? And so on.
More details here are absolutely essential.). In
identifying and evaluating this part of the argument, our work would appear as follows:

support space	main argument space	evaluation space
	1. ...	
	2. ...	

1. Look at the work of Mother Teresa in Cal-cutta. } → 3. Religion fosters a ← more support needed
sense of brotherhood
and a tolerance of
other people.

4. ....
. . ...

Even when a main premise is supported by several considerations, these considerations in turn may each need more support if they are to gain accept-ance and so contribute to our willingness to assent to the main premise. Consider, for instance, the following excerpt from a much long-er argument:

(e) ....Secondly, the study of religion should be a compulsory subject in the curricula of all public schools. After all, for one thing, religious people act better than non-religious people. And, for another, the study of religion should make or at least aim at mak-ing people religious....

In this excerpt, main premise 2 is supported by two mini-premises. Each of these mini-premises is highly controversial and each is unsupported. As the mini-argument stands, it is unlikely to gain any acceptance. The mini-premises need support. We would indicate this as follows:

support space   main argument space   evaluation space

1. ...

1. Religious people act better than non-religious people.
2. The study of religion should make or at least aim at making people religious.

2. The study of religion should be a compulsory subject in the curricula of all public schools. — support needed

— support needed

3. ...
. . ...

170

In pointing out that <u>support</u> or <u>more support</u> is
needed, we do not presume to answer the question,
how much support is needed? (or, how much more
support is required?). There is no one general
answer to questions concerning the necessary
amount of support. It's a matter which depends
very much on the particular circumstances in
which the argument is offered--how much support
is needed <u>in that context</u>. For example, it is
one thing to argue the guilt or innocence of
someone while riding in a taxi; it is quite another matter to argue this in the context of a
law court. So, too, arguing the pros and cons
of one political party over another may be one
thing with friends and acquaintances in a bar;
quite another matter on a talk show on national
TV. So, too, with arguing about the extent of
pollution in the Great Lakes. It is one thing
to argue about this with a friend; quite another,
to argue your point before an environmental
review agency. And so on. In each case the
particular circumstances in which the argument is
offered will affect how much support or additional support it is reasonable to expect. This
often calls for considerable judgment, expertise,
and general familiarity with what's expected in
each kind of circumstance.

When support for premises, or more support, is
called for, the defect can be readily remedied.
All that needs to be done is for the arguer to
provide the needed back-up or additional support
for his premises.

3.   Step #2

Step #2
Look at the language used in the premises
and conclusion and with respect to the
basic key words and expressions needed
to make sense of the argument, draw
attention to words and phrases which
(a) are vague
(b) are ambiguous

(c) exhibit an unhelpful use of language, or

(d) represent an undiscussed controversial definition.

This step focuses our critical attention on the <u>language</u> of the argument. It is, after all, the medium in which argumentation occurs, and it is an important vehicle for communication. It would be unreasonable, of course, to expect that all the words that occur in an argument will be precise and sufficiently pinpointed so that no shadow of doubt as to their meaning lingers. No one can be that precise all the time, nor, for the most part, is there any dire necessity to do so. We usually attempt to tailor our level of precision and specificity to the particular circumstances of the argument.

Recognizing, then, that we cannot be precise and specific all the time, it is not unreasonable, however, to demand that at least the basic key words and expressions will be clear and specific. Words that relate centrally to the topic or issue under discussion, words that deal with the advantages or merits of one approach over another that we may be recommending, words that articulate the traits or characteristics of whatever it is that we are talking about, and so on--these key words and expressions need to be clearly drawn so that we can grasp what the arguer is saying and what claim he is making. Failure to provide this in an argument serves to impede or block understanding. When this lack of clarity occurs in basic words and phrases needed to make sense of the argument, we should draw attention to this fact.

There are several features of language that can affect our ability to grasp accurately what is being said in an argument. Four such features are particularly noteworthy.

(a) vague words and expressions

A word or expression is <u>vague</u> when it lacks even

one clear meaning in the passage under discussion. The word 'infant' is an example of a vague word, for it is by no means clear what range in age is encompassed by this term. Other vague words and phrases include: peace with honor, death with dignity, right to life, wrestling inflation to the ground, peace of mind, the free enterprise system, the meaning of life, personal fulfillment, a meaningful relationship, and so on. (Such expressions can be made specific, by providing discussion and details, but as they stand, they are vague).

It is not unusual, of course, for an argument to contain vague words and phrases, and there is no need for us to draw attention to each and every vague word. Vagueness is a flaw in an argument only when the key words and phrases of the argument are left unclear, expressions that have to do basically with the topic being discussed, the claims being made, and so forth. If we are advocating euthanasia, for instance, and claim that people have "the right to die with dignity," we had better discuss this if we expect people to understand exactly what it is we are saying. Or, if we advocate that our country should adopt "a more aggressive attitude" towards the Soviet Union, we should make clear what we mean by this phrase. In any argument the basic words and phrases need to be made clear if people are to grasp accurately what is being claimed. It is vagueness in these circumstances for which we should be on the alert.

When an argument contains basic words and phrases that are vague, we should indicate this in the evaluation space of the format by making the comment "vague expression." Notice how vagueness has been handled in the following two sketches:

(f) <u>support space</u>   <u>main argument space</u>   <u>evaluation space</u>
         1. ...
         2. People who take
            vitamin E lead
            healthier, more _____ vague expressions
            fulfilled, more
            authentically
            human lives than
            those who do not.
         . . ...

(g) <u>support space</u>   <u>main argument space</u>   <u>evaluation space</u>
                                1. ...
1. Govt. should   2. ...
be responsive to   3. Governments should ___ vague expressions
the wishes of its   sponsor more law
decent and produc-   and order legis- _____ vague expression
tive citizens.   lation.
                     . . ...

Vagueness can be overcome: the arguer should
simply be more explicit about what his key
expressions mean.

(b) ambiguous words and expressions

A word or expression is ambiguous when it possess-
es <u>two or more</u> distinct meanings and when it is
unclear from the context which meaning is intended. (Note how ambiguity differs from vagueness).

With no context given, the word 'bank' in the
sentence "I'll meet you by the bank" is ambiguous:
it may mean the side of some river or else it
might mean a specific kind of financial institution. The word is ambiguous because it has two
distinct meanings and there is no way of telling
which meaning is intended in this instance.
Similarly, the word 'boom' is ambiguous in the
sentence: "Watch out for the boom!" The boom
referred to may be either the boom of a yacht,
the boom in stock market sales, or perhaps the
boom of an airplane breaking the sonic barrier

174

over-head. Again the word is ambiguous because
it has several distinct meanings and it is impossible to discern from the context which meaning is
intended.

Usually context (either the other words in the
passage or the actual situation in which the
expression occurs) will serve to disambiguate
expressions. On occasion, however, we will
encounter arguments in which expressions are
used ambiguously. When this happens, we will
place the comment "ambiguous expression" in evaluation space, drawing a line to the expression in
question, and mentioning the various possible
meanings the expression or term can have in the
passage under examination. Consider, for example,
the following argument, and let us suppose that
what the arguer has said in the premises does not
help us understand whether he means active euthanasia (actively removing life support systems) or
passive euthanasia (allowing nature to take its
course, without resorting to any extraordinary
life support systems to prolong life).

(h) support space   main argument space   evaluation space

                        1. ...
                        2. ...
                        3. ...   ambiguous expre-
                     ∴. The government ought   ssion (means
                        to permit doctors to   passive euthan-
                        practice euthanasia   asia? or active
                        on willing patients.   euthanasia?)

Ambiguity can be remedied by the arguer making
clear which of the several possible meanings for
the expression he intends.

(c) unhelpful use of language

Both vagueness and ambiguity are unhelpful uses
of language, at least from the point of view of
making clear what issues are to be resolved in
a controversy and what the main lines of support
are for particular positions.

175

There are, however, many other unhelpful uses of
language. On some occasions, an arguer may use
language which does not serve to support the
point at issue but rather is designed to irritate
or to inflame other arguers in the dispute or
else to attack the character or integrity of
another arguer in the controversy. Compare the
following:
  (A) My opponent advocates greater govern-
       mental involvement in controlling big
       business.
  (B) He stupidly suggests greater govern-
       mental involvement in controlling big
       business.
Statement (A) sticks to the position the arguer's
opponent is putting forth. Statement (B) serves
to deflect attention away from the position the
arguer's opponent is maintaining towards the
arguer's assessment of his mental perspicacity.
Unless the person arguing wants to show (i) that
his opponent advocates greater governmental invol-
vement in controlling big business and (ii) that
he does so stupidly, then (B) involves an unhelpful use of language. The phrase "stupidly
suggests" draws attention away from the issue at
hand towards a much lesser concern.

If statement (B) occurred in the context of an
argument, we would place the comment "unhelpful
use of language" in evaluation space, drawing a
line to the word or phrase in question. This
kind of defect can be remedied simply by eliminating the unhelpful language in question and by
focusing instead on the issue at hand.

(d) undiscussed controversial definitions

In the course of offering an argument, many arguers will introduce definitions into the discussion, either to clarify what they mean by a particular word or else to give an old word some new
specific twist. Such a move is often helpful,
especially if the controversy is in danger of
becoming bogged down in semantics.

The definitions that are incorporated into an argument, need, however, to be carefully intro- duced. They should, on one hand, be clearly worded, with all vague, ambiguous or unhelpful words eliminated. On the other hand, they need to be plausible. Making sure that a definition is plausible involves some discussion on the part of the arguer, to ensure that other participants in the controversy will regard the definition as appropriate and legitimate. Definitions, in other words, and particularly controversial definitions, need to be supported.

If an arguer introduces a controversial defini- tion into the discussion that plays an important role in the argument and yet fails to back it up with adequate discussion, we should note this shortcoming in evaluation space. We would write "undiscussed controversial definition" as our comment and draw a line to the definition which is unsupported.

Consider, for instance, the following argument:
(i) The heart of the abortion issue is the ques- tion: what is a person? In my judgment, a human organism is a person only when it is capable of interacting actively with other people and the world, and when it is capable of rational thought. A fetus isn't a person: a fetus can't interact actively with other people and the world, and it isn't capable of rational thought. Therefore aborting a fetus isn't the same thing as killing a person.
The entire argument turns on the definition of 'person'. Yet, it is an undiscussed definition. The definition may be a good one but the point is however, that the arguer has not backed it up nor made it at all plausible. In addition, it is cluttered with vague expressions: "interacting actively with other people and the world," and "rational thought." Before this definition can be of much use in ascertaining whether or not a fetus satisfies its conditions, these vague expressions would have to be extensively clarified

by discussion. In evaluating this argument's
worth in terms of Step #2, our critical comments
would appear as follows:

support space	main argument space	evaluation space
	1. The heart of the abortion issue is the question: what is a person?	
	2. A human organism ◄——— is a person only when it is <u>capable of interacting actively with other people and the world</u>, and when it is <u>capa-ble of rational thought</u>.	undiscussed controversial definition vague expressions
	3. A fetus isn't a ◄——— person: fetus can't interact actively with other people and the world and it isn't capable of rational thought.	support needed
	∴ Aborting a fetus isn't the same thing as kill-ing a person.	

The remedy for this kind of shortcoming in an
argument is obvious: discuss, support and clarify
the undiscussed controversial definition.

4. <u>Step #3</u>

<u>Step #3</u>
Look for missing premises (needed to
establish the conclusion).

Usually an arguer will proceed point by point in
offering his argument, leading us gradually up to
his conclusion. To do otherwise would be to place
our acceptance of his conclusion in jeopardy.
Occasionally, however, we may come across a

puzzling gap in an argument - it seems as though
the arguer has left something out, something needed to establish his conclusion. When this happens
we can usually tell not only that something is
missing but also what is missing. That is, we
can usually put our finger on what the arguer
should have said explicitly (but didn't). The
context in which the argument is offered often
makes this clear. The arguer may simply have
taken for granted that under the circumstances
we'd naturally read into his argument the point
he neglected to mention.

We should make it explicit, however. Where a
premise needed to establish a conclusion has been
omitted from an argument, we draw attention to
this in our critical evaluation of it. We do
so as follows:
- in evaluation space we make the comment
  "missing premise"
- in the body of the argument, we supply the
  premise we say has been omitted, placing
  it in wedges (< >) to indicate that it is
  something we have read into the argument.
  (Different argument analysts will word this
  missing premise somewhat differently, of
  course).
- along with our comment we indicate briefly
  why we think a premise has been omitted.

Consider the following argument:
(j) (presented at a Right-to-Life, anti-abortion,
    rally dealing with various forms of threats
    to human life in society today.)
    ...Euthanasia, too, in all its forms, would
    be a denial of the right to life. So, then,
    euthanasia should also be rejected.
As this argument stands, it has 1 premise and a
conclusion. But something seems to be missing.
What connects a denial of the right to life
(premise 1) with the rejection of euthanasia (in
the conclusion)? The context - a Right-to-Life
rally-would appear to indicate that what is absent
is a premise to the effect that any denial of the
right to life should be rejected. The arguer

probably assumed that everyone present would hold this view and would automatically read it into the argument. It is something we should make explicit - it's a point that we, the argument analyst, might wish to challenge by way of response. Our work would appear as follows:

support space	main argument space	evaluation space
	1. Euthanasia, too, in all its forms, would be a denial of the right to life.	missing premise (evident from
	2. < any denial of the right to life should be rejected. >	context of a Right-to-Life rally)
	.˙. Euthanasia should also be rejected.	

What we called an "unexpressed assumption" in Part One of this text fulfills the role of a missing premise in an argument. As you will recall, such assumptions were positions the arguer has taken for granted in the course of making his argument, which he has not explicitly stated, and which plays an important role in understanding the argument or in assessing its worth. It is time now to incorporate these assumptions into the body of an argument, as a missing premise. Consider the following argument:

(k)   The present Grade Five reading materials should be discarded. For one thing, they portray girls in dependent and domestic roles, boys in active and career-oriented roles. Such role stereotyping, moreover, is blatantly sexist.

As it stands, the argument contains 2 premises and a conclusion. But it omits something, an unexpressed position which in this day and age the arguer has taken for granted, namely that what is sexist should be discarded. It certainly seems evident from what he says that he's opposed to sexism. Rather than placing this unexpressed position in left space, we can now proceed to insert it into the main body of the argument, thereby recognizing more fully the role that such an unexpressed position plays. It is, simply, a missing premise.

Our work would be displayed as follows:

support space	main argument space	evaluation space
	1. They portray girls in dependent and domestic roles, boys in active career-oriented roles.	
	2. Such role stereotyping is blatantly sexist.	
	3. < What is sexist < ─────── should be discarded.>	Missing premise (evident from context).
	∴ The present Grade Five reading materials should be discarded.	

By pointing out the missing premise, we have thereby rectified the shortcoming we've detected, making explicit what is implicit. In doing this, however, we have supplied yet another premise to be subjected to critical scrutiny. The missing premises furnished in arguments (j) and (k) need to be submitted to other steps in argument evaluation - Step #1, for instance.

5. Step #4

Step #4
Look for absent qualifiers in the premises and conclusion.

Often premises or conclusions omit important qualifiers (such as "all," "some," "most," "rarely," "always," "never," "for the most part," etc.) which would serve to qualify the point being made. Consider, for example, argument (d) above that contains the following third premise:
3.   Religion fosters a sense of brotherhood and a tolerance of other people.
This premise would become much less contentious, and require much less support, if it were to be constructed as containing an important qualifier: "on some occasions." We should pinpoint such

181

areas of clarification and indicate the proposed
emendation in right space, drawing a line to where
the insert should be placed:

support space	main argument space	evaluation space
	1. ...	
	2. ...	
	3. Religion fosters a sense of brother-hood and a tolerance of other people	qualifier omitt-ed? insert: "On some occasions."
	. . ...	

When qualified, premise 3 would be compatible with
there being occasions on which religion has not
fostered a sense of brotherhood and a tolerance
for other people. It would represent a much less
extreme position than the statement with the
qualifier omitted.

6. Summary

The first 4 steps in argument evaluation are as
follows:

#1	Look at the premises in the argument and draw attention to those that need support or more support.
#2	Look at the language used in the premises and conclusion and with respect to the basic key words and expressions needed to make sense of the argument, draw attention to words and phrases which (a) are vague (b) are ambiguous (c) exhibit an unhelpful use of language, (d) represent an undiscussed controversial definition.
#3	Look for missing premises (needed to establish the conclusion).
#4	Look for absent qualifiers in the premises and conclusion.

Let's apply these 4 steps to an argument. Bear

in mind that not all arguments exhibit all defects and that each step, moreover, should be applied to mini-arguments as well as the main argument.

(1)   Kids in school today can't read as well as those of 25 years ago. Moreover they lead lives that are less rich and less fulfilling then those of yesteryear. In addition, the school curriculum today is unbalanced. Kids, after all, have too many options and there is, moreover, less emphasis today on math, science, and reading and more emphasis on social studies. Schools, therefore, should return to a more structured curriculum.

The structure of this argument should be readily apparent: 3 main premises (the third being supported by 2 mini-premises) and a conclusion. It exhibits a variety of defects, however: premises 1 and 2 are unsupported; the mini-premises of premise 3 need support; some words and phrases in premise 2 are vague; and there seems to be an unexpressed position to the effect that a structural school curriculum would remedy the deficiencies mentioned by the arguer in premises 1, 2 and 3. So: our work would appear as follows:

support space	main argument space	evaluation space
	1. Kids in school today ←— support needed	
	can't read as well as	
	those of 25 years ago.	
	2. They lead lives that ←— support needed	
	are less rich and less	
	fulfilling than those — vague expressions	
	of yesteryear. —— support needed	
1. Kids... options. 2. There is less...social studies.	3. The school curriculum is unbalanced.	
	4. < a structured school — vague expression	
	curriculum would ← missing premise	
	remedy the deficiencies (evident from	
	mentioned above > context)	
	∴ Schools should return to a more structured curriculum.	

183

Recall Quiz

(1) In what space of the standard format is argument evaluation placed?

(2) In identifying and evaluating arguments, which task should we do first: argument evaluation or argument identification? Why?

(3) What are some of the main purposes of argument evaluation? (mention 5)

(4) What is an offered argument, a genuine argument, a bogus "argument"?

(5) What kinds of defectiveness are there? (mention 2). How do they differ?

(6) How many steps in argument evaluation will be presented in this text?

(7) Does argument evaluation apply to mini-arguments as well as to main arguments? Why?

(8) What are the first 4 steps in argument evaluation?

(9) With respect to each of the first 4 steps, what sorts of comments are made in evaluation space?

(10) With respect to each of the first 4 steps, how can each kind of defect be remedied?

(11) How do vagueness and ambiguity differ?

Exercise #1

Examine the arguments already identified in the exercise at the end of Chapter One. Critically evaluate these arguments in terms of steps 1, 2, 3 and 4.

Exercise #2

Examine the arguments already identified in Exercise #1 at the end of Chapter Two. Critically evaluate these arguments in terms of steps 1, 2, 3 and 4.

CHAPTER SIX

ARGUMENT EVALUATION: FALLACIES I

1.   Introduction

fallacies

In this chapter and the next we will be concerned
with what have traditionally been called "fall-
cies." Simply put, fallacies are errors in
reasoning. They include a great many different
sorts of mistakes and flaws that affect arguments
in a number of important ways. Because of this,
fallacies are difficult to systematize in any
comprehensive manner and there is no one generally
accepted framework of classification.

In this text we will approach this material in
three steps, each step focusing on a different
aspect of argument evaluation and including within
its scope a different cluster of those errors and
shortcomings called "fallacies." In this chapter
we will introduce Step #5: in the next chapter,
Steps #6 and #7.

bogus premises

In a genuine argument, the premises support the
conclusion. On occasion we come across arguments
where this relationship of support between premises and conclusion is disrupted. We find that
some offered arguments contain premises which fail
to support the conclusion. Such offered premises
may masquerade as genuine premises. Indeed, they
may be intended by the arguer to be genuine: they
may have been put forward as bona fide premises.
But where an offered premise fails to support the
conclusion, it ought to be rejected as a premise.

Premises which are offered as support for a

conclusion but which, upon examination, are found
to give no support to the conclusion, are called
"bogus" (or "spurious") premises. Bogus premises
give no support to the conclusion of the argument;
hence they are not genuine premises at all. If
the offered argument consists entirely of bogus
premises, then it fails to be a genuine argument:
it consists only of an unsupported claim. If the
offered argument consists of a mixture of bogus
and genuine premises, then we should delete the
bogus ones from the argument, retaining only the
genuine ones.

There are many reasons, of course, why an offered
premise may be bogus. Some of these reasons are
indicated below. If we advocate in evaluation
space the deletion of a premise from an argument,
then it is incumbent upon us to state our reason
for this recommendation. The general form this
recommendation takes is as follows:

support space	main argument space	evaluation space
	1. ... ←———————	Delete: the prem-
	2. ...	ise is bogus
	————————————————	because...
	∴ ...	

This annotation in evaluation space indicates that
we advocate deleting premise 2; the reason on
which we base this recommendation is indicated in
the "..." slot following the 'because'. Some
standard reasons for advocating deletion of a
premise because it is bogus are indicate below.

Suppose all the offered premises are bogus. Then
we would also indicate beside the conclusion that
the offered argument fails to be a genuine argument (because, being bogus, all the offered premises have been deleted). The general form this
annotation takes is as follows:

support space	main argument space	evaluation space
	1. ... ←———————	Delete: the prem-
		ise is bogus
		because...

186

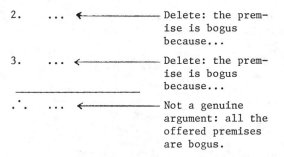

2.　　...　←————————— Delete: the prem-
　　　　　　　　　　　　ise is bogus
　　　　　　　　　　　　because...

3.　　...　←————————— Delete: the prem-
　　　　　　　　　　　　ise is bogus
　　　　　　　　　　　　because...
　————————————————
∴　　...　←————————— Not a genuine
　　　　　　　　　　　　argument: all the
　　　　　　　　　　　　offered premises
　　　　　　　　　　　　are bogus.

The next step in argument evaluation is to examine
the argument for bogus premises, deleting them
from the argument where they occur.

2. Step #5

Step #5
Look at the premises offered by the arguer
to ascertain if any are bogus. If any
are, then recommend deletion of the premise and state the reason. A premise may
be bogus for any of the following reasons:

(a) because it is ad hominem (AH)

Suppose there are two arguers. For ease of reference, let's call them "E" and "B". Suppose E has
put forward the following argument which we have
reconstructed as follows:
E's argument

support space	main argument space	evaluation space
	1. Abortion is the killing of a fetus.	
	2. Fetuses are human.	
	3. Killing humans is murder.	
	4. Murder should not be allowed by society.	
	∴ Abortion should not be allowed by society.	

187

Suppose, furthermore, that arguer B offers the following argument in reply:

B's argument

support space	main argument space	evaluation space
	1. Arguer E is a Roman Catholic.	
	∴ What E says about abortion should be disregarded.	

The argument B offers is seriously defective, for in premise 1, B simply draws attention to E's religious commitments without coming to grips with the argument E has offered. The premise of B's argument fails to support the conclusion: pointing out E's religious affiliation does not, in and of itself, support the claim that E's position ought therefore to be set aside. It is especially ludicrous when, in context, E has offered an argument on behalf of his position. E's argument may not be particularly good (and this is a matter for argument evaluation). The point is, however, that B has not responded to E's argument at all: he has simply attacked E himself.

B's offered argument is defective. It is defective because the premise offered fails to support the claim made. In this case, because premise 1 is the only premise offered, the argument presented by B fails to constitute a genuine argument. Because the offered premise focuses its attention on a personal characteristic of the opposing arguer, it is said to be bogus because it is ad hominem (that is, directed towards the person, not the position put forward by the person).

An offered premise is bogus because it is ad hominem when the offered premise simply attacks the person argued against. In general, an offered premise that is bogus because it is ad hominem has the following structure:

1. The opposing arguer is a ...

∴ What the opposing arguer says ought to be disregarded.

In the "..." slot of premise 1 would appear some
personal characteristic of the opposing arguer.
The conclusion, of course, may be expressed in a
variety of ways, all serving to dismiss from
serious consideration the position the opposing
arguer has put forward.

In annotating B's argument, we should make the
following comments in the evaluation space:

support space	main argument space	evaluation space
	1. Arguer E is a Roman ←—Catholic.	Delete: the premise is bogus because it is AH
	∴ What E says about ←——abortion should be disregarded.	Not a genuine argument: all the offered premises are bogus

It should be noted carefully that bogus premises
may occur alongside genuine premises in an offered argument. In this case, only the bogus premises are deleted from the argument, and the
strength of the argument rests solely on the
remaining genuine premises. Also notice that
because mini-arguments are offered arguments,
mini-premises may be bogus. When this occurs,
the same sort of annotation should appear in
evaluation space and a line drawn to the mini-
premise in support space indicating the recommended deletion.

An argument that is defective because it contains
a bogus ad hominem premise may be remedied in
several ways:
     (1) The arguer could attempt to establish
        a connection between the opposing
        arguer's personal characteristics and
        the unacceptability of his position.
In terms of B's argument above, this would require
B to establish (if he can) the connection between
E's being Roman Catholic and E's position being
disregarded. Even if this is possible, this
option is unlikely to result in a good argument.
B could modify his argument by adding this premise:

what Roman Catholics say about abortion should be
disregarded. With the addition of this premise,
premise 1 would serve to support the conclusion.
But this ad hoc tactic simply shifts the defect
in the argument to support for the new second
premise.

A better approach is this:
          (2) the arguer could start afresh, with a
               different argument.
This new argument could, for instance, attack one
of the premises in the opposing arguer's position.
Or, it could introduce new considerations on
behalf of a conclusion that is the negation of
the opposing arguer's position. In terms of B's
argument above, this would require B to stop
name-calling and to start arguing. B could attack
one of E's premises. Or B could take a different
line of thought, constructing a new argument which
would have as its conclusion: therefore, abortion
should be allowed by society (This is the negation
of E's conclusion).

Common to all ad hominem bogus premises is the
attack on the person, not on the position put forward by the person, and the dismissal of that
person's position just because of that individual's
personal characteristics. There are many ways in
which an ad hominem attack can occur. The following are some common ways:

          (1) by character assassination.
This occurs when an arguer Y uses a derogatory
phrase about his opposing arguer X in order to
dismiss X's position. A typical ad hominem attack
using character assassination would go as follows:
Y might argue:
     1. Arguer X is stupid (or arrogant, conniving, a
        liar, a liberal, a chauvinist, a racist, a
        sexist, certifiable, incompetent, etc.)

     ∴. The position X put forward should be disregarded.
Just because X is what Y says X is (even if true)
is no reason to dismiss the position X has put
forward. The premise is bogus because Y has

engaged in an ad hominem attack on X.

(2) by attacking origins.
This occurs when an arguer Y cites X's origin in
order to set aside X's position. A typical ad
hominem attack using an attack on an arguer's
origins would go as follows. Suppose Y argues:

1. Arguer X is a Yankee (or a Wasp, a
    Southerner, an immigrant, a rural hick, etc.)

∴. The position X put forward should be
    disregarded

Just because those are X's origins (even if true) is
no reason to dismiss the position X has put forward. The premise is bogus because Y has indulged
in an ad hominem attack on X.

(3) by attacking affiliations.
This occurs when an arguer Y mentions the religious or political or social or professional
affiliations and commitments of an opposing arguer
X in order to discount the position X has put
forward. A typical ad hominem approach by attacking affiliations would go as follows. Suppose
arguer Y maintains:

1. Arguer X is a Baptist (or Roman Catholic,
    scientist, Republican, car salesman, an
    industrialist, a crusader for Free Enterprise,
    etc.)

∴. The position X has put forward should be
    disregarded.

Just because arguer X has the affiliations Y
alleges (even if true) is no reason to discount
the position X has put forward. The premise is
bogus because Y has committed an ad hominem attack
on X.

(4) by suggesting guilt by association.
This occurs when arguer Y cites an organization
of dubious merit to which X is alleged to belong
and when Y uses the unacceptability of this organization and X's alleged membership in it to impugn
the position X has put forward. It is unimportant
whether or not the organization is of dubious
merit; it is simply sufficient for Y to suppose

this, and even to suppose that his audience will share his supposition. A typical ad hominem attack using a guilt by association slur would go as follows: Suppose Y reasons that

1. Arguer X is a member of the Flat Earth Society (or the KKK, the Communist Party, the Anti-vivisectionists, or any other organization Y deems of dubious merit).

∴ The position X has put forward should be disregarded.

Just because arguer X is a member of the organization Y alleges (even if true) and even if this organization should be unacceptable to Y and to his audience, this is no reason to discount the position X has put forward. The premise is bogus because Y has engaged in an ad hominem attack on X.

These four ways, then, are some common instances of ad hominem attacks. In each case the premise is bogus because it serves to dismiss the conclusion just because of some personal characteristic of the opposing arguer. An ad hominem attack represents a serious defect in reasoning. When all premises offered are bogus, then no argument has been made at all, although the arguer has attempted to foist off his argument as genuine. Even when an argument contains some genuine premises in addition to bogus ones which we have deleted, the high emotional energy generated by personal ad hominem attacks deflects attention away from the issue at hand and the evidence pro and con.

An ad hominem premise has traditionally been treated as an attack on an opposing arguer to discredit his position. It should be equally clear that any premise that just appeals to the personal character (or origins or affiliation) of an arguer in order to gain acceptance of the conclusion put forward by that arguer is similarly bogus. In this extended sense of ad hominem, the premise in the following argument schema is bogus:

1. Arguer X is a ...

.˙. What X says ought
to be accepted.

Just because X is what he is alleged to be is no
reason either to accept (or reject) what he says.

From what has been said above about ad hominem
attacks, it should not be supposed that all
attacks on a person's character are illegitimate
in argumentation. There are some situations in
which the character of an arguer is at stake. In
courtroom situations, for example, a lawyer may
attack the character of a witness: his reliability,
his competence, his expertise, the accuracy of
his memory, his vested interests, his political
and professional affiliations and commitments,
etc. Such attacks on a witness's character may
be purely ad hominem -- that is, using a personal
characteristic just to discredit his testimony
before a judge or jury. Or they may represent
serious attempts to have what the witness says
discounted.

In the latter case, impugning what a witness says
requires much more than a simple allegation that
he is incompetent, unreliable, not an expert,
unduly biassed, or unqualified to testify, etc.
Suppose a lawyer wants to set aside the testimony
of witness P on the grounds that P is incompetent.
In this case, the lawyer must first of all defend
(i.e. support) the view that P is incompetent.
Secondly, the lawyer must contend that only compe-
tent testimony in this matter should be heeded.
(In normal courtroom situations, premise 2 would
probably simply be assumed, as part of customary
courtroom procedures). In this case, the lawyer's
argument would have the following general structure:

support space	main argument space	evaluation space

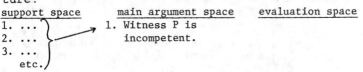

1. ...   1. Witness P is
2. ...   incompetent.
3. ...
   etc.

```
1. ...  ⎫ ─────────→  2. Only competent
   etc. ⎭                testimony in this
                         matter should be
                         heeded.
                      ─────────────────
                   .˙. The testimony of
                       witness P should
                       be disregarded.
```

An argument of this sort differs from an ad
hominem attack: the allegation (premise 1) is
supported by considerations [which in standard
format are placed in support space] and the personal characteristics of the witness are made germane
to the issue under discussion (in premise 2).
Neither premise is bogus. The lawyer has made an
argument.

In addition to an ad hominem attack, consider a
second reason why a premise may be bogus:

(b) because it begs the question (BQ)

An offered premise may be bogus because it states
the same information, perhaps in slightly different words, as the conclusion. When this occurs,
the offered premise "begs the question" -- that
is, it assumes ("begs") the very point ("question")
at issue in the discussion. Such arguments are
often said to be "circular," for what they reason
from is the same as what they reason to, and vice
versa. The offered premise gives no support to
the conclusion (it is the conclusion). It therefore should be deleted from the argument.

An offered premise is bogus because it begs the
question when it states or contains the same
information as the conclusion of the argument.
Such a defect may occur in a variety of ways:

> (1) when the premise and conclusion state
>   the same information, with only minor
>   stylistic variations.

A blatant example of this would be the following

concocted argument:

support space	main argument space	evaluation space
	1. If you smoke, you're ← likely to get lung cancer.	Delete: the prem- ise is bogus because BQ
	∴ You're likely to get ← lung cancer if you smoke.	Not a genuine argument: all the offered premises are bogus.

In this offered argument, both premise and the
conclusion state the same information with only a
minor stylistic variation. Such blatant examples
of begging the question rarely occur. Usually
the matter is much subtler.

> (2) when the premise and conclusion state
> the same information, although worded
> quite differently.

Usually begging the question occurs because in the
course of making an argument, the arguer has
mistakenly incorporated into his argument as one
of his premises the very conclusion he is trying
to support. The arguer himself may be misled
because on first hearing or first reading the two
points (premise and the conclusion) do not appear
to be the same: the different wording may throw
off the arguer from realizing that he has stated
the same information twice, once as a premise and
once as a conclusion. When worded differently,
the two sentences are probably not going to be
strictly synonymous: it is usually more a matter
of containing more or less the same information.
Consider the following argument.

support space	main argument space	evaluation space
	1. Welfare, government hospital schemes, unemployment insur- ance, legal aid, old age pensions are all socialist schemes of a degenerate democra- tic system.	

1. Many university and government economists spout socialistic platitudes.

〈 this is undesirable 〉

〈 this is undesirable 〉

1. Socialist schemes undermine democratic attitudes.

2. Our country is currently being led by socialist thinkers.

3. (2) has had serious repercussions:

a) on the economy of the country by bleeding taxpayers, and

b) on fostering an attitude of dependency on the government.

4. (3b) sets up unhealthy expectations in citizens of what a government is and what a government should do.

5. All socialist schemes such as those cited in (1) ought to be rejected by legislators bent on maintaining the merits of our system.

6. The values of individuality, freedom and self-sufficiency far outweigh the cries for compassion for those who can't make it in our system.

7. Such compassion is misplaced compassion anyway: it only enslaves its recipients to further governmental beneficience.

∴ For preserving the good of our system, welfare, government hospital schemes, unemployment insurance, legal aid, and old age pensions ought to be rescinded by our representatives.

Compare closely the conclusion and premise 5: both items identify pieces of legislation (those named in premise 1) that ought to be rejected by legislators for the well-being of the present

196

system. Although worded differently, premise 5 and the conclusion state the same information. Therefore premise 5 is bogus. We should recommend its deletion from the argument.

So, next to premise 5, in evaluation space: we would place the annotation: Delete: the premise is bogus because BQ. In this case, the offered argument is still an argument, because there are other premises besides 5 which has been deleted. The strength of the argument, of course, rests on the remaining premises.

Suppose in the above example, with all 7 premises listed, the conclusion were as follows:

.˙. Socialist schemes erode
basic democratic values.

In this argument, too, there is an example of a bogus premise. It is mini-premise 1 on behalf of the main premise 5 which, while worded differently, more or less states the same information as the conclusion.

Arguments containing premises that beg the question can readily be improved. The offending premise should be stricken from the argument and a new premise (or premises) added which would support the conclusion.

In addition to begging the question and ad hominem attacks, consider another reason why a premise may be bogus:

(c) because it appeals to authority (AA)

It is perfectly legitimate, in the course of making an argument or case, to introduce opinions other than one's own and to cite authorities for the point of view one is developing. The point to be careful about, however, is not to rest the weight of what one is saying just upon the sheer say-so of the authority but rather upon the evidence the authority has to support the position.

This point is often overlooked and often unappreciated because of an overly generous and often unwarranted assumption made by arguers that authorities do have evidence to support their positions. This is not always so: the authority, for instance, may be bluffing. Or the authority may be expressing a point of view in an area in which the evidence is conflicting. Or, indeed, the authority may be speaking well outside of his area of expertise, allowing his image as an authority to lend weight to his point of view. In any case, what makes an authority an authority is not his personage: rather it is the evidence he has marshalled on behalf of his position. Careful reasoning takes pains to incorporate into the argument not only the name of the authority but also the general lines of considerations the authority has to back up his position. This preserves what is truly authoritative in argumentation: the evidence, not the personage.

Some offered premises are seriously defective when they simply name an authority and report the position he holds <u>without</u> indicating the evidence the authority has to support the position. Such offered premises are bogus, contributing nothing to the development of the argument. What follows from the statement that authority A holds position P is that A holds P, not that P is true.

An offered premise is bogus, then, when it rests solely on the authority of the person or group expressing the point contained in the premise. The general form of an appeal to authority is as follows:

1. <u>Authority A holds position P.</u>

∴ Position P is true.

Note in passing that the reason for the conclusion ("Position P is true") is that authority A advocates this position. It would be incorrect there-

fore, to represent the general schema of this type
of reasoning as follows:

support space	main argument space	evaluation space
Authority A ⟶	1. Advocates position P.	

∴ P is true.

This representation would not capture that the
reason for the conclusion is authority A's maintaining position P. Furthermore, it would imply
that such arguments beg the question, by definition, and this is false. There is a crucial
difference between saying "authority A advocates
P" and saying "P is true."

The authority appealed to may be any of the following: for example:
  (1) an author (e.g. a published expert in
      some field, a scientist, a famous person
      from history, etc.).
  (2) a leader, a public figure, a spokesper-
      son for some group, etc.
  (3) a group or institution (e.g. "the AMA
      says ...," "the DAR maintains ...," "the
      AFL/CIO contends ...," etc.)
  (4) society generally (e.g. "Society today
      holds that ...," "Everybody now believes
      that ...," etc.)
  (5) a book (e.g. "As Future Shock points out,
      ..." or as Plato maintains in The Repub-
      lic, ..." etc.)
And so on. Just because any of these authorities
advocate position P does not support the claim
that position P is true. What is lacking are the
evidential considerations that lie behind the
position the authority cited is maintaining. This
indicates the broad general lines along which the
appeal to authority can be rectified: where the
authority cited is an authentic authority, and has
evidence to support the position being touted,
then the general outlines of the authority's case
should be cited. In this way, the weight of the
conclusion of the argument would rest not upon the
authority himself, but upon the case he has
assembled on behalf of the position he maintains.

Offered premises which simply appeal to the say-so
of some authority without indicating the lines of
support the authority has for the position should
be deleted from the argument. We should single
out such bogus premises, annotating them in evaluation space as follows:
    Delete: premise is spurious because AA.

<u>There is, however, the following exception.</u> Where
it is reasonable for us to suppose that the
authority is indeed an authority, and that he is
speaking within the general orbit of his competence, and that he has evidence to support the
position being made, then we may urge not just the
deletion of the premise but also mention that the
defect could be rectified by support for the position put forward in the premise. In this case, we
should write in evaluation space of the standard
format next to the offending premise the following
annotation:
    Delete: premise is bogus because AA. Could
    be rectified by support for position stated.
This recommendation for rectification has the
effect of eliminating the appeal just to the
authority cited, placing the weight of the case on
the evidential considerations the authority has
for the position stated.

Consider the following examples of appeals to
authority:

support space	main argument space	evaluation space
	1. Linus Pauling says that massive doses of Vitamin C can help prevent colds.	
	∴ Massive doses of Vita- min C can help prevent colds.	

As it stands, premise 1 is bogus because it simply
appeals to authority: the authority of Linus Pauling. No reasons are given to support the view
that massive doses of Vitamin C can help prevent
colds other than the fact that Linus Pauling says
so. Yet it is reasonable to suppose that Linus
Pauling, being a leader in Vitamin C research, has

considerable evidence to support this position. Presumably, then, this argument could easily be rectified by incorporating into the argument support for Pauling's position on Vitamin C. This we should point out in evaluation space. (Also notice that the expressions "massive doses" and "can help prevent" are vague key expressions). This argument would be annotated in evaluation space as follows:

support space	main argument space	evaluation space
	1. Linus Pauling says ◄——— that <u>massive doses</u> of Vitamin C <u>can</u> <u>help prevent</u> colds.	Delete: premise is bogus because AA. Could be rectified by support for position stated.
	————————————————	vague expressions
	∴ Massive doses of ◄——— Vitamin C can help prevent colds.	Not a genuine argument unless rectified as suggested: all the offered premises are bogus.

Consider next this argument:

support space	main argument space	evaluation space
	1. Xaviera Hollander ◄——— claims that Dr. Spock's latest child-rearing techniques are a step <u>in the right direction.</u>	Delete: premise is bogus because AA.
	∴ Dr. Spock's latest ◄——— child-rearing techniques are a step in the right direction.	Not a genuine argument: all the offered premises are bogus.

Premise 1 is bogus: it rests solely on the say-so of Xaviera Hollander. The premise should be deleted. Furthermore, since Xaviera Hollander is not an acknowledged authority in the area of child-rearing, it is unlikely that producing evidence on behalf of her point of view is going to improve the situation.

201

Consider these additional appeals to authority:

support space	main argument space	evaluation space
	1. Most geologists and meteorologists now say that ice ages can occur very rapidly and that another one is probably due any time.	Delete: premise is bogus because AA. Could be rectified by support for position stated.
	∴ We're likely to have an ice age pretty soon.	Not a genuine argument unless rectified as suggested: all the offered premises are bogus.

Another example:

support space	main argument space	evaluation space
	1. Society today generally approves of abortion.	Delete: premise is bogus because AA.
	∴ Abortion is right.	Not a genuine argument: all the offered premises are bogus.

All that follows from the statement that society today generally approves of abortion is that . abortion is approved of by present-day society. This is uninformative -- indeed, if intended as an argument, it would beg the question. It does not support the conclusion that abortion is right (unless 'right' is defined as "what society approves of." In this case, though, the argument would beg the question.)

Another example, similar to the one above:

support space	main argument space	evaluation space
	1. 78% of people in society today are in favor of abortion on demand.	Delete: premise is bogus because AA.

202

```
∴  Abortion on demand ◄── Not a genuine
     is right.              argument: all
                            the offered
                            premises are
                            bogus.
```

All that follows from that statement that 78% of
people in society today favor abortion on demand
is that abortion is favored by 78% of the people
in present-day society: the premise does not
support the conclusion that abortion on demand is
right. Premise 1 is therefore bogus.

Even if 'right' were to be defined as "what most
people in society favor," the argument would still
be defective since it would then beg the question.
It would also introduce into the argument an
undiscussed controversial definition. Also notice
that matters are not helped by placing the following support for premise 1 in support space: Gallup
Poll, June 28th, 1980. The premise would still
be spurious, appealing just to the authority of
public opinion to settle the rightness of an issue.
The argument needs to be completely reworked,
examining critically the arguments being advanced
in that society in favor of abortion on demand.

In addition to begging the question, ad hominem
attacks, and appeal to authority, consider another
reason why a premise may be bogus:

(d) because it represents an irrelevant reason (IR)

An offered premise is irrelevant to the conclusion
of an argument when it contributes nothing by way
of evidential worth to the argument. Such premises fail to support the conclusion and are therefore bogus. They should be deleted from the argument. In general, we should make the following
annotation in evaluation space of the standard
format:

support space	main argument space	evaluation space
	1. ... ←———————	Delete: the
	2. ...	premise is bogus
		because IR.
	————————————	
	.	
	. . ...	

While devoid of evidential worth, premises which
represent an irrelevent reason (irrelevant, it
should be noted, to the conclusion of the argument)
often have persuasive worth. They may work effectively on us, perhaps even to the point of getting
us to accept the position stated in the conclusion.
Such arguments may have considerable persuasive
worth. They are effective not because evidence is
presented on behalf of a conclusion but because
what is said in the offered premises is designed
to manipulate or compel us into accepting the
position stated. Such offered arguments are not
genuine arguments -- that is, they are not devices
that serve the interests of rational decision-making by bringing forth evidence to support positions. Rather they serve the purposes of coercive
persuasion and intimidation, to the exclusion of
evidential considerations.

There are many sorts of irrelevant reasons that
arguers may appeal to in the course of offering
an argument. In a sense, the defects already
labelled "ad hominem," "begging the question,"
and "appeal to authority" constitute irrelevant
reasons, although these are given separate names
because of their prevalence in argumentation.
There are a great host of other irrelevant reasons
that can collectively be grouped under this broad
category heading. They include at least the
following:

(i) irrelevant reason (appeal to force)

Some offered premises, rather than supporting the
conclusion, serve to threaten the person argued
against in order to coerce acceptance of a particular position. Because such a reason fails to
support the conclusion, it is called an irrelevant
reason (appeal to force) and it should be stricken

204

from the argument as bogus. For example, imagine
the following exchange between father and 14-year
old daughter:

daughter: But I want to go steady with
            Harry.
father: No way.
daughter: I'm old enough to make up my
            own mind.
father: Look, if you don't do as I
            say, I'll make sure you never
            see Harry again.

As reconstructed, the father's argument would
appear as follows:

support space	main argument space	evaluation space
	1. If you don't do as I ◄── say, I'll make sure you never see Harry again.	Delete: the premise is bogus because IR (appeal to force).
	∴. You can't go steady ◄── with Harry.	Not a genuine argument: all offered premises are bogus.

The offered premise is irrelevant to the conclusion: it has nothing to do with the merits or
demerits of the daughter going steady with Harry.
It appeals to force, at least to the threat of
force, since it suggests that if the daughter does
not comply with the father's position, he will
prevent her from ever seeing Harry again.

Consider another example, this time, an exchange
between a major stockholder in a company and a
member of the board of directors. The scene is an
annual meeting of the company.

stockholder: The company's mining operations
               in South Africa help support
               an apartheid regime.
director: Nonsense. They help provide a
               much needed source of employ-
               ment for South African Blacks.
stockholder: The company ought to cease all
               operations in South Africa.

205

director: That seems a bit rash.
stockholder: If you don't do as I say, I'll
               muster other like-minded stock-
               holders and we'll take over
               the company and put in a board
               of directors that'll do as we
               say.

As reconstructed, the stockholder's argument
would appear as follows:

support space	main argument space	evaluation space
	1. The company's mining ←—	premise needs
	operations in South	support
	Africa help support	
	an apartheid regime.	
	2. If you don't do as I ←—	delete: premise
	say, I'll muster other	is bogus because
	like-minded stockhold-	IR (appeal to
	ers and we'll take over	force).
	the company and put in	
	a board of directors	
	that'll do as we say.	

  ∴. The company ought to
     cease all operations
     in South Africa.

Premise 2 constitutes an irrelevant reason: it
does not support the conclusion. It simply tries
to pressure the director by intimidation tactics
into accepting the stockholder's position.
Premise 1 is relevant to the conclusion, although
it needs considerable support. Also there are
some premises missing that would serve to connect
the alleged effects of the company's operations in
South Africa with ceasing operations there alto-
gether. Even if the arguer could substantiate
premise 1 it would in no way dictate that the
company must cease operations. There are other
alternatives: e.g. to revise company policy to
engage in corporate pressure tactics upon the
South African government, etc.

Another type of irrelevant reason is the following:

    (ii) irrelevant reason (appeal to pity)

Some offered premises, instead of supporting the conclusion, contain statements that appeal directly to the pity of the person argued against. Because such a reason fails to support the conclusion, it is called an irrelevant reason (appeal to pity); it should be deleted from the argument as bogus. Consider, for example, the following exchange.

> Prof. Smith: Sorry, John, you only scored D on this test.
>
> John: Gosh, Dr. Smith, that's really awful. I really need an A on the course. You see, I want to go to Law School, and this is a required course.
>
> Prof. Smith: That's all very well and good, John, but ... .
>
> John: Please. It really means a lot to me. Just raise my mark to an A. Just this once.

As reconstructed, John's argument would appear as follows:

support space	main argument space	evaluation space
1. I want to go to Law School. 2. This is a required course.	1. I really need an A ⟵ on the course.	Delete: premise is bogus because IR (appeal to pity).

< A D isn't good enough to get into Law School. >

∴. Raise my mark on the ⟵ test to an A.　Not a genuine argument: all offered premises are bogus.

Main premise 1 is bogus because it represents an appeal to Prof. Smith's pity. It provides no reason to support the position that John's test grade should be raised from a D to an A.

Another sort of irrelevant reason is the following:

(iii) irrelevant reason (appeal to "two wrongs make a right")

An offered premise represents an irrelevant reason (by appealing to "two wrongs make a right") when the arguer appeals to the practice or policy of some other group or person to support the very practice or policy he himself is advocating. While it may be interesting that some other group or person likewise adopts a similar stance, it is in no way germane to the conclusion. Just because some other group or person does, approves of or rejects some particular position is no reason to do, approve of, or reject it. The reason is an irrelevant one. Basically it represents an attempt to manipulate us into accepting the conclusion on the grounds that the arguer is not alone in his conviction.

A typical example of this sort of irrelevant reason can be found in the following exchange between a mother and her 6-year old son.

mother: You shouldn't take money from my purse.

son: Why not? Jimmy does it all the time.

As reconstructed, the son's argument would go as follows:

support space	main argument space	evaluation space
	1. Jimmy does it (i.e. ⟵ takes money from his mother's purse) all the time.	Delete: the premise is bogus because IR (appeal to "two wrongs make a right").
	∴ < I should be allowed ⟵ to take money from my mother's purse. >	Not a genuine argument: all the offered premises are bogus.

A more sophisticated version of the same line of thought is the following:

208

support space	main argument space	evaluation space
	1. In dealing with ←——— foreign companies, it is common business practice to bribe favorably-disposed individuals in order to gain contracts.	Delete: the premise is bogus because IR (appeal to "two wrongs make a right").
	∴ Government should ←——— likewise bribe favorably-disposed officials in foreign countries to get what it wants.	Not a genuine argument: all the offered premises are bogus.

Just because companies bribe is no reason to
think that governments ought to engage in the same
sort of behavior. The offered premise fails to
support the conclusion. It represents an irrelevant reason. Because it appeals to what another
group does to support what the government ought
to do, it constitutes an appeal to "two wrongs
make a right."

In the phrase "two wrongs make a right," not too
much significance should be attached to the word
'wrong'. The defect in this line of reasoning
is not that one wrong policy or practice is justified on the basis of another wrong policy or practice: rather it is that a particular position is
bolstered by appeal to what another group or
individual does. The appeal is to what someone
else (or even most people or even "everybody")
approves of or disapproves of in order to gain
acceptance of a conclusion. It doesn't indicate
that both the practice advocated and the practice
appealed to are necessarily "wrongs".

Other examples of this sort of line of reasoning
at work include the following:
- Sparta approved of infanticide: therefore
  infanticide must be fine.
- Everyone pilfers stationery. Therefore
  pilfering stationery is all right.

- Most spouses cheat. Consequently
  spouse cheating is perfectly acceptable.
In each case the premise should be deleted as
bogus because IR (appeal to "two wrongs make a
right").

Appealing to force, to pity, or to "two wrongs
make a right" are only some of the major ways in
which irrelevant reason can occur. In each
instance, the move within an argument which makes
use of irrelevant reason is to by-pass the conclusion and to work directly on us, the hearer/read-
er of the argument, in order to gain acceptance
of the conclusion by other than evidential considerations.

In such arguments, these premises should be
entirely forfeited. The argument cannot be
improved by their retention. To remedy an argument containing irrelevant reason, the arguer
needs to be directed back to the position stated
in the conclusion and asked to come up with premises which support that position. This will
necessitate re-focusing on the issue at hand and
devising new premises. It will also mean that
the arguer will have to drop his attempt to
persuade without evidence and to adopt a different format, one that attempts to persuade with
evidence.

Consider, finally, another way in which the offered premise of an argument may be bogus:

(e) because it represents an appeal to ignorance (Ig)

In a series of books, Erich von Daniken contends
that the earth has been visited in historical
times by beings from outer space and that this
explains a lot of the art and mythology of earlier
cultures. In considering his point of view, we
occasionally hear arguments that go as follows:
    Well, after all, no one has been able to
    show that what he says is wrong. Therefore

        I guess he may have a point.
or
        Well, he hasn't really made a case for his
        position, has he? I guess that he's wrong.
In both instances, the arguer is making an appeal
to ignorance.

There are two main forms of an appeal to ignorance.
Schematically they can be represented as follows:

form #1	form #2
1. Position p hasn't been shown to be false.	1. Position p hasn't been shown to be true.
∴ Position p is true.	∴ Position p is false.

Notice in form #1 that premise 1 states that
position p hasn't been shown to be false. This
is not the same as saying that p isn't false. It
is just saying that p hasn't been shown to be
false, a much milder claim about what people have
or have not been able to demonstrate. Just
because a position has not been shown to be false
does not mean that the position is true. All that
follows from the statement that position p hasn't
been shown to be false is that it hasn't been
shown to be false, not that it's true. Consequently the premise offers no support for the conclusion. It is bogus and should be deleted from the
argument.

The same sort of reasoning applies to form #2.
Just because a position hasn't been shown to be
true does not mean that the position is false.
Premise 1 (in form #2) doesn't say that position
p isn't true: all it says is that it hasn't been
shown to be true. The premise is directed towards
what people have or have not been able to establish about the position in question, not whether
or not that position is true. Again the premise
is bogus, offering no support to the conclusion.
It should be deleted from the argument.

We should reject such premises in evaluation space.
In form #1 and in form #2, the appeal basically is
to ignorance, that is to what hasn't been shown to

justify what is to be accepted. Absence of support for a position is simply that: absence of support. In evaluation space, we should make the following remarks:

form #1

support space	main argument space	evaluation space
	1. Position p hasn't ◄——— been shown to be false.	Delete: premise is bogus because Ig.
	∴ Position p is true. ◄———	Not a genuine argument: all the offered premises are bogus.

An example of this sort of appeal to ignorance would be the following line of thought about Erich von Daniken's positon:

support space	main argument space	evaluation space
	1. No one has been able ◄——— to show that what von Daniken says is wrong.	Delete: premise is bogus because Ig.
	∴ What von Daniken says ◄——— is right.	Not a genuine argument: all the offered premises are bogus.

form #2

support space	main argument space	evaluation space
	1. Position p hasn't ◄——— been shown to be true.	Delete: premise is bogus because Ig.
	∴ Position p is false. ◄———	Not a genuine argument: all the offered premises are bogus.

An example of this kind of appeal to ignorance:

support space	main argument space	evaluation space
	1. von Daniken hasn't ◄——— really made a case for his position.	Delete: premise is bogus because Ig.

$\therefore$ von Daniken's position ⟵——— Not a genuine
    is wrong.   argument: all
                                      the offered
                                      premises are
                                      bogus.

Arguments of this sort are best abandoned. If the
premise were revised to make a stronger claim,
then difficulties still occur. In form #1 of this
sort of appeal, for instance, the arguer might
revise the first premise to read: position p isn't
false. This move has the merit of taking attention away from what has or has not been shown to
what is or is not the case. But it runs into the
following difficulty: the argument now begs the
question, the "is not false" in the premise meaning the same as "is true" is the conclusion.
Instead of modifying the premise, the arguer could
seek to modify the conclusion. If the situation
is such that no evidence one way or the other has
been found to support or undermine the position
stated in the conclusion, perhaps the appropriate
conclusion might be that more inquiry is needed
before the matter can be known. This, however,
changes the conclusion substantially, resulting
in a quite different line of reasoning.

3. Summary

In this chapter we have presented Step #5. It
focuses on one specific aspect of argument evaluation: whether the premises are bogus or genuine.
Five major reasons have been discussed why a
premise may be judged to be bogus. Because they
are counterfeit, such premises should be stricken
from the argument.

Putting all the pieces together, Step #5 goes as
follows:

    Step #5
    Look at the premises offered by the arguer
    to ascertain if any are bogus. If any are,
    then recommend deletion of the premise and
    state the reason. A premise may be bogus

for any of the following reasons:
(a) because it is <u>ad hominem</u> (AH), for
    example
    (i)   by character assassination
    (ii)   by attacking origins
    (iii) by attacking affiliations
    (iv)   by suggesting guilt by association
(b) because it begs the question (BQ)
(c) because it appeals to authority (AA)
    (for example, the authority of an
    author, a leader, a group or institu-
    tion, society generally, a book, etc.)
(d) because it represents an irrelevant
    reason (IR)
    (i)   appeal to force
    (ii)   appeal to pity
    (iii) appeal to "two wrongs make a
           right"
(e) because it represents an appeal to
    ignorance (Ig).

Recall Quiz

(1) What is a "bogus premise"? How does it
     differ from a genuine premise? Why is it
     important to detect bogus ones?

(2) If all the premises of an argument are found
     to be bogus, is the argument itself genuine?

(3) What is Step #5?

(4) When is a premise bogus because <u>ad hominem</u>?
     How are such premises annotated? How is such
     a defect remedied? What are some of the
     common ways in which a premise may be <u>ad
     hominem</u>?

(5) When is a premise bogus because it begs the
     question? How are such premises annotated?
     How is such a defect remedied? What are some
     of the common ways in which a premise may beg
     the question?

(6) When is a premise bogus because it appeals to
     authority? What sorts of authorities may be
     appealed to? How are such premises annotated?

214

How is such a defect remedied?

(7) When is a premise bogus because it represents an irrelevant reason? How are such premises annotated? What sorts of irrelevant reasons may be appealed to (cite 3)? Why are they irrelevant? How may such a defect be remedied?

(8) When is a premise bogus because it represents an appeal to ignorance? What two forms does this defect take? How is such a defect annotated? Can this defect be remedied?

Exercise #1

Using standard format, identify the arguments contained in the following selections. Then critically evaluate them in terms of Step #5.

(1) Everyone cheats on their income tax form. Besides, it's O.K. as long as you're not caught. What's more, the government's an ass. It's O.K. therefore to cheat on your income tax form.

(2) Most scientists today think that sooner or later there will be a devastating earthquake along the San Andreas Fault in California. Consequently, people would be ill-advised to move to California.

(3) Fags shouldn't be teachers. After all, most people don't want them to be. They represent, moreover, a distinct danger to young children. And Anita Bryant wants them barred from public life.

(4) Well, no one has proved conclusively that God doesn't exist. So it's reasonable to suppose that he does exist.

(5) According to a recent public opinion poll, most people over the age of 30, in fact 71% of those polled, favored nude sunbathing and nude swimming areas in national parks. Therefore nude sunbathing and nude swimming areas ought to be set up in national parks.

(6) The Bible is the inspired Word of God. This is so because many passages in the Bible say that God has inspired it.

(7) Scientists say that there's another Ice Age coming. So people had better get in a good supply of fuel and blankets.

(8) In the current controversy I take a definite stand. My stand is this: we ought to retain capital punishment for major crimes. And my reasons are likewise crystal clear: for serious crimes in this country, we shouldn't abolish capital punishment. Do I make my point?

(9) All the evidence indicates that life does exist elsewhere in the universe. For one thing, most space scientists today admit the possibility that life has developed on other planets, perhaps in galaxies other than our own. For another thing, no one has ever shown beyond a shadow of a doubt that life does not exist elsewhere. It should not be forgotten, moreover, that those who pooh-pooh this idea are simply self-seeking, stupid fundamentalists who cling to the position that life is unique to this planet.

(10) The Bible says, "An eye for an eye, a tooth for a tooth." Revenge is therefore morally justifiable.

(11) Winston's commitment to progressive social change is really suspect. He's from the Old Deep South, don't forget. Moreover, his father is a prominent right-winger. Besides that, Winston's an utter jerk.

(12) The fetus is not a person. The evidence for this is overwhelming. According to a recent national poll, 68% of those interviewed stated that they do not believe that the fetus is a person. Then, too, many Hollywood TV personalities have gone on the record against the view that the fetus is a person. Also, don't forget, no one has ever shown that the fetus is a person.

(13)　You'd better vote for the Welfare Reform package. If you don't then I'll dredge up all the sordid details of your "working holiday" in San Juan with your lovely administrative assistant.

(14)　His economic forecasts are completely for the birds. He's a follower of Keynes, after all.

Exercise #2

Look at various print ads in several popular magazines. Select 5 that present arguments. Identify each argument, using standard format. Then critically evaluate them in terms of Steps #1 - 5 inclusive.

Exercise #3

Select 2 print ads from popular magazines that (1) present an argument and (2) exhibit a flaw detected by Step #5.

CHAPTER SEVEN

ARGUMENT EVALUATION: FALLACIES II

1. Introduction

In the previous chapter we examined Step #5, one
which scrutinized the premises offered by the arguer to see if they were genuine or bogus. A bogus
premise is a serious matter, for it is a counterfeit item pretending to be the real thing. It
provides <u>no</u> support for the conclusion. We have
now learned how to unmask these impostors.

Step #6 also focuses on the premises offered by
the arguer, but with a different purpose in mind.
In Step #6 the task is to assess the genuine premises to see if they give <u>enough</u> support to the
conclusion. Of course, being genuine premises,
they must provide <u>some</u> support for the conclusion.
They may, however, contain a defect that seriously
affects the amount of support they provide. Step
#6 focuses on these defects - flaws which genuine
premises exhibit which <u>reduce</u> the amount of support
they provide the conclusion.

Step #6 differs considerably, then, from Step #5.
In Step #5 we're hunting for bogus premises, for
those that provide <u>no</u> support for the conclusion.
In Step #6, on the other hand, our search is for
genuine premises which fail (because of a defect)
to provide <u>enough</u> support for the conclusion.

2. Step #6

Step #6
Look at the genuine premises to ascertain if
they give sufficient support to the conclusion.
A genuine premise may fail to give sufficient
support to the conclusion for any of the
following reasons:

A list of reasons follows. In evaluating the
argument, we will indicate in evaluation space
that such premises are defective and will give the
reason for the defect. Detecting where and how
premises are defective in this manner provides an
important clue in understanding how the argument
can be improved.

(a) because it represents a false dilemma (FD)

A dilemma is a statement of mutually exclusive
alternatives, that is, a statement that contends
that x must be either A or B (but not both). Many
arguments contain premises that state alternatives,
for example:
- Either I'm pregnant or I'm not
- Either I'll vote for the incumbent or
  I'll vote for his opponent.
- Israel and the Palestinians have two
  choices: either to continue acts of
  terrorism to the bitter end or else to
  sit down and negotiate a settlement.
- In the current monetary situation, the
  investor has two alternatives: either
  to put his money in government bonds or
  else to tuck it away in a high interest
  rate savings account.

And so forth. Such expressions state alternatives:
x is either A or else B. Arguments which contain
such statements often go on to reflect on these
alternatives, perhaps advocating one of them (e.g.
an argument that advocates what Israel and the
Palestinians should do given the two alternatives
that confront them) or else perhaps settling upon
a course of action based on one of the alternatives (e.g. an argument that sets forth a course
of action should the girl prove pregnant).

There is of course, nothing wrong in and of itself
with premises that contain the word 'or' or that
state alternatives. Nor is there anything wrong
with arguments which use such premises to reflect
on the alternative options and to advocate positions that rest on the options suggested. Such

premises, properly used, may support the conclusion. There is, however, a matter that the wary argument analyst will observe. A statement of alternatives (a) should provide genuine alternatives, and (b) should state all the reasonable options open.

(b) is particularly important in argumentation. If the point of the argument is to advocate one alternative over another, or to urge adoption of one particular course of action that depends on one of the alternatives, then unless all other reasonable options are ruled out, the argument is weak. Some of the premises mentioned above state all reasonable options (e.g. either I'm pregnant or not), while others do not. In the statement, "either I'll vote for the incumbent or I'll vote for his opponent " one possible additional alternative might be: or I'll not vote at all. Also, there are additional choices confronting Israel and the Palestinians, for instance, to have an all-out war, to create a Palestinian state on Arab territory, etc. Similarly, unless more is forthcoming about the exigencies of the current monetary situation, the investor probably has more than just the two choices mentioned -- for instance, investing in mortgages, precious metals, stamps, coins, etc.

The defect known as "false dilemma" occurs when a premise in an argument fails to state all the reasonable alternatives about x. It is a false dilemma because, given the range of options, it would be false to say that x is either A or B when it could very well be C (or even D, E, etc.). The general pattern of a false dilemma, with our annotation in evaluation space, is as follows:

support space	main argument space	evaluation space
	1. ...	
	2. ...	
	3. x is either A or else ←—	False dilemma: x
	B.	could also be C.
	. . ...	

221

In contending that a dilemma is a false one, we should cite an alternative the premise omits.

Consider the following argument:

support space	main argument space	evaluation space
	1. Either man is free and responsible for his actions or else he is determined and not responsible for his behavior.	
	2. If the latter, then human behavior lacks moral value and man would be no better than an animal.	
	3. But man is better than an animal.	
	∴. Man is free and responsible for his actions.	

Note carefully the way in which the argument is developed. Premise 1 states alternatives: either man is this (free and responsible) or else he is that (determined and not responsible). According to the first premise, those are the two alternatives. Premise 2 picks up on the second option, exploring its consequences. It mentions that it would deprive human behavior of moral worth and that it would make man no better than an animal. In premise 3 new information is given that would serve to reject the consequences cited in the second premise, thereby cancelling out the desirability of the whole second alternative indicated in premise 1. With the whole second alternative disposed of, the arguer concludes that man is free and responsible. The arguer, in other words, concludes that the first option, cited in premise 1, is the case.

There are, of course, some notable defects in this argument. For one thing, premise 3 would need considerable support. Also premise 2 would need support: the arguer would have to show that these

alleged consequences are indeed consequences of
the second option stated in the first premise.
Also, it would be particularly helpful if such
vague words as 'responsible,' 'free,' and 'determined' were defined. A prudent arguer, moreover,
might qualify the alternatives somewhat, perhaps
with the use of either the expression "totally"
(as in "totally free" or "totally determined") or
else "to some extent" or "to a large extent" (as
in, man is "to some extent free" or "to some
extent determined").

Even if all these flaws are remedied, however,
there is still another important defect. The
argument rests upon there being only two alternatives, namely, the ones mentioned in the first
premise. If these aren't the only two ways of
construing human behavior, then the argument loses
much of its strength. In this particular case,
there is an alternative that has not been included in the first premise, namely, the position
that many have argued for, that man is determined
and yet is responsible for his actions. This
third alternative would maintain (somehow) that
determinism is compatible with responsibility.
Exactly how and why an arguer would defend this
position is not particularly relevant here. The
point is that such a position is reasonable and
has been put forward. And yet, in the context of
the argument in question, it has not been considered, let alone guarded against. Thus the first
premise represents a false dilemma. The options
stated are not the only two alternatives open.
When evaluated, the argument would appear as
follows:

support space	main argument space	evaluation space
	1. Either man is _free_ ⟵	False dilemma:
	and _responsible_ for	perhaps man
	for his actions or	could be both
	else he is _determined_	determined and
	and not responsible	yet responsible
	for his behavior.	for his actions.
		vague words

223

2. If the latter, ←—— needs support
then behavior (show that these
lacks moral value are indeed conse-
and man would be quences of the
no better than an latter alternative)
animal.

3. But man is better ← needs support
than an animal.

∴ Man is free and
responsible for
his actions.

Another example:

support space	main argument space	evaluation space
	1. Either archeological ←—— puzzles such as the Pyramids, the lines on the Plain of Nasca, the statues on Easter Island, and so forth must remain mysteries or else we must postulate visits to earth by space men.	False dilemma: perhaps earlier civilizations were technologically sophisticated.
	2. No one but space men, with superior technology, could have constructed these items.	
	3. There is no need, given that there is a readily available explanation, for these items to remain mysteries.	
	∴ The earth has been visited by space men.	

In scanning the argument, we should note carefully
that premise 1 represents a statement of alternatives. Whenever this happens, we should consider
whether all reasonable options have been stated.

In this case they have not been. Another possible
option would be that earlier civilizations were a
great deal more sophisticated technologically than
we give them credit. Or, to consider yet another
alternative, each of these archeological puzzles
might have a separate explanation. Premise 1 is
a false dilemma and should be annotated as such.

A false dilemma can be rectified. The arguer
could modify the argument so as to include the
broader list of alternatives and then discuss them
in the course of the argument.

(b) because it exhibits slippery slope reasoning (SS)

In the course of argumentation, it is perfectly
legitimate for the arguer to consider what would
happen if another event or course of action were
to happen. Arguers often make statements such as
the following in the course of presenting an argument: "If this were to happen, then ... would also
happen." In making such statements, arguers are
speculating on the probable consequences of a
particular proposed set of circumstances. Actions
have consequences, and in considering the appro-
priateness of a particular course of action, it is
not only rational but prudent to consider the
likely consequences.

To give proper support to the conclusion, however,
reasoning of this sort requires not only the simple
assertion that such-and-such will probably happen
if a particular action or event occurs; it also
requires that the arguer make a case that these
are indeed the likely consequences of just such a
set of circumstances. In other words, the contention that such-and-such are the likely consequences
of some proposed action or event needs to be
supported.

The defect of slippery slope reasoning occurs when
the consequences of an event or course of action
are just asserted as consequences and are not

225

supported. The flaw detracts from the evidential worth of the argument. Where the adoption or rejection of some course of action recommended in the conclusion rests upon a statement of the probable consequences of just such an event happening, then that statement needs substantial support. Where such support is lacking, the argument exhibits a slippery slope defect.

There are two main forms to slippery slope reasoning.

form #1	form #2
1. If A happens, then so will B, C, D, E, etc.	1. If A happens, then so will B, C, D, E, etc.
2. < B,C,D,E, etc. are undesirable.>	2. < B,C,D,E, etc. are desirable.>
∴ not-A.	∴ A.

Form #1 contends that if something happens (or is allowed to happen), then all hell will break loose. An example of a premise that exhibits slippery slope reasoning would be:

1. If euthanasia is allowed, then the way would be paved for killing genetic defectives, old age persons, people who are mentally retarded, and even people who were just considered a burden to society.

Such indeed may be the consequences of euthanasia, but, in this particular statement, that they are consequences of euthanasia is not argued for. The statement lacks support. It represents slippery slope reasoning. This premise, coupled with another one that is frequently unstated:

< 2. These consequences are undesirable.>

could be used to advocate the following position:

∴ Euthanasia should not be allowed to happen.

Next to premise 1, in evaluation space, we would write:

slippery slope reasoning (support needed)

Another example of slippery slope reasoning is the following:

	#1		#2

<table>
<tr><td colspan="2" align="center">#1</td><td colspan="2" align="center">#2</td></tr>
</table>

#1	#2
1. If the Philippines fall to the communists, then so will Malaya, Thailand, Indonesia, Australia, and New Zealand	1. If the Philippines fall to the communists, then so will Malaya, Thailand, Indonesia, Australia, and New Zealand
2. < These consequences are undesirable >	2. < These consequences are desirable >
∴Let's ensure that the Philippines do not fall.	∴Let's help ensure that the Philippines do fall.

#1 may be articulated from a Western perspective; #2 from a communist perspective. Regardless of the particular ideological perspective, premise 1 in both instances exhibits slippery slope reasoning. In both instances, consequences are alleged to follow from a certain event happening, with no support whatsoever to back up the contention. Next to premise 1 in both instances we should write: "slippery slope reasoning (support needed)."

Slippery slope reasoning can be remedied. The premise picked out as exhibiting slippery slope reasoning should be supported: the arguer should show (if he can) that the event happening will have the consequences he alleges. If the arguer cannot, or indeed has no supporting evidence, then the premise should be disregarded as simply a scare tactic without substance. Indeed many a slippery slope premise is primarily designed to scare or shock us into awareness of the seriousness of the proposed event. If such consequences are not in the offing, however, such scare tactics are without foundation.

(c) because it leads to a hasty conclusion (HC)

A conclusion is hasty when it is insufficiently supported by relevant premises. The defect in this sort of argumentation is that although the premises are on the right track, supporting the conclusion, the argument terminates prematurely. The argument lacks some crucial premises that

227

would serve to tie in the premises already advanced
with the desired conclusion. Suppose an arguer
were to offer the following argument:

support space	main argument space	evaluation space

1. National   1. 72% of all high
Poll, 1978, of   school students admit
15,000 randomly   engaging in sexual
selected high   intercourse at least
school students.   once a week.

∴ High schools should
set up birth control
clinics.

Premise 1 is well supported, and its meaning is
clear. It represents an interesting finding of
a rather large sampling of high school students.
Yet what follows from the finding that 72% of all
high school students admit engaging in sexual
intercourse at least once a week? Certainly not
the conclusion. The conclusion is a hasty one,
for several additional premises would have to be
added to the argument to move from premise 1 to
the desired conclusion. The arguer would have to
consider the contraceptive practices of these
students, the possibility of bravado in this age
group, and certainly the various alternative
possibilities for handling whatever problem the
arguer thinks the finding stated in premise 1 poses
for society. We should annotate the argument as
follows:

support space	main argument space	evaluation space

1.National   1. 72% of all high
Poll, 1978, of   school students admit
15,000 randomly   engaging in sexual
selected high   intercourse at least   premises omitted
school students.   once a week.   (contraceptive
practices of
this group;
alternative means
of handling pro-
blem, etc.)

∴ High schools should ←— hasty conclusion
set up birth control
clinics.

This sort of annotation indicates that the conclusion is hasty and suggests where and how the argument has omitted crucial information.

Consider next this example in which part of an argument has been sketched:

support space	main argument space	evaluation space
	1. ...	
	2. ...	
	3. The welfare system is open to abuse.	premises omitted (examples of actual abuse of the welfare system)
	4. ...	

∴. The welfare system
has been abused

and it should be
scrapped.

← hasty conclusion

From the contention that the welfare system is open to abuse the conclusion that it has been abused does not follow (let alone that it should be scrapped). The mere possibility of abuse does not automatically mean that abuse actually has occurred. The conclusion is hasty. What is missing from the argument are examples and instances of actual abuse of sufficient magnitude as to warrant scrapping the whole system. In evaluation space we would draw attention to the hasty conclusion and would indicate that a premise (or premises) has been omitted.

It should not be forgotten that mini-arguments are arguments in their own right and that they are subject to all steps in argument evaluation. This applies to hasty conclusions as well. In a mini-argument, the conclusion, even though it is a premise of the main argument, is the conclusion of the mini-argument and it may very well be hasty. Consider, for example, the following mini-argument and the evaluation in right space:

229

```
                        1. ...
                                                   mini-premises
                                                   omitted (exam-
1. The welfare  ⎞   2. The welfare system         ples of actual
   system is open⎬      has been abused and        abuse)
   to abuse.    ⎠      it should be scrap-
                       ped.                        hasty conclusion
   ←───────────────  3. ...
                        . . ...
```

A hasty conclusion can be easily rectified by
supplying the missing premises that served to make
the conclusion hasty.

summary

In sum, Step #6 goes as follows:

> Step #6
> Look at the genuine premises to ascertain
> if they give sufficient support to the
> conclusion. A genuine premise may fail to
> give sufficient support to the conclusion
> for any of the following reasons:
> (a) because it represents a false dilemma (FD)
> (b) because it exhibits slippery slope
>   reasoning (SS)
> (c) because it leads to a hasty conclusion
>   (HC)

3.   Step #7

An argument may in and of itself be impeccable:
well-supported premises, free of defects, careful
attention to language, good support for the conclusion, and so forth. Such an argument is a
delight! It has passed successfully through our
rather formidable gauntlet. But, even so, all is
not finished. So far argument evaluation has
focused exclusively on the argument itself--its
composition, its structural elements, its flaws

and omissions, and so forth. The argument has been viewed quite narrowly, in isolation from other arguments and the controversy of which it is a part.

Step #7 takes us into the broader context in which an argument occurs. It is not a step which we can automatically apply to all arguments; it is applied only to those that occur in a controversy, where we can see the other arguments that are made, either by the same arguer or by the other participants in the discussion. It is a step to be applied whenever we come across an exchange of arguments.

Step #7
Look at the argument in relation to other arguments in the controversy (either by the same arguer or by others) to ensure the following: (3 considerations to follow)

(a) that no misrepresentation has occurred

Misrepresentation occurs when one arguer distorts what another arguer has said, either as a premise or as a conclusion. Suppose arguer X says the following:

support space	main argument space	evaluation space
	1. There are more starving people than well-fed people in the world today.	
	2. We must discriminate between helping one child in Korea on the Foster Parent Plan for $17 a month and helping 9 people in Chad for the same amount.	
	3. Generally speaking, we must help as many people as possible given limited resources.	

231

$$\therefore \quad \text{\$17 per month is better}$$
spent on helping 9 people
in Chad than on helping
1 person in Korea.

Suppose arguer Y says in reply:
1. Arguer X wants to dis-
   criminate against
   Koreans.

$$\therefore \quad \text{Arguer X is anti-Korean}$$

In premise 1, arguer Y has misrepresented (distorted) what arguer X has said. Apart from changing
the meaning of 'discriminate,' arguer Y has failed
to grasp the point X is trying to make. In evaluation space, next to premise 1 of Y's argument, we
should write:
    misrepresents premise 2 of X's argument.

In considering arguments in their broader perspective, another factor we should consider is the
following:

(b) that the arguer has not attacked "a straw man"
                     position

A "straw man" position is one that is easier to
attack than the one actually set forward by the
opposing arguer in the controversy. The arguer
who sets up a straw man position, and then proceeds
to demolish it, has only succeeded in replying to a
flimsy version of the position the opposing arguer
has put forward. In context, the attack is weak,
even though the arguer may have made a good argument attacking the straw man position. Unfortunately, however, the straw man position the arguer
has set up for attack is not the point at issue in
the controversy.

Suppose arguer X puts forward the following position, which he defends with a variety of premises:
    Without a religious perspective, an
    individual often cannot develop a sense of

> self-worth and a feeling of being a
> significant part of the world in which
> he lives.

Note that arguer X is not maintaining that religion
always does this. Nor is he maintaining that
people who lack a religious perspective cannot
achieve a sense of self-worth. His point is a
more moderate one, simply saying that without a
religious perspective, a person often cannot develop this sense of self-worth.

Suppose arguer Y misconstrues what X is saying.
Suppose Y construes X as having put forward the
position that a religious perspective is necessary
for the formation of a sense of self-worth and a
feeling of being a significant part of the world
in which he lives. This is a much more extreme
position, and one that is easier to attack (e.g.
by advancing case after case where a religious
perspective adopted has failed to do this, or
where people have achieved a sense of self-worth
independent of a religious perspective). Y could
have a field-day advancing premise after premise
on behalf of this conclusion.

> Religion doesn't always help an individual
> develop a sense of self-worth or a feeling
> of being a significant part of the world
> in which people live.

Y may advance a perfectly good argument on behalf
of this conclusion. The difficulty, however, is
that Y has distorted the position X has put forward. Y has attacked a much more extreme (and
therefore easier) position than X has put forth,
thereby setting up a "straw man" position. In
context, Y has failed to respond satisfactorily to
what X has contended. We should mark in evaluation
space, next to the conclusion of Y's argument:

> attacks a straw man position (X did not say
> religion always does this but only that if
> often does).

The straw man position is the position Y attacks.
Y's error is that, in context, the position he
attacks is not the position X has put forward.

Y has distorted what X has said, setting up an
easier position to demolish. In so doing, Y's
response to X is beside the point. Once convinced
of the irrelevancy of his reply, Y should more
accurately state X's position and then develop a
proper counter-argument (one that responds to what
X really stated).

Another important factor we should take into
account when considering arguments in their broader perspective is the following:

(c) that the arguer has not been inconsistent

Many arguments are chain-linked. Many arguments,
that is, form part of a case the arguer is making.
Cases are rather intricate creations. They draw
together many arguments that develop, explore,
and probe different aspects of the general over-all
position being advanced by the arguer. In such an
undertaking, there are often many loose-ends, e.g.
pieces of information not fully developed, difficulties glossed over or skirted entirely, positions
made more precise or modified in some manner as
the case unfolds, etc. Such loose-ends are not
surprising, given the complex nature of a case,
and unless the arguer has had extensive time to
reflect upon all aspects of the case -- indeed to
brood over it -- it is unlikely that all the
details of the case will be patched up.

One defect that is of importance in the development
of a case is the occurrence of an inconsistency.
Inconsistency is a serious defect, for it impairs
understanding the position being advanced by the
arguer. An inconsistency noted must be repaired,
or else comprehension is vitiated.

There are many ways in which inconsistency may
occur. The following are some of the commonest:

(i) through contradiction
Suppose a father is engaged in a hotly-contested

234

divorce action. In the course of presenting his case, he may on one occasion have claimed that he wants custody of the child; on another, that access is all he wants. This arguer has contradicted himself: he has claimed both that he wants custody and that he doesn't want custody. A contradiction occurs when an arguer asserts position P and then also asserts not-P. Until the arguer clears up the contradiction, we are unable to grasp what the arguer wants to say. We should note an inconsistency of this sort.

(ii) through words changing meaning

In the pressure of developing a case, an arguer will occasionally deviate in his use of language. He may, for instance, use a word with one meaning in one instance and another meaning in another instance, without intending to inject ambiguity into the discussion. Suppose an arguer is advocating euthanasia. Should he use the word 'euthanasia' in the sense of active euthanasia in one instance, and then employ the word to indicate passive euthanasia in another instance, then he has inadvertently changed the meaning of the word. The arguer has been inconsistent in what he means by the words he uses. We should note such shifts in meaning, for they introduce a lack of clarity into the case being made.

(iii) through change in details

In an intricate case, where many details must be remembered or marshalled in defense of a position, it is not unusual for an arguer to slip up on some of the details, perhaps even getting some of them wrong. An inconsistency of this sort is often minor, particularly when one can discern from the context of the case what was intended. Such changes in details do not affect the substance of the argument.

A much more serious form of this defect, however, occurs when details of a substantial nature change in the course of making a case. Suppose an arguer is advocating euthanasia. In any such discussion, an important question concerns who has the right to participate in deciding whether or not a patient should be allowed to die: the doctor, several doctors, the patient, relatives, beneficiaries of the patient's estate, a representative of society, a lawyer, a clergyman, etc. Suppose an arguer has, in one instance, asserted that it is the right of the patient in consultation with his doctor to choose euthanasia. Suppose, however, that in another instance, in the course of developing his case, he contends that it is the right of the patient, in consultation with his doctor, and with the consent of his relatives, to select euthanasia. In this latter instance, a significant detail has been added. An inconsistency has developed, and the arguer should clarify exactly who has the right in question.

These, then, are some of the common ways in which inconsistency can occur in the presentation of a case. There are others: e.g. by changing qualifiers in the statements made, etc. Whenever we encounter inconsistency in a controversy, we should note both that an inconsistency has occurred and what this inconsistency is. Our comment in evaluation space would appear as follows:
    inconsistency (...is inconsistent with....)

in sum

Piecing the parts together, Step #7 goes as follows:
    Step #7
Look at the argument in relation to other arguments in the controversy (either by the same arguer or by others) to ensure:
(a) that no misrepresentation has occurred
(b) that the arguer has not attacked "a straw man" position
(c) that the arguer has not been inconsistent, e.g.
    (i) through contradiction
    (ii) through words changing meaning

(iii) through change in details

4. The Steps So Far

So far the following steps in argument evaluation have been presented:

#1   Look at the premises in the argument and draw attention to those that need support or more support.

#2   Look at the language used in the premises and conclusion and with respect to the basic key words and expressions needed to make sense of the argument, draw attention to words and phrases which
(a) are vague
(b) are ambiguous
(c) exhibit an unhelpful use of language
(d) represent an undiscussed controversial definition.

#3   Look for missing premises (needed to establish the conclusion).

#4   Look for absent qualifiers in the premises and conclusion.

#5   Look at the premises offered by the arguer to ascertain if any are bogus. If any are, then recommend deletion of the premise and state the reason.
A premise may be bogus for any of the following reasons:
(a) because it is <u>ad hominem</u> (AH), e.g.
    (i) by character assassination
    (ii) by attacking origins
    (iii) by attacking affiliations
    (iv) by suggesting guilt by association
(b) because it begs the question (BQ)
(c) because it appeals to authority (AA)
    (e.g. the authority of an author, leader, group or institution, society generally, a book, etc.)
(d) because it represents an irrelevant reason(IR)
    (i) appeal to force
    (ii) appeal to pity

237

(iii) appeal to "two wrongs make a right"
    (e) because it represents an appeal to ignorance
       (Ig)

#6   Look at the genuine premises to ascertain if they
give sufficient support to the conclusion.
A genuine premise may fail to give sufficient
support to the conclusion for any of the following
reasons:
(a) because it represents a false dilemma (FD)
(b) because it exhibits slippery slope reasoning
    (SS)
(c) because it leads to a hasty conclusion (HC)

#7   Look at the argument in relation to other arguments
in the controversy (either by the same arguer or
by others) to ensure:
(a) that no misrepresentation has occurred
(b) that the arguer has not attacked "a straw man"
    position
(c) that the arguer has not been inconsistent, e.g.
    (i) through contradiction
    (ii) through words changing meaning
    (iii) through change in details

Recall Quiz

(1) What is Step #6?

(2) How does Step #6 differ from Step #5?

(3) When does a genuine premise fail to give
sufficient support to a conclusion because it
represents a false dilemma? What is a
dilemma? How is a false dilemma annotated?
How can this defect be rectified?

(4) When does a genuine premise fail to give
sufficient support to a conclusion because
it exhibits slippery slope reasoning? What
two forms does this defect take? How is such
a defect annotated? How can this defect be
remedied?

(5) When does a genuine premise fail to give
sufficient support to a conclusion because it
leads to a hasty conclusion? How is a hasty
conclusion annotated? How can this defect

238

be remedied?

(6) What is Step #7?

(7) What is "misrepresentation"? a straw man position"? and "inconsistency"? How are such defects annotated? How are such defects improved?

Exercise #1

Using standard format, identify the arguments contained in the following selections. Then critically evaluate them in terms of Step #6.

(1) Death is either a peaceful sleep or else it is utter oblivion. If it's the latter, then we know and feel nothing. If it's the former then it's refreshing and delightful. Either way death is not painful. Consequently we should not fear death.

(2) I contend that all the criticisms of the mail service are totally unfounded. Why, just yesterday, I received in New York a letter that had been sent from San Francisco just the day before.

(3) George: It's really appalling how rapes have dramatically increased in the last year.
Walter: How do you know?
George: Well, my sister got raped last month.

(4) Everyone should take vitamin E daily. For one thing, vitamin E increases the sex drive. I've noticed this myself, having taken vitamin E faithfully now for 8 months. For another thing, vitamin E strengthens the heart muscle. Studies in many leading hospitals confirm this finding. Moreover, if you don't take vitamin E regularly, then your cells will lose precious oxygen, your body will be deprived of important restorative powers, and your health will generally deteriorate.

(5)   IQ tests tend to penalize the culturally-
disadvantaged. Therefore IQ tests should be
abolished.

(6)   In the current hard economic times, I can
make money either by investing in stamps or
else in bonds. If I invest in stamps, however, I'll have to wait years to realize a
profit. Thus I'll invest in bonds.

(7)   If the government forces people to wear
seatbelts while driving, then pretty soon
the government will be telling us what to
wear, what to eat, where to live, what to
think, and so on and so on. It's high time
we called a halt to legislation that meddles
in the private lives of citizens. I maintain, therefore, that people shouldn't be
forced by government to wear seatbelts while
driving.

(8)   According to a recent public opinion poll,
72% of the people surveyed favored the
immediate return of the death penalty.
Moreover, of these, clearly a full 89%
favored administering death by means of a
humane procedure. Therefore the death
penalty should be restored promptly and the
mode of death should be a fast-acting, pain-
less, lethal injection.

(9)   Either we'll acquiesce and accept their
ridiculous offer or else we'll strike and
tie up the works. If we succumb and
accept their outrageous offer, then we're
setting a bad precedent. Bad precedents
should be avoided at all costs. Consequently
we'll strike and tie up the works.

(10)   Smoking causes all sorts of diseases. Therefore people who smoke should bear the full
financial burden of their hospital and
medical treatments.

Exercise #2

Identify the **arguments** contained in the **following**
selections. Then critically evaluate them in

terms of Steps #5 and #6.

(1) I'll be damned if I'll help you with the
housework. Other working wives can do it--
why, just look at what Gloria across the
street does. If you expect me, vice-presi-
dent of Zee Corporation, to move dirt, then
you're a raving bloody idiot. Besides, in
a recent public opinion poll, most husbands
of working wives stated very clearly that
they don't think they should have any part
in doing the housework. Housework, moreover,
has always been what women have traditionally
done in a marriage, and no one has shown
that this concept is outdated. Besides,
what would happen if I were to start: Bert
across the street would call me a sissy. our
son Bill would grow up thinking I'm queer,
and I'd probably become an alcoholic.

(2) Dear Joan,
I think I should make it perfectly clear
at the outset that I want you to stop dating
Bill.
According to Marg, Bill's a no-good
speed addict, and you deserve better than
that. Rumor has it he's freaked out more
than once on the stuff.
Besides, you can never tell what's going
to happen with a speed addict: he's likely
to become violent, irrational, and perhaps
even rape or murder you.
Your mother, too, is sick to death of
this whole sorry mess, worried, upset, unable
to sleep, pacing around, and very very hurt
by your actions.
If you have any respect and regard for
your old dad, you'll take my advice to heart.
Besides, if you don't stop seeing Bill,
I'll cease the monthly subsidy on which you
depend.
                              Your loving father.

(3) My accuser is a damn, stinking, lying son-
of-a-bitch. Moreover, he took bribes from
XYX Corporation, so why can't I? Everyone

does that sort of thing in politics. Only
a naive hick from Porcupine Junction would
think otherwise. That sort of thing happens
in business all the time. I'm innocent, I
tell you--you can take my word on that! If
I'm ruined, then many other members of the
House will be brought down with me. So
you see: there's simply no point setting up
an Inquiry to investigate the charge that
XYX Corporation bribed me and other members.

Exercise #3

Identify the arguments presented by each arguer
in the selections below. Critically evaluate
them in terms of Step #7.

(1) Mary: The Bible should be interpreted
            literally. It is, after all, the
            inspired Word of God. It contains,
            moreover, a complete guide to faith,
            morals, and human history. Further-
            more, if it's not interpreted liter-
            ally, then anybody can make it say
            whatever they want it to say.

     Lisa: I don't think the Bible should be
            interpreted literally. For one
            thing, in many places God is portray-
            ed in human terms as a walking,
            talking, breathing entity. For
            another thing, in many places God is
            depicted as engaged in behavior
            pretty unbecoming to Divinity: chang-
            ing his mind, being angry, experimen-
            ting with human lives (consider Job),
            and so on.

     Mary: I don't think you understand my posi-
            tion. I'm simply contending that the
            important passages of the Bible
            should be interpreted literally, for
            the reasons I've already given.

(2) Alice: I tend to favor an open and honest
            relationship, especially among people
            who are close. Such a relationship
            is particularly important among

242

married people where trust, encourage-
ment, and support should flourish.
If one partner, for example, has been
unfaithful, then he or she should
confide in the other and talk out the
situation. Such openness and honesty
is more important in the long run to
the stability and permanence of a
relationship than the occasional
infidelity. A mature relationship,
moreover, ought to be able to with-
stand such confidence and to build
upon it. So I recommend that people,
especially married persons, should
take the time to confide in one
another and to share their innermost
concerns and activities.

Carol: You're just going to encourage extra-
marital sex. After all, when you say
that sexual cheating makes for an
open and honest relationship, you
know nothing about people.

Alice: But I didn't say that, Carol,....

(3) Ralph: You should give me a raise. I'm the
best designer you've got. And I'm
also the hardest working employee in
the whole section.

Phil: Sorry, you can't have a raise.
George scored higher than you did on
the Job Performance Evaluation Proce-
dure (JPEP). So you aren't the best.
George also logged in more over-time.
So you aren't the hardest working.

Ralph: I still think you should give me a
raise. I am, after all, the most
deserving.

(4) Sue: We're a nation of addicts. After all,
84% are addicted to caffeine and 61%
to nicotine.

Sarah: That's a bit sweeping. What do you
mean by addiction? And where did you
obtain these figures.

Sue: Well, before I answer your questions,
let me point out one further piece of

support for my claim that we're a
bunch of addicts. A full 100% of
us are addicted to food.

Sarah: I guess there's no hope for us then.

Exercise #4

(1) Examine various letters to the editor from a
local newspaper. Select 5 that present arguments. Identify these arguments using standard format and then critically evaluate them
in terms of Steps #1-6 inclusive.

(2) Identify and evaluate 2 letters to the editor
from a local newspaper that exhibits a flaw
mentioned in Step #6.

CHAPTER EIGHT

DEDUCTIVE AND INDUCTIVE KINDS OF ARGUMENT

1. Introduction

There's a difference in argument evaluation
between Steps #1 through #6 on the one hand, and
Steps #7 through #10 on the other. Steps #1
through #6 apply to all arguments. Steps #7
through #10, however, are restricted ones: they
apply only to some arguments. This was evident
in Step #7: we didn't apply it to all arguments but
only to arguments that occur in the context of
other arguments. It's not the sort of step we
would apply to an argument in isolation from the
broader controversial context in which some arguments are found. In a similar way, the next 3
steps are also restricted. To explain Steps #8
and #9, however, we need to learn about two basic
kinds of arguments.

There is a fundamental distinction made in the
Study of Argument between deductive and inductive
kinds of argument. These are the only two kinds
of argument. An argument is either deductive, or
inductive, but it's not both. There is no suggestion, of course, that one sort of argument is
better than another: they are simply different.

Their differences are important, however, especially in argument evaluation. For, as we shall shortly see, the kind of argument an argument is determines what we, as argument analysts, should consider about the way in which its premises relate to
the conclusion. The kind of argument the argument
is determines the appropriate criteria we should
employ in looking at how the premises support the
conclusion.

In reasoning about issues, arguers may present both
deductive and inductive arguments together. The
main argument may be of one sort (deductive or
inductive), the mini-arguments may be of the same

or another sort (deductive or inductive). A
variety of combinations are possible:

main argument may be	while the mini-arguments are
deductive	deductive
deductive	inductive
deductive	mixed (some deductive, some inductive)
inductive	deductive
inductive	inductive
inductive	mixed (some deductive, some inductive)

This variety should raise no eyebrows. Main
arguments and mini-arguments are each arguments
in their own right, and each may be of either the
deductive or inductive kind. The important point
is to recognize which is which.

The distinction between deductive and inductive
arguments gives rise to two different aspects of
an argument which we should carefully evaluate.
Both have to do with the support the premises give
the conclusion, a very important relationship
indeed. In a deductive argument, we examine the
deductive validity of the argument. In an inductive argument it is its inductive strength we
examine.

In this chapter and the next three we will be
concerned with these matters. In this chapter we
will discuss two important distinctions already
mentioned.
> (1) deductive and inductive kinds of
>   arguments.
> (2) deductive validity and inductive
>   strength.

Just before we begin, you should note that the
distinction between deductive and inductive arguments has given rise to two very substantial
fields of inquiry in the Study of Argument.
Symbolic logic (also called "deductive logic" or
"formal logic") studies deductive argument and
ways of evaluating validity. Inductive logic
studies inductive arguments and ways of evaluating

inductive strength. You should be aware that in
this text only some of the elementary considerations from each of these fields is presented so
as to provide a general, reasonably comprehensive
overview without demanding detailed specialization.

2. Deductive and Inductive Arguments

the contemporary distinction

The distinction between deductive and inductive
arguments used to be made as follows. It was said
that a deductive argument was one in which the
reasoning went from general premises to particular
conclusions, while inductive reasoning went from
the particular to the general. This way of
differentiating the two types of argument is still
to be found in many dictionaries and even in some
texts in the field. This view, however, is no
longer generally accepted.

In every genuine argument, the premises provide
some support for the conclusion. The way in which
the premises support the conclusion is now used
to distinguish the two main types of argument. In
broad, general terms, the contemporary distinction
is basically this: in a deductive argument, the
reasons cited purport to provide conclusive
grounds for the conclusion, while in an inductive
argument they provide only probable grounds for
the conclusion. Inductive arguments may vary
considerably in the amount of strength the premises furnish the conclusion: from very little
support which makes the conclusion rather unlikely
to exceptionally strong support which renders the
conclusion highly likely. In a deductive argument,
however, either the premises provide conclusive
support to the conclusion or else they fail to:
there are no degrees of conclusive support.

deductive arguments

A more precise account and some examples will help

clarify the distinction. Consider, first of all,
deductive arguments.

> A <u>deductive</u> argument is one in which the
> conclusion of the argument, as put forward
> by the arguer, purports to follow conclu-
> sively from the information contained in
> the premises.

The conclusiveness that is referred to in this
delineation of a deductive argument has nothing
to do with the vehemence or confidence with which
the arguer presents his argument. That is, it is
not a characteristic of the manner in which the
argument is offered. Nor does it have anything to
do with the degree of certainty the arguer has
about the position he is advocating. That is,
the conclusiveness in question is not a characteristic of the arguer. Rather it is an attribute
of the argument itself. The conclusiveness has to
do with what <u>must</u> follow from the information
contained in the premises of the argument, suppos-
ing it to be true. The conclusion in a deductive
argument represents a helpful sorting out of
information already contained implicitly within
the premises.

Consider the following examples of deductive
arguments:

(a) <u>support space</u>   <u>main argument space</u>   <u>evaluation space</u>
                    1. All lawbreakers will
                       be punished.
                    <u>2. Jones is a lawbreaker.</u>

                    .˙. Jones will be punished.
The conclusion follows conclusively from the
information contained in premises 1 and 2. It
makes explicit what is already contained implicitly in the information of premises 1 and 2. In a
sense, the conclusion adds nothing new: it simply
makes explicit. The argument is a deductive one.

(b) <u>support space</u>   <u>main argument space</u>   <u>evaluation space</u>
                    1. If there are bees
                       buzzing, then there
                       is honey in the tree.

2. <u>There are bees buzzing.</u>

.˙. There is honey in the
     tree.

One does not have to be Pooh-Bear to recognize
that the conclusion follows conclusively from the
information contained in the premises. The information may, of course, be wrong, and there may
indeed be no honey in the tree. But whether or
not the premises and conclusion state true information is a separate matter from whether or not
the argument is deductive. From the information
presented in premises 1 and 2, the conclusion
follows conclusively. The argument is deductive.

(c) <u>support space</u>   <u>main argument space</u>   <u>evaluation space</u>
                1. Viruses are living.
                2. All living things are
                   conscious.

.˙. Viruses are conscious.

Again, the conclusion follows conclusively from
the information contained in the premises. The
argument is deductive. Again you should note
that determining whether or not an argument is
deductive is a different matter from determining
whether or not the premises and conclusion are
true. In this instance, the truth of premise 1 is
debatable, and premise 2 is false, as is the conclusion.

It is very important to note that in saying an
argument is deductive, we're not saying anything
about the truth or falsity of the premises or
conclusion. We are only saying that the conclusion follows conclusively from the information
contained in the premises.

(d) <u>support space</u>   <u>main argument space</u>   <u>evaluation space</u>
                1. There are only five
                   people who could have
                   killed Jones: A, B,
                   C, D, or E.
                2. B could not have
                   done it.

3. C could not have
   done it.
4. D could not have
   done it.
5. E could not have
   done it.

∴ A killed Jones.

The conclusion that must follow from the information contained in the premises is that "A killed
Jones." It follows conclusively. The argument
is deductive.

Note in passing that saying an argument is deductive does not mean that it is a good argument.
In (d), for instance, premise 1 may represent a
false dilemma unless substantial support is
forthcoming to support the position that only
these five individuals could individually have
committed the crime in question. Similarly,
premises 2 to 5 inclusive would require support.
Again, in saying that an argument is deductive
we're simply indicating the way in which the
conclusion follows from the premises offered,
namely, that it follows conclusively from the
information stated therein.

(e) support space   main argument space   evaluation space
1. Abortion is killing
   a human being.
2. Killing a human being
   is murder.
3. Murder is wrong.

∴ Abortion is wrong.

Regardless of whether or not one agrees with the
first premise (or any of the others, for that
matter), the conclusion follows conclusively from
the information contained in the premises. The
conclusion simply brings out explicitly what is
implicitly stated in premises 1, 2 and 3. The
argument is deductive.

(f) support space   main argument space   evaluation space
1. ABC is a triangle.
2. Angle A is 70°.

3. Angle B is 40°.
4. The sum of the angles
   of a triangle is 180°.

$\therefore$ Angle C is 70°.

The conclusion makes explicit information already contained in what is stated in premises 1 to 4 inclusive. The argument is deductive.

In some deductive arguments, the conclusion is so obvious that in many instances, the arguer would not bother to utter it but would assume we would automatically fill in what follows. In other instances, however, stating the conclusion is helpful, drawing our attention to information implicitly stated in the premises. Some further examples of deductive arguments are the following:

(g) <u>support space</u>   <u>main argument space</u>   <u>evaluation space</u>

1. If God exists, then there would be no evil in the world.
2. There is evil in the world.

$\therefore$ God does not exist.

(h) <u>support space</u>   <u>main argument space</u>   <u>evaluation space</u>

1. If country X goes to war with country Y, then X must break treaties with countries D and C.
2. If X breaks treaties with country C, then X must raise tariffs and reduce imports from country M.
3. If X reduces imports from country M, then X must either increase its balance of payments to M or else take out a further loan from the World Bank.

251

        4. X will not take out a
           further loan from the
           World Bank.
           _____

        ∴. If country X goes to
           war with country Y,
           then it must increase
           its balance of payments
           to country M.

As this chapter and the next unfolds, further
examples of deductive arguments will be provided.

To sum up our discussion of deductive arguments
to date, you should observe the following points
carefully:
    (1) A deductive argument is one in which
        the conclusion of the argument, as
        put forward by the arguer, purports to
        follow conclusively from the information
        contained in the premises.
    (2) In a deductive argument, the conclusion
        represents a helpful sorting out of
        information already contained implicitly
        within the premises.
    (3) In saying that an argument is deductive,
        we are not saying that the information
        contained in the premises is in fact
        true.
    (4) In saying that an argument is deductive,
        we are not saying that the argument is
        a good one.
In saying that an argument is deductive, all we
are saying is that it is an argument of a certain
kind, one in which the conclusion purports to
follow conclusively from the information contained
in the premises. That's _all_ we're saying.

                inductive arguments

Next let us consider inductive arguments. Since
there are only two types of arguments, any argument which is not deductive is inductive.
Furthermore, since an argument, in order to be an
argument, must have premises which support the
conclusion, a more precise account of inductive

                        252

argument can quickly be given.

An <u>inductive</u> argument is one in which the premises of the argument provide some support for the conclusion but where the conclusion does not follow conclusively from the information contained in the premises.

In an inductive argument, the conclusion is what is <u>probably</u> the case, given the information cited in the premises. In such arguments, the premises provide some support for the conclusion. In some instances, what they provide constitutes good support, in other instances, only minimal support. In inductive arguments, the conclusion always surpasses the evidence presented in the premises. There is always the <u>risk</u> that further testing or information will show the conclusion to be wrong. Examine the following examples carefully.

(a) <u>support space</u>   <u>main argument space</u>   <u>evaluation space</u>

                1. During the past three
                    winters, the heaviest
                    snowfall has occurred
                    in February.

               ∴ It is likely that in
                    this coming year the
                    heaviest snowfall will
                    occur in February.

This is an inductive argument: the premise provides some support for the conclusion and the conclusion does not follow conclusively from the information contained in the premise. What the conclusion states is only probably what will happen. There is the risk that the snowfall pattern of the previous three years may not be repeated in the forthcoming winter.

(b) <u>support space</u>   <u>main argument space</u>   <u>evaluation space</u>

                1. Since 1894 when snow-
                    fall levels were first
                    recorded, the heaviest
                    snowfall has tended to
                    occur in February.

                    ∴. It is likely that in
                        this coming year the
                        heaviest snowfall will
                        occur in February.
In this instance, there is some quite considerable
support for the conclusion. There is still the
chance, however, that the snowfall pattern during
the time it has been recorded is atypical or that
for some reason the snowfall pattern in the forthcoming year will be different. The argument is
inductive.

In (a) and (b) the reasoning has moved <u>from a</u>
<u>statement in the premises concerning what has been</u>
<u>the case in the past to a statement in the conclu-</u>
<u>sion concerning what is likely to happen in the</u>
<u>future</u>. Such reasoning is characterically induc-
tive: there is always the risk that the future
will be unlike the past.

(c) <u>support space</u>   <u>main argument space</u>   <u>evaluation space</u>
                        1. 119 randomly selected
                            samples of surface
                            moon substance corres-
                            pond in taste, texture
                            and chemical composi-
                            tion to cheddar cheese.

                    ∴. The surface of the moon
                        is made of cheddar cheese.
If what premise 1 reports were the case, then it
would provide considerable support for the conclusion. Even so, there is still the chance that
the selection is unrepresentative or that the
comparison tests are faulty. The argument is
inductive.

(d) <u>support space</u>   <u>main argument space</u>   <u>evaluation space</u>
                        1. Ever since I started
                            taking 400 inter-
                            national units of
                            vitamin E daily last
                            Fall, I've had fewer
                            colds and much more
                            energy.

                            254

$\therefore$ Vitamin E helps prevent
colds and raise energy
levels.

Even apart from the vagueness in premise 1 concerning "fewer colds" and "much more energy," the argument appeals for its strength only to the personal testimony of one person. While this supports the conclusion, it does so only in a minimal way. The effects of vitamin E on this one person may not be typical of its effects on others. The argument is inductive.

In (c) and (d) the reasoning has moved <u>from selected examples of a particular phenomenon to a generalization about the phenomenon in question</u>. In (c) the reasoning went from selected examples of surface moon substance to a generalized statement about the composition of the moon's surface. In (d), the reasoning went from the personal experience of one vitamin E user to a generalized statement about the effects of vitamin E on people. Reasoning in which some limited or restricted portion of what is being discussed is used to support a generalized statement about it all is characteristically inductive: there is always the risk that the limited selection is atypical.

Consider next this argument:

(e)   <u>support space</u>   <u>main argument space</u> evaluation space

<u>McKim Study</u>
- 1979
- survey of
medical
records of
asbestos
workers

1. Doctors have found
the following in-
cidence of lung
cancer in asbestos
mine workers:
over 25yrs in
the mine ... 26%
20-24yrs ... 21%
15-19yrs ... 18%
10-14yrs ... 12%
5-9yrs ... 8%
1-5yrs ... 5%
2. This compares with
an incidence of
lung cancer in the
general population

<u>of 4.5%.</u>

.˙. There is something in
asbestos that contributes
to the development of
lung cancer.

Assuming that the medical records of the mine workers examined are not unrepresentative of all those
of all asbestos mine workers, the argument provides some good reasons for the conclusion: the
incidence of lung cancer is higher in the mine
workers than in the general population, and the
incidence of lung cancer increases with increased
duration as an asbestos mine worker. The premises
provide strong support for the conclusion. The
conclusion, however, does not follow conclusively
from the information contained in the premises.
It is still only what is probably the case. There
is always the chance that there is some other
factor than asbestos that accounts for the higher
incidence of lung cancer in the mine worker population. The argument is inductive.

(f) (The following appeared in <u>Psychology Today</u>,
     November 1976, p. 116)
        Fat babies are likely to end up as
     fat adults. Researchers at the University
     of Rochester School of Medicine compared
     the weight of 366 adults between 20 and 30
     years of age with the weights their doctors
     recorded for them at six weeks, three months,
     and six months of age.
        The researchers also questioned the young
     adults about their weight and length at
     birth, educational level, social class, and
     the present weight of their parents. Over-
     weight was defined as more than 10 percent
     above the median for a person's height and
     age, obesity as over 20 percent.
        One-third of the infants who were over-
     weight at birth grew up to be fat adults,
     whereas only one-fifth of the thin or
     average newborns did....

As reconstructed, using standard format, the

argument appears as follows:

support space	main argument space	evaluation space

Univ. of Roch-
ester Medical
School Study
- 366 adults
  between ages
  20-30
- present
  weight com-
  pared with
  weight at
  6 wks., 3
  mos., and
  6 mos.
- defined
  'overweight'
  as more than
  10% above
  median for
  person's
  height and
  age.

1. One-third of the
   infants who were
   overweight at birth
   grew up to be fat
   adults, whereas only
   one-fifth of the thin
   or average newborns
   did.

∴ Fat babies are likely
to end up as fat adults.

The premise states one of the findings of the
University of Rochester Medical School's study.
It supports the conclusion. The conclusion, however, does not follow conclusively from the information contained in the premise. There is always
the chance that the 366 persons selected for this
study are unrepresentative of people in general.
There is, moreover, always the chance that the
finding of this study is not typical of what
happens to fat, thin and average infants. The
argument is inductive.

In (e) and (f) the reasoning went from what was
found to be the case in one or more studies to what
is generally the case. In (e) the reasoning went
from a recent report about the incidence of lung
cancer in asbestos mine workers to a general statement about the relationship of asbestos to lung
cancer. In (f) the reasoning went from a study on

257

overweight conducted on 366 persons to a general
statement about the relationship between being fat
as an infant to being fat as an adult. Such
reasoning is characteristically inductive: there
is always the chance that the study (or studies)
is unrepresentative.

Unlike deductive arguments which simply sort out
in the conclusion pre-existing information already
contained in the premises, inductive arguments
involve conclusions that go beyond what is contained by way of information in the premises. Both
extend knowledge -- deductive arguments, by making
information explicit, and inductive arguments, by
providing information of a more general sort than
what a study, or a selected example, or a previous
experience would cover in and of itself. Both
kinds of argument have their place in argumentation.

To sum up this discussion of inductive argument,
you should note carefully the following points
that have been mentioned.
  (1) An inductive argument is one in which
      the premises of the argument provide
      some support for the conclusion but
      where the conclusion does not follow
      conclusively from the information
      contained in the premises.
  (2) In an inductive argument, the conclusion
      always surpasses the information present-
      ed in the premises.
  (3) The following sorts of reasoning are
      characteristically inductive:
      a) moving from a statement in the
         premises concerning what has been
         the case in the past to a statement
         in the conclusion concerning what is
         likely to happen in the future.
      b) moving from selected examples of a
         particular phenomenon (in the premises)
         to a generalization about the phenomen-
         on in question (in the conclusion).
      c) moving from what was found to be the
         case in one or more studies (in the

258

                    premises) to what is generally the
                    case (in the conclusion).
    (4) In saying that an argument is inductive,
        we are not saying that the information
        contained in the premises is in fact true
        nor are we saying that the argument is
        necessarily a good one.
In saying that an argument is inductive, all we
are saying is that it is an argument of a specific
sort, one in which the premises give some support
for the conclusion and where the conclusion does
not follow conclusively from the information contained in the premises. That's <u>all</u> we're saying.

3. Deductive Validity and Inductive Strength

a review

The contemporary distinction between deductive and
inductive arguments is drawn in terms of the <u>two</u>
<u>very different kinds of relationship premises and</u>
<u>conclusions can have to each other</u>. To repeat:
in a deductive argument, conclusions are put forward in such a way that they receive or are intended to receive conclusive support from the information contained in the premises, whereas, in an
inductive argument, they receive only probable
support.

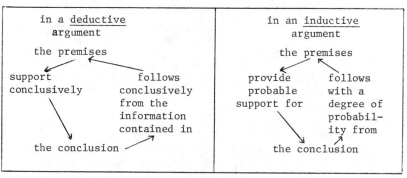

Not all deductive or inductive arguments are good
ones. All arguments, whether deductive or inductive, are subject to defects outlined in Steps #1
through #7 of argument evaluation. In addition
to these steps, however, there is another aspect
of an argument to consider, namely, the relationship between premises and conclusion.

The relationship between premises and conclusion
is, of course, an important aspect of an argument.
Indeed, since premises are specifically intended
to back up conclusions, this relationship is the
most important one in an argument. Regardless
of what other flaws an argument may have, if it
fails to have premises which support the conclusion, then it is seriously defective. The
relationship between premises and conclusion is
one that has been extensively examined in the
Study of Argument.

In looking at the relationship between premises
and conclusion in an argument, there are two
distinct considerations to ponder:
   (a) In a deductive argument, does the
       conclusion follow conclusively from
       the information contained in the
       premises, as purported, or has some
       error been made?
   (b) In an inductive argument, do the
       premises give sufficient support to the
       conclusion or do they contain flaws
       that reduce or call into question the
       amount of support they actually give
       the conclusion?
Question (a) concerns deductive validity;
question (b), inductive strength. Let us examine
each in turn.

deductive validity

Consider question (a) above: does the conclusion
of the deductive argument follow conclusively
from the information contained in the premises,

260

as purported? If so, the argument is said to be valid. If not, the argument is said to be invalid. To summarize:

A deductive argument is said to be valid when the conclusion of the argument, as put forward by the arguer, purports to follow conclusively from the information contained in the premises and actually does so.

A deductive argument is said to be invalid when the conclusion of the argument, as put forward by the arguer, purports to follow conclusively from the information contained in the premises but fails to do so.

A deductive argument is either valid or invalid.

The notion of validity simply labels successful deductive reasoning. Saying that a deductive argument is valid only means that its conclusion follows conclusively from the premises, as alleged by the arguer in putting forward the argument as a deductive one. It indicates successful sorting out of information already contained in the premises.

This is an extremely important feature for a deductive argument to have, for it indicates that the conclusion follows from the information contained in the premises, as intended by the arguer because of the way in which he designed his argument. It does not, of course, mean that the premises are true, or that the conclusion is true, nor does it exempt the argument from argument evaluation in terms of other criteria (such as those indicated in Steps #1 through #7 inclusive).

Examples (a) to (h) of deductive arguments (on pages 248-252 above) are also examples of valid deductive arguments. Occasionally, however, a mistake can occur in deductive reasoning that violates the intended link between premises and conclusion. The arguer, in putting forward the

261

argument, may cast it in a deductive framework, making the conclusion appear to draw out information already contained in the premises, and yet not succeed in so doing. The arguer may fail to draw out what properly should be concluded conclusively on the basis of the information expressed in the premises. Such arguments are said to be "invalid." Saying that an argument is invalid simply means that the information contained in the premises has not been properly sorted out in the conclusion of the offered argument. It represents a serious flaw in deductive reasoning, for it indicates that the premises do not support this particular conclusion in a deductive fashion as intended by the arguer.

Consider these examples:

(a) 1. If I smoke two packages of cigarettes a day, then I'll get lung cancer.
   2. I smoke two packages of cigarettes a day.

∴ I'll get lung cancer.

(b) 1. If I smoke two packages of cigarettes a day, then I'll get lung cancer.
   2. I have lung cancer.

∴ I smoke two packages of cigarettes a day.

In (a) the conclusion follows conclusively from the information contained in the premises. The argument is deductive and it is valid. Example (b) looks suspiciously like (a). It is cast in a deductive framework and it would appear that the arguer intends the conclusion to follow conclusively from the information contained in the premises. The argument is deductive. But the conclusion does not follow conclusively from the information contained in the premises. Even if the premises are accepted as true, the conclusion does not follow. There may be many other reasons why the person in question has lung cancer apart from his smoking two packages of cigarettes a day. The argument is invalid.

Consider two more examples:

(c) 1. All rapists are mentally ill.
2. Brown is a rapist.
_____
∴ Brown is mentally ill.

(d) 1. All rapists are mentally ill.
2. Brown is mentally ill.
_____
∴ Brown is a rapist.

Argument (c) is deductive and the conclusion actually does follow from the information contained in the premises. It therefore is a valid deductive argument. Argument (d) is deductive, but the conclusion does not follow from the information contained in the premises. It therefore is an invalid deductive argument.

Some further contrasting examples:

(e) 1. If there is God, then he created everything in the universe.
2. If he created everything in the universe, then he created evil.
3. If he created evil, then he is responsible for evil.
_____
∴ If there is a God, then he is responsible for evil.

(f) 1. If there is a God, then he created everything in the universe.
2. If he created everything in the universe, then he created evil.
3. If he created evil, then he is responsible for evil.
_____
∴ God did not create evil and he did not create everything in the universe.

The argument in (e) is deductive, and, since the conclusion does follow from the information contained in the premises, the argument is valid. The argument in (f) is deductive, but, since the conclusion does not follow conclusively from the information contained in the premises, the argument is invalid.

For these short deductive arguments it is relatively easy to "see" which ones are valid and which are invalid. For longer ones, however, the process of inspection is much more complicated.

263

The field of Symbolic Logic has fortunately developed some useful, easily applied procedures for ascertaining quickly if a deductive argument is valid or invalid, and in the next two chapters some basic methods will be outlined.

It is important for you to recognize that the validity of an argument is different from the truth or falsity of its component premises and conclusion. A valid deductive argument, for instance, can have a false conclusion. Likewise, an invalid deductive argument can have a true conclusion. The following cases and examples may make clearer the difference between truth and falsity on the one hand and validity and invalidity on the other:

case 1: true premises, a true conclusion

(a) 1. All humans are mortal.   (b) 1. All humans are mortal.
    2. Einstein is human   2. Einstein is mortal.

∴ Einstein is mortal.   ∴ Einstein is human

      (valid)   (invalid)

case 2: false premises, a false conclusion

(c) 1. All cats are plants   (d) 1. All cats can fly.
    2. All plants can fly.   2. All plants can fly.

∴ All cats can fly.   ∴ All cats are plants.

      (valid)   (invalid)

case 3: false premises, a true conclusion

(e) 1. All rocks are human   (f) 1. All human beings are
      beings.   rocks.
    2. Einstein is a rock.   2. Einstein is a rock.

∴ Einstein is a human   ∴ Einstein is a human
   being.   being.

      (valid)   (invalid)

This leaves only one final case: case #4 - true premises, a false conclusion. It is impossible for a valid deductive argument to have true premises and a false conclusion. All such arguments are invalid.

case 4:   true premises, a false conclusion.

(g) no valid arguments of   (h) 1. All humans are mortal.
    sort.   2. Flipper (a dolphin) is
                                      mortal.
                                   ∴. Flipper is human.

                                   (invalid)

The absence of valid deductive arguments with
true premises and a false conclusion calls for an
explanation. The reason is quite apparent:

> It is a characteristic of all valid deductive
> arguments that it would be contradictory to
> accept as true the information expressed in
> the premises and then not accept the conclu-
> sion of the argument.

Examine any of the valid deductive arguments
mentioned so far.   For instance, in the following example:

1. All lawbreakers will be punished.
2. Jones is a lawbreaker.

∴. Jones will be punished.

It would be contradictory to accept as true the
premises and then deny the conclusion.   The conclusion follows "automatically" from the information expressed in the premises.   Similarly for
other examples of valid deductive arguments, such
as:

1. All cats are plants.
2. All plants can fly.

∴. All cats can fly.

If one accepts as true the information contained
in the premises of this argument, then one must
accept the conclusion as well, as following
conclusively from the information expressed
therein.   Note the claim here is not that the
information expressed in the premises has to be
true.   Rather the claim is a conditional one:
if one accepts the information expressed in the
premises as true, then in valid deductive argument the conclusion must also be accepted as true
(or else one contradicts oneself).

Another example:
> 1. If Jesus rose from the dead, then
>   resurrection is possible.
> 2. Jesus rose from the dead.
> ∴. Resurrection is possible.

This is a deductive argument, and, because the
conclusion does follow conclusively from the
information expressed in the premises, it is
valid. Again notice an important characteristic
of deductive arguments: if one accepts as true
the information contained in the premises, then
one must also accept as true the information
contained in the conclusion.

This trait is absent in invalid deductive arguments. That is, in invalid deductive arguments
it is not contradictory to accept the information contained in the premises and then not
accept the conclusion of the argument. In this
example of an invalid deductive argument, for
instance,
> 1. All humans are mortal.
> 2. Flipper the dolphin is mortal.
> ∴. Flipper is human.

It is not contradictory to accept premises 1 and
2 while not accepting the conclusion. That is,
just because all humans are mortal and Flipper
the dolphin is mortal does not automatically mean
that Flipper is human. That does not follow from
the information contained in the premises. There
would be no inconsistency incurred by accepting
the premises and yet denying the conclusion. The
same is true of all other invalid deductive arguments.

In sum, then, the following points should be
carefully noted about deductive validity:
> (1) Validity indicates that in a deductive
>   argument the conclusion follows conclu-
>   sively from the information contained
>   in the premises.
> (2) Every deductive argument is either valid
>   or invalid. There are no degrees of

266

validity. (The notion of validity functions very much like the notion of pregnancy: a girl is either pregnant or not pregnant; there are no degrees of pregnancy.)

(3) The validity of an argument is a different notion from the truth or falsity of the individual statements that make up the argument. For example, both valid and invalid arguments may have all true statements or all false statements.

(4) It is impossible, however, for a valid deductive argument to have true premises and a false conclusion. The reason for this is that it is characteristic of valid deductive arguments that it would be contradictory to accept as true the information expressed in the premises and then not accept the conclusion of the argument.

inductive strength

The corresponding notion for inductive arguments is strength. "Strength" refers to the amount of probable support the premises give the conclusion. 'Amount' here has to be loosely interpreted, for it is often impossible to quantify accurately the amount of support given the conclusion by the premises. With this in mind, the following characterizations can be given of types of inductive strength:

An inductive argument exhibits good inductive strength if the premises provide substantial support for the conclusion.

Such an argument is said to be "inductively strong." By contrast

An inductive argument exhibits poor inductive strength if the premises provide minimal support for the conclusion.

Such arguments are said to be "inductively weak." There are degrees of inductive strength, from weak, through moderate, to strong support.

There exist no rigorous procedures for determining
the precise degree of inductive strength premises
provide conclusions with. In areas where inductive arguments are employed, there exist numerous
disagreements over such fundamental matters as:
how much support is sufficient to warrant acceptance of the conclusion? how much support constitutes good support? and so on. Inductive logic
simply provides the argument analyst with guidelines for help in judging the approximate amount
of inductive support the premises provide the
conclusion. These will be examined in Chapter
Eleven.

4.   Steps #8 and #9 (A Preview)

An argument is either deductive or inductive.

If the argument is deductive, then we must examine its validity. Validity indicates successful
deductive reasoning, and, as such, it constitutes
the most basic and central feature of a deductive
argument. It is a feature of a deductive argument that we, as conscientious argument analysts,
must examine. If the deductive argument is valid,
then it has passed an important step in assessing
its worth. If, on the other hand, the deductive
argument is found to be invalid, then we have
noted an extremely serious defect in its worth as
an argument. In such an instance what we have
found is that the premises do not support the
conclusion in the manner intended.

Step #8
In deductive argument, determine if the
argument is valid or invalid.

How this can be done is the subject matter of the
next two chapters. Chapter Nine will discuss
"truth table methods" while Chapter Ten will
indicate common patterns of deductive reasoning.

If the argument is inductive, then we must examine its inductive strength. Again, inductive

strength is the most fundamental feature of inductive arguments, for it concerns the degree of support the premises provide the conclusion. As has already been indicated, the specific degree of support the premises provide the conclusion is often a matter of judgment and dispute. Nonetheless, there are certain specific features of an inductive argument that we, as argument analysts ought to be aware. These will be discussed in Chapter Eleven in setting out Step #9 of argument evaluation.

Because an argument is either deductive or inductive, we will either apply Step #8 or Step #9 (but not both) to each argument we meet. This applies not only to the main argument, but also to each mini-argument which are also arguments in their own right.

Recall Quiz

(1) How many different kinds of argument are there? What are they called?

(2) In an argument consisting of a main argument and several mini-arguments, can
   a) the main argument be deductive, while the mini-arguments are inductive?
   b) the main argument be inductive, while the mini-arguments are deductive?
   c) the main argument be either deductive or inductive, and each mini-argument be one or the other?

(3) On what basis is the distinction between deductive and inductive argument now made?

(4) What is a deductive argument?

(5) If we say that an argument is deductive, what are we saying about that argument? Are we saying, for instance that the argument is a good one? Are we saying that it contains all true information?

(6) What is an inductive argument?

269

(7) What sorts of reasoning are characteristically inductive (give 3 sorts)?

(8) If we say that an argument is inductive, what are we saying about that argument?

(9) When is an argument said to be valid? invalid?

(10) Can a valid deductive argument contain false information? Can an invalid deductive argument contain true information? Can a valid deductive argument have true premises and a false conclusion?

(11) Why is it impossible for a valid deductive argument to have true premises and a false conclusion?

(12) To what does "inductive strength" refer?

(13) In a deductive argument, what crucial feature ought we to consider in evaluating its worth as a deductive argument? Why is this feature important?

(14) In an inductive argument, what crucial feature ought we to consider in evaluating its worth as an inductive argument? Why is this feature important?

Exercise #1
Re-examine the arguments contained in the selections in Exercise #1 of Chapter One (pages 31-38 above). State whether each argument is deductive or inductive

Exercise #2
Re-examine the arguments found in selections on the following pages of this text. State whether each argument is deductive or inductive.

page 17, (b)	page 59, (k)
page 20, (c)	page 62, (m)
page 22, (e)	page 65, (1)
page 24, (f)	page 67, (7)
page 26, (i)	page 100,(j)
page 28, (k)	page 102,(k)
page 40, (a)	page 109,(6)
page 56, (h)	

CHAPTER NINE

ARGUMENT EVALUATION: DEDUCTIVE ARGUMENT I

1. Step #8

Step #8
In a deductive argument, determine if the
argument is valid or invalid.

One way of determining the validity or invalidity
of a deductive argument is known as the "truth
table method." This method will be presented in
this chapter.

Before this method can be explained, however, there
are three important matters that must be probed
first:
    (1) you must learn some symbols
    (2) you must learn some definitions (5 in all)
    (3) you must gain some experience in trans-
        lating expressions from our language into
        the symbolic language used in evaluating
        the worth of deductive arguments
In this chapter we'll discuss these matters first
and then move on to the application of Step #8 to
deductive arguments.

2. Some Symbols

visualizing structure

Let us consider once again the following familiar
argument:
    1. If God exists, then there would be
       no evil in the world.
    2. There is evil in the world.

    `. God does not exist.
Notice carefully some things about the structure
of this deductive argument. For one thing, note
that premise 1 has an "if...then..."structure. It

271

reads: "If God exists, then there would be no evil in the world." "If...then..." sentences are called conditional sentences. The part after the "if" is referred to as the antecedent of the sentence; the part after the "then" is called the consequent. So, in premise 1 above, "God exists" is the antecedent; "there would be no evil in the world" is the consequent.

Notice also the places where 'no' and 'not' are to be found. Such words indicate information which is negated (or denied). In the argument above, 'no' is to be found in the consequent of premise 1, while 'not' is found in the conclusion. Note, too, that the conclusion negates the antecedent of premise 1 and that the consequent of premise 1 negates premise 2.

In other words, this argument exhibits an intricate internal pattern of interrelationships among the various bits of information that make up the argument. This is not unusual for a deductive argument. Indeed, you may have noticed in the last chapter that deductive arguments tend to repeat portions of the information expressed in the sentences of the argument, to combine bits of information in different ways in different premises, and to sort out pieces of the same information within the conclusion. This indicates that the structure of a deductive argument is very important.

A symbolic language has been devised to help us visualize much more clearly the structure of deductive arguments. It is a language that helps us see at a glance what the bits of information being expressed are, how they are being combined, and what's being sorted out in the conclusion. It shows us the structure in a much less cumbersome manner than simply talking about it as we did in the example above.

We need to learn how to use two sorts of symbols in order to learn the truth table method for ascertaining the validity of deductive arguments:
    (1) symbols for informative sentences

        (2) symbols for words that connect or
            negate informative sentences.
Let us consider each in turn.

symbols for informative sentences

Informative sentences are basically sentences that
are capable of being either true or false--the
sorts of sentences, in other words, that figure in
most of the arguments we are likely to encounter.

Note here that the requirement is that the sentences
be _capable_ of being either true or false. For our
purposes here it is not necessary for us to know
which particular bit of information is which. In
addition, although the following are interesting
questions, they are not germane to our exposition
of truth table method:
        (1) what is the meaning of 'true,'
            'false'?
        (2) how can one tell whether or not
            something is true or false?
        (3) what sorts of sentences are not
            informative?
We will not consider these philosophical issues
here.

We will use _alphabetical letters_ (either small or
large case) as symbols for informative sentences.
Any alphabetical letter may stand for any sentence,
although it is usually convenient to select a letter
from one of the key expressions in the sentence as
an aid to memory. It makes no difference, however,
what alphabetical letter is selected.

Just so that we work together in this text, suggested
letters for symbolizing sentences will be underlined.
For example, for the purposes of working together,
the sentence "There is considerable evidence that
space men visited earth within historical times"
will be symbolized as "v".

Here are some further examples. Note the letters
underlined:

273

sentence	symbolization
(1) I had an automobile accident on July 8, 1980.	a
(2) The OPEC nations increased the price of oil to Western nations by 65% in September 1980.	i
(3) One way of solving the problems of inflation is to engage in deficit financing.	d
(4) Amniocentesis is often helpful in pregnancy.	h
(5) Women have been oppressed for centuries.	o

And so on.

Alphabetical letters, then, are one type of symbol we will use. They stand for informative sentences. Technically speaking, what is being symbolized are not sentences but rather what-sentences-express. Two sentences, for instance, may express the same information. "It is raining" and "Il pleut" express the same information, although they are two separate sentences (in two different languages). Likewise, "John killed Mary" and "Mary was killed by John" are two separate sentences, although they convey the same information. Some have proposed the word 'proposition' to stand for what-sentences-express. We won't enter into the interesting philosophical ramifications of this proposal here.

Let us now consider the second sort of symbol we use.

symbols for words that connect or negate informative sentences

Words that connect or negate sentences are key words that play an important part in showing up the structure of deductive arguments. Five such key words are of particular importance, and they have been given symbols of their own. These 5 basic key words and their symbols are as follows:

(1) <u>not...</u>

The word 'not' is used to negate a sentence, and it is symbolized by a curl: '~'.

For example, if the sentence "It is raining" is symbolized as 'r', then the sentence "It is <u>not</u> raining" would be symbolized as '~r'.

Consider some further examples.

	sentence	symbolization
(1)	It is not <u>i</u>cy on the streets of San Francisco today.	~ i
(2)	Deficit financing is not a viable option for most charitable institutions.	~ o
(3)	Vitamin E does not affect the heart beneficia<u>l</u>ly.	~ a
(4)	The moon is not <u>m</u>ade of green cheese.	~ m

(2) <u>...and...</u>

The word 'and' serves to connect sentences, and it is symbolized by a dot: '·'. The dot is placed between the two sentences connected by 'and'.

For example: suppose we symbolize the sentence "I went to the doctor's office this morning" by 'w' and the sentence "I got the car fixed this afternoon" by 'g'. In this case, the whole sentence "I went to the doctor's office this morning <u>and</u> I got the car fixed this afternoon" would be symbolized as: 'w · g'.

Some further examples of dot at work:

	sentence	symbolization
(1)	<u>E</u>uthanasia discriminates against old people and <u>i</u>nfanticide penalizes children.	E · i
(2)	<u>C</u>apital punishment is not <u>j</u>ustifiable and those who support it are simply <u>v</u>indictive.	~j · v
(3)	I won't go to <u>j</u>ail and I won't pay my <u>f</u>ine.	~j · ~f

(3) ...or...

The word 'or' also serves to connect sentences, and it is symbolized by a wedge: 'v'. The wedge is placed between the two sentences connected by 'or'.

For example: suppose we use 'B' to stand for the sentence "I'll have a Bloody Mary" and 'd' to stand for the sentence "I'll have a dry Martini." Then, in this case, the entire sentence "I'll have a Bloody Mary or I'll have a dry Martini" would be symbolized as 'B v d'.

Some further examples:

sentence	symbolization
(1) Indians in North America will become assimilated or they'll experience a resurgence of ethnic pride.	a v r
(2) I'll go to Club Med for Spring Break or I won't spend any money at all.	g v ~s

Notice how the next sentence is symbolized:

| (3) Women are equal and are required to pay alimony or they are not equal and are not required to pay alimony. | (e · r) v (~e · ~r) |

The parentheses are useful here in showing that it is one thing or the other.

Notice, too, the next sentence:

| (4) I'll have a cheddar cheeseburger, and I'll have beer or I'll have milk. | c · (b v m) |

The parentheses here are useful in preventing ambiguity. Without them, the sentence might mistakenly be read as: (c · b) v m -- in other words, "I'll have a cheddar cheeseburger and I'll have a beer, or else I'll have milk." This says something quite different than sentence (4) says. In such instances where ambiguity is apt to occur, parentheses are used to show what is grouped with what.

(4) if...then...

The expression "if...then..." is used to connect
sentences, one sentence (after the 'if') being the
antecedent, the other (after the 'then') being the
consequent. The expression "if...then..." is symbolized by a horseshoe: ' ⊃ '. The horseshoe (⊃) is
placed between the antecedent and the consequent.

For example: if we use 'r' to symbolize the sentence
"Snodgrass will resign" and 'c' for the sentence
"I'll have a chance for the presidency," then the
entire sentence "If Snodgrass will resign, then I'll
have a chance for the presidency" would be symbolized as: r ⊃ c.

Some further examples:

sentence	symbolization
(1) If capital punishment is reinstituted, then there will be executions each week.	r ⊃ e
(2) If inflation is not beaten, then the poor people in this country will become even poorer.	~b ⊃ p
(3) If TV continues to escalate violence and if it continues to associate sex with violence, then society will have inflicted upon it a brutal generation.	(v · s) ⊃ b
(4) If I plan to go to law school, then I'll have to excel in logic and I'll have to do well in economics.	g ⊃ (l · e)
(5) If I plan to go to law school, then I'll have to excel in logic or be good at debating.	g ⊃ (l v d)
(6) If I plan to go to law school and if I am to get a good job with a senior law firm, then I'll have to have outstanding grades.	(g · j) ⊃ o
(6) If I plan to go to law school and if I am to get a good job	

277

with a senior law firm, then
I'll have to have outstanding
grades and I'll have to have $(g \cdot j) \supset (o \cdot r)$
excellent references.

(5) ...is equivalent to...

The expression "...is equivalent to..." is used to
connect two sentences and it is symbolized by three
bars: '$\equiv$'. The symbol ($\equiv$) is placed between the
two sentences it connects.

For example: suppose we use '$(m \supset \sim c)$' to stand for
the sentence "If I get married, then I won't have a
career" and '$(\sim m \supset c)$' to stand for the sentence
"If I don't get married, then I will have a career."
In this case, saying that the one sentence "If I
get married, then I won't have a career" is equivalent
to the other sentence "If I don't get married, then
I will have a career" would be symbolized as follows:
$(m \supset \sim c) \equiv (\sim m \supset c)$.

in sum

Using 'p' and 'q' to stand for any informative sentence whatsoever, the following are the symbols we
have discussed:

expression	symbol	symbol name	example
not...	$\sim$	curl	not-p $\sim$p
...and...	$\circ$	dot	p and q p $\cdot$ q
...or...	v	wedge	p or q p v q
if...then...	$\supset$	horseshoe	if p then q p $\supset$ q
...is equi- valent to...	$\equiv$	three bars	p is equivalent to q p $\equiv$ q

278

application to arguments

These two sorts of symbols are exceptionally useful
in helping us to inspect and evaluate the worth of
deductive arguments. In fact they help us do two
very important things.

First of all, they help us to see the <u>pattern</u> the
argument exhibits. Let's go back to the argument
with which we started this chapter:
      If God exists, then there would be no <u>e</u>vil
      in <u>t</u>he world. But there is <u>e</u>vil in the world.
      Thus <u>G</u>od does not exist.
Using the letters underlined, this argument would
be symbolized as follows:
$$1. \; G \supset \sim e$$
$$2. \; e$$

$$\therefore \; \sim G$$

We can see at a glance what bits of information the
sentences contain, how they are connected, what is
negated, and what's sorted out in the conclusion.
The structure of the argument is readily apparent.
(Just note in passing that in symbolizing an argument we must be consistent in what we use to symbolize each bit of information).

Secondly, these symbols can help us see <u>similar</u>
<u>patterns</u> of argument. Compare, for instance, the
following two arguments:

argument #1	argument #2
If there is an Ice Age coming, then there'll be a gradual <u>d</u>ecline in the average ye<u>a</u>rly tempera-ture. There is a gradual <u>d</u>ecline in the average ye<u>a</u>rly temperature. Thus there is an Ice Age <u>c</u>oming.	If people from space visited earth in remote <u>h</u>istorical times, then they would have <u>l</u>eft be-hind traces of t<u>h</u>eir visit (statues, landing pads, inscriptions,pictures,etc). Visitors from space have <u>l</u>eft behind traces of t<u>h</u>eir visit (statues... pictures). Consequently, people from space <u>v</u>isited earth in remote hi<u>s</u>torical times.

279

Using the letters under-   Using the letters underlined, argument #1 would   lined, argument #2 would
be symbolized as follows: by symbolized as follows:
    1. c ⊃ d   1. v ⊃ l
    2. d   2. l
    ∴ c   ∴ v

These two arguments have the same pattern, even
though they deal with quite different topics. Symbolizing the argument helps us see the sameness of
pattern readily. Seeing patterns in deductive
reasoning will become more important as we progress
in the study of deductive arguments.

Exercise #1
Using the letters underlined, symbolize the
following expressions:
(1) President John F. Kennedy was not
    killed by Oswald.   _____
(2) If I go to Key West for the Spring
    Break, then I'll have a good time. _____
(3) If I don't go to Key West for the
    Spring Break, then I won't have
    a good time.   _____
(4) If I go to Key West for the Spring
    Break, then I won't have a good
    time.   _____
(5) If I don't go to Key West for the
    Spring Break, then I won't have
    a good time.   _____
(6) If pornographic material is not
    censured, then children will be
    exposed to potentially harmful
    literature.   _____
(7) Mediums are frauds and seances
    are hoaxes.   _____
(8) Reincarnation does not occur
    and death is the end.   _____
(9) Earth was visited by space men
    in remote times and ancient man
    was not more advanced than we
    currently give him credit.   _____
(10) Venus hasn't any oxygen and
    Mars hasn't any water.   _____

(11) I won't go to medical school
and I won't go to business school.   _____

(12) I'll go to Arizona or I'll go
to Oregon.   _____

(13) Saying "if you are in favor of
abortion then you are in favor of
euthanasia" is equivalent to saying
"if you are in favor of euthanasia
then you are in favor of abortion.   _____

(14) If New York City collapses and the
State takes over, then the country
is in serious economic trouble.   _____

(15) If I buy a new sports car, then
I'll have sex appeal and I'll have
a huge debt.   _____

(16) If I don't get a job or if I
don't get accepted by the army,
then I won't have much of a
future.   _____

(17) If you don't go to graduate
school or if you don't get a job,
then your parents will support
you or society will support you.   _____

Exercise #2
Using the letters underlined, symbolize the expressions in the following arguments.
(1) If Snodgrass resigns, then I'll have a chance
for the presidency. Snodgrass does not resign.
Thus I won't have a chance for the presidency.

(2) I'll have a Bloody Mary or I'll have a dry
Martini. If I have a Bloody Mary, then I'll
have to tolerate the tomato juice and I'll
break out in hives. If I have the dry Martini,
then I'll have to suffer the bartender's in-
competence and I'll taste too much Vermouth.
I won't tolerate the tomato juice. Thus I'll
have a dry Martini.

(3) If I'm to excel in my job, then I'll have to
become more outgoing. I won't become more outgoing. Hence I won't excel in my job.

(4) If there is life after death, then some people
are in for a big surprise. There is life after

281

death. Thus some people are in for a big surprise.

(5) If vitamin E is effective, then the blood of
people who use vitamin E will contain less
cholesterol. The blood of people who use vitamin
E does not contain less cholesterol. Thus vitamin E is not effective.

(6) If amniocentesis is already a widely-used medical procedure, then doctors are now in the
position of making life-and-death decisions.
Amniocentesis is already a widely-used medical
procedure. Thus doctors are now in the position
of making life-and-death decisions.

(7) If unions were truly committed to the liberation
of women, then they would espouse feminist causes.
Unions do not espouse feminist causes. Therefore unions are not truly committed to the liberation of women.

(8) Do any of the above arguments exhibit the same
pattern? If so, which ones?

3. Some Definitions

Having now become familiar with the basic symbols
of the language of deductive logic, the next step
is to learn some definitions. These are important
definitions, and they must be carefully learned.
They play a central role in the truth table method
which we're gradually approaching. The definitions
in question are the definitions of each of the 5
symbols that connect or negate informative sentences
which we've just learned how to use.

In what follows, we're not going to talk about
specific informative sentences. Rather we're going
to discuss matters a bit more generally (we'll
come back to specific sentences and arguments a
little later on). We're going to speak about any
two informative sentences -- let's refer to them
as 'p' and 'q'. In our discussion here it makes
no difference what particular informative sentences
'p' and 'q' symbolize. We just need two informative
sentences for the sake of discussion.

Informative sentences, you will recall, are those that are capable of being true or false. We need not know which. All we need note here is that they are sentences which are capable of being true or false. 'True' and 'false' here are called <u>the truth values</u> of informative sentences.

So: the two informative sentences we're considering ('p' and 'q') are each capable of being true or false. In other words, 'p' has two truth values (true, false) and so does 'q' (true, false). In talking about 'p' and 'q' in what follows and in arriving at the definitions of the five symbols, we're going to ask questions like the following:

(1) When 'p' is negated, how does this change the original truth value of 'p'?

(2) What is the truth value of the new expression that is created when two informative sentences -- 'p' and 'q' -- are connected by such words as 'and', 'or', 'if...then...', and 'is equivalent to'? In other words, what is the truth value of the following expressions:

$$p \cdot q$$
$$p \lor q$$
$$p \supset q$$
$$p \equiv q$$

The definitions we're about to give of each of the five symbols are definitions in terms of their truth values.

negation

The negation of informative sentence 'p' is expressed as NOT-p. As we already know, this is expressed in symbolic terms as $\sim p$.

The expression "$\sim p$" translates the following expressions which also serve to indicate the negation of sentence 'p':

NOT-p
IT IS NOT THE CASE THAT p

IT IS FALSE THAT p
p IS FALSE (WRONG, UNTRUE)

If 'p' is an informative sentence (that is, one that can be either true or else false), then under what circumstances is '~p' true or false? The answer is easy to discern:

When 'p' is true, NOT-p is false; when
'p' is false, NOT-p is true.

This, after all, is the meaning of negation. Using 'T' to stand for 'true' and 'F' to stand for 'false' this information can be succinctly encapsulated in the following table:

p	~p
T	F
F	T

Reading across the table horizontally, the table simply indicates that when 'p' is true, '~p' is false, and when 'p' is false, '~p' is true. This table is referred to as <u>the truth table definition</u> of '~p'. It represents the logical definition of negation.

Before moving on to the standard truth table definitions of the other symbols, some help is needed in learning how to symbolize expressions containing 'not' and "it is not the case that...". Consider the following expressions and their indicated translations into the language of symbolic logic:

(1) not p or q

This expression is ambiguous as it stands, for it is not clear exactly what the 'not' is negating. On the one hand, 'not' might simply be negating the 'p' which follows it. On the other hand, 'not' might be negating the whole expression which follows it, namely "p or q". As it stands, we simply cannot tell.

To avoid this ambiguity, the following convention is adopted in symbolic logic:

'not' negates the shortest expression
which follows it.

Following this convention, then, in "not p or q"
the 'not' is taken as simply negating the 'p'.
The following, then, is the correct translation:
    not p or q $\sim$p v q

    (2) it is not the case that p or q
This expression is also ambiguous as it stands, for
"it is not the case that" might simply negate either
the 'p' only or else the whole expression "p or q".
As it stands, we simply cannot tell. Again a convention has been adopted in symbolic logic so as to
avoid the ambiguity. The convention is this:
    "it is not the case that..." is inter-
    preted as negating the whole expression
    which follows it.
Following this convention, then, in "it is not the
case that p or q" the phrase "it is not the case
that" is construed as negating the entire expression
"p or q". So the following is the correct translation:
    it is not the case that
    p or q $\sim$ (p v q)
The parentheses are needed here in order to indicate
that the "it is not the case that" negates the
whole of what follows.

Some more examples of expressions with "it is not
the case that" prefixed:
    it is not the case that
        p and q $\sim$ (p $\cdot$ q)
    it is not the case that
        if p then q $\sim$ (p $\supset$ q)
    it is not the case that
        if p then not q. $\sim$ (p $\supset$ $\sim$q)
    it is not the case that
        if not p then q $\sim$ ($\sim$p $\supset$ q)

    (3) not p and not q
This is correctly symbolized as follows:
        not p and not q $\sim$ p $\cdot$ $\sim$ q
In a similar fashion, the sentence "Jack did not
go up the hill and Jill did not go up the hill"
would be symbolized as follows:
         $\sim$a $\cdot$ $\sim$i

It should be noted that the following expressions are not equivalent:

$$\sim p \cdot q$$
$$\sim(p \cdot q)$$
$$\sim p \cdot \sim q$$

Why this is so will be discussed in the next chapter.

conjunction

The next symbol to be discussed and defined is '·' ('and' in English), known technically as "conjunction." The sentences which make up a conjunction are referred to as "conjuncts." Thus, in the expression "p AND q" 'p' is a conjunct and so is 'q'.

The conjoining of any two informative sentences 'p' and 'q' is symbolized as:

$$p \cdot q$$

The expression "p · q" symbolizes other words in English which also express conjunction:

            p AND q
            p; MOREOVER q
            p; ALSO q
            p BUT q
            p; HOWEVER q
            p ALTHOUGH q
            BOTH p AND q
            p IN ADDITION q

Note the following translations from English into the language of symbolic logic:

sentence	symbolization
(1) Susan wants to go downtown but Mary doesn't.	$S \cdot \sim M$
(2) I would like to go to the opera, but John wants to go to the symphony.	$o \cdot s$
(3) I would like to go to the opera, although if it rains then I'd like to go for a walk.	$o \cdot (r \supset w)$

(Note that in (3) the parentheses are needed to prevent ambiguity)

286

(4) I'll have pie for dessert and
    I'll also have ice cream.   p · i
(5) I will take you to the movies
    but if you whine, then we'll   m · (w ⊃ h)
    just stay home.
(Again note the use of parentheses in (5) to prevent
ambiguity)

In the expression "p · q" the letters 'p' and 'q'
stand for any informative sentences whatsoever.
Sentence 'p' could be either true or false. Similarly 'q' could be either true or false. When put
in combination, there are four possible arrangements of "trues" and "falses" for the two informative sentences 'p' and 'q'. Using 'T' for 'true'
and 'F' for 'false' these can be arranged in
tabular form as follows:

p	q
T	T
T	F
F	T
F	F

Reading across horizontally, all the table above
says is:

           p is true, q is true
           p is true, q is false
           p is false, q is true
           p is false, q is false
In other words, the table simply indicates the only
four possible combinations of T's and F's for the
two sentences 'p' and 'q'.

Consider the whole expression "p · q". When is it
(the whole expression) true and when is it false?
In other words, what is the definition of conjunction
in terms of truth values? The answer is as follows:
    The whole expression "p AND q" is true
    when both 'p' and 'q' are true; otherwise
    the whole expression is false.
This definition represents the usual meaning of
'and': unless both parts of the expression containing 'and' are true, then the expression as a
whole contains falsehood and ought to be indicated
as such. Bearing in mind that the definition of the

287

whole expression "p AND q" is true when both conjuncts are true, otherwise false, we can portray
this succinctly in terms of the following table:

p	q	p . q
T	T	T
T	F	F
F	T	F
F	F	F

This table states the truth table definition of
"p . q". Reading across horizontally, all this
table says is:

          when p is T and q is T, p . q is T
          when p is T and q is F, p . q is F
          when p is F and q is T, p . q is F
          when p is F and q is F, p . q is F

In other words, the truth table definition of
"p . q" simply states in shorthand form the definition of "p AND q", namely, that the whole expression
is T when both 'p' and 'q' are true, otherwise the
whole expression is F.

Note that the dot in the expression "p . q" represents simply the conjunctive sense of 'and' (and
associated words that express conjunction), that
is, the linking together of two informative sentences.
In ordinary usage, however, these words often have
additional sense than simply the conjunctive. For
example, in the sentence

          Jack fell down and broke his crown

the 'and' not only expresses conjunctive sense: it
also expresses causal sense (Jack broke his crown
as a result of his falling down).

Our symbol--dot--captures only the conjunctive sense
of an expression, not any causal sense that may also
be present. In addition, in a language like English,
the order of the conjuncts may be important on some
occasions. For example, the sentence

          Joan became pregnant and got married

differs somewhat from the sentence

          Joan got married and become pregnant

In the former sentence, the 'and' may convey to
some readers a causal sense (Joan's pregnancy

being the cause of her getting married) as well as
a conjunctive sense. While the order of the conjuncts
may be important in English, it is not important in
the symbolic language. Either (p . q) or (q . p) may
be written. The order doesn't matter, since the two
expressions are equivalent (as will shortly be shown).

In the following sentence
    I'll take the chocolate chip cookie, although
    I also like vanilla wafers
the 'although' serves to express <u>contrastive sense</u>
in addition to conjunctive sense. In a similar
manner, 'however' and 'but' usually serve to express contrastive sense in addition to conjunctive
sense.

The point to note is this: the expression "p . q"
translates only the <u>conjunctive</u> meaning of "p AND
q". Whatever additional sense (e.g. causal or contrastive senses) is conveyed in ordinary English
occurrences of 'and' and related conjunctive words
is not captured in the language of symbolic logic.
As in any translation between languages, the fit
is not perfect. "p . q" expresses fully but only
the conjunctive sense of 'and'. That's its job,
nothing more.

disjunction

So far, two truth table definitions have been advanced: one for negation and one for conjunction.
The next symbol to be discussed is "or"--technically
known as <u>disjunction</u>.

The disjunction of any two informative sentences
"p OR q" is symbolized as
$$p \lor q$$
The sentences which make up a disjunction are referred to as "disjuncts." Thus, in the above expression, 'p' is a disjunct and so is 'q'.

The expression "p v q" symbolizes the following
expressions in English which express disjunction:

p OR q
EITHER p OR q
p OR ELSE q

In a language such as English, 'or' is ambiguous.
In the following sentence
    A newborn baby is either male or fe-
    male
the 'or' is being used in an <u>exclusive</u> sense: the
newborn baby is either male, or else female, but
not both. Similarly, the 'or' in the following
sentence
    An argument is either deductive or
    inductive
is also being used in an exclusive sense: an argument is either deductive, or else inductive, but
not both. The exclusive sense of 'or' prevents
both disjuncts from applying.

On the other hand, in the following sentence
    A person is homosexual or heterosexual
the 'or' is being used in an <u>inclusive</u> sense: a
person may be homosexual, or heterosexual, or perhaps both (bisexual). Another example of the inclusive sense of 'or' occurs in the following sentence:
    Applications from Blacks or women will
    receive preferential treatment
The sentence indicates that preferential treatment
will be given to Blacks, or to women, or to those
who are both (i.e. to Black women). The inclusive
sense of 'or' leaves open the possibility that
both disjuncts apply.

In the <u>exclusive sense of 'or'</u> the meaning is
clear: either one disjunct is true, or else the
other is true, but not both are true. This differs
from the <u>inclusive sense of 'or'</u> which has the
following meaning: either one disjunct is true,
or else the other is true, or perhaps both are
true. English leaves open this ambiguity in 'or,'
although some languages, such as Latin, have two
words for 'or': <u>vel</u> for the inclusive sense, and
<u>aut</u> for the exclusive sense.

At this point, only the inclusive sense of 'or'
will be defined. To repeat, the meaning of "p or q"
in the inclusive sense of 'or' is:

    either one disjunct is true, or else
    the other is true, or perhaps both
    are true.

This is easily encapsulated in a truth table definition of "p or q" in the inclusive sense of 'or'.
Remember that 'p' and 'q' are informative sentences,
and, as such, can be either true or false. As we
saw when we discussed conjunction, for two informative sentences, there are 4 possible combinations
of T's and F's, namely

p	q
T	T
T	F
F	T
F	F

Now, remember the meaning of the whole expression
"p or q" (in the inclusive sense of 'or'):

    either one disjunct (p) is T, or
    else the other disjunct (q) is T,
    or perhaps both (p, q) are T.

So, to find the truth table definition of "p or q"
simply go down the 4 possible arrangements of T's
and F's and mark the whole expression T when p is
T, q is T, and when both p and q are T. The results
are as follows:

p	q	p $\vee$ q
T	T	T
T	F	T
F	T	T
F	F	F

This is the truth table definition of "p or q" in
the inclusive sense of 'or'. It represents the
meaning of disjunction.

So far, then, three symbols have been given a
truth table definition.(mentally review negation,
conjunction, disjunction so that they become firmly
fixed in your mind). This leaves only two more to
consider.

291

material equivalence

The material equivalence of any two informative sentences, "p is equivalent to q", is symbolized as follows: p ≝ q.

The expression "p ≝ q" symbolizes the following English expressions:

> p IS EQUIVALENT TO q
> p IF AND ONLY IF q

Two expressions are said to be materially equivalent when they have the same truth value. Two expressions have the same truth value when both are T or when both are F. The following, then, is the truth table definition of "p ≝ q".

p	q	p ≝ q
T	T	T
T	F	F
F	T	F
F	F	T

Using the symbols hitherto advanced, the following translations should be carefully noted:

p is not equivalent to q	∼ (p ≝ q)
it is not the case that p is equivalent to q	∼ (p ≝ q)

Four symbols have so far been defined (again review them mentally so that they sink in). Only one symbol left to define.

material implication

what p ⊃ q symbolizes

The material implication of any two informative sentences, in English "if p then q", is symbolized as follows: p ⊃ q.

"If...then..." sentences are referred to as "conditional sentences," the expression coming after the "if" being referred to as the "antecedent" and the expression coming after the "then" being called the "consequent." For example, in the following sentence, the antecedent and consequent are as indicated:

If <u>I win the contest</u>, then <u>I'll take a trip</u>
     antecedent   <u>around the world</u>.
                         consequent

The usual pattern is:
    if (antecedent) then (consequent)
In an ordinary language such as English, however, conditional sentences are subject to a variety of purely stylistic variations. For instance, on some occasions, the 'then' in conditional sentences is not expressed, although it is clearly understood. This is the case in the following example:

If <u>I win the contest</u>, <u>I'll take a trip</u>
    antecedent   <u>around the world</u>.
                   consequent

Moreover, on some occasions, the consequent is expressed first. For example:

<u>I'll take a trip around the world</u>, if <u>I win</u>
      consequent   <u>the contest</u>
                       antecedent

Such purely stylistic matters should not serve to confuse us: what follows the "if" is the antecedent, and what follows the "then" (either expressed or understood) is the consequent. In sum, the following expressions are the same:
$$\text{if p then q}$$
$$\text{if p, q}$$
$$\text{q, if p}$$

The expression "$p \supset q$" symbolizes the following expressions in English which express material implication:
$$\text{IF p THEN q}$$
$$\text{IF p, q}$$
$$\text{q, IF p}$$
$$\text{q, PROVIDED THAT p}$$
$$\text{p IMPLIES q}$$

293

q IS IMPLIED BY p
q FOLLOWS FROM p

some examples

The following are some conditional sentences in
English translated into the language of symbolic
logic (using the letters underlined):

sentence	symbolization
(1) If I have a headache, then I'll take aspirin.	h ⊃ a
(2) If I have sinusitis and heartburn, then I'll take an aspirin and a glass of milk.	(s . h) ⊃ (a . g)
(3) If I have a cold and a headache, I'll take aspirin and vitamin C.	(c . h) ⊃ (a . v)
(4) I'll go to Israel for the summer if it's not at war.	~w ⊃ g
(5) I'll go to Israel for the summer provided that it's not at war.	~w ⊃ g
(6) My not paying the mortgage this month implies that I'm not honoring my agreement with you.	~p ⊃ ~h
(7) If Bob and Judy divorce, they can't come on a camping trip with us.	d ⊃ ~c
(8) If the world is spherical, then if a person walks in a straight line towards the west, he will return to the same spot from the east.	s ⊃ (w ⊃ r)
(9) If he's a liberal and if he's consistent, then he'll vote for increased immigration from the Third World nations.	(l . c) ⊃ v
(10) If he's a liberal but either confused or not informed, then he cannot be counted on to vote for increased immigration from the Third World nations.	[l . (c v ~i)] ⊃ ~c

294

(11) If a person favors abortion
but not euthanasia, then
that person is not con-   (a . ~ e) ⊃ ~ c
sistent.

implicative sense

A fundamental characteristic of all conditional
sentences is that they are used to express "implicative sense." That is, conditional sentences are
used to assert a relationship between the antecedent
in a sentence and its consequent.

In expressing implicative sense, conditional sentences maintain that if one thing is the case
(namely, what the antecedent expresses), then another thing is the case (namely, what is expressed
in the consequent). Put rather loosely, in conditional sentences, what is said in the antecedent
is alleged to imply what is said in the consequent.
The state of affairs expressed by the consequent
is dependent upon the state of affairs expressed by
the antecedent. Implication, then, is concerned
with the relationship expressed between antecedent
and consequent.

In the following sentence, for example,
        (1) If the Brontosaurus is a dinosaur,
            then it died out before there were
            human beings on earth.
what is being asserted is not that the Brontosaurus
is a dinosaur (although that is true). Nor is it
being asserted that the Brontosaurus died out before there were human beings on earth (although
that, too, is true). Rather what is being asserted
is the relationship of implication between antecedent and consequent: if the Brontosaurus is a
dinosaur, then it died out before there were human
beings on earth. Its dying out before there were
humans is contingent upon its being a dinosaur.
The sentence expresses implicative sense.

Similarly, in the following sentence:
        (2) If the U.S.A. took over the Gov-
            ernment of Canada in 1980, then

> an American Democratic Administration
> in Ottawa would explain Canada's
> economic plight of 1980.

it is not being asserted that the U.S.A. took over
the Government of Canada in 1980 (although that is
false). Nor is it being asserted that an American
Democratic Administration in Canada's capital city,
Ottawa, would explain Canada's economic plight in
1980 (although that, too, is false, since there
was no American administration in Ottawa in 1980).
What is being asserted is that if the U.S.A. took
over the Government of Canada in 1980, then an
American Democratic Administration in Ottawa would
explain Canada's economic plight of 1980. In other
words, what is being expressed is again a relationship between the antecedent of a sentence and its
consequent. The sentence expresses implicative
sense.

Note, too, the following sentence:
> (3) If Charles Reich wrote The Third
> Wave, then it is concerned with
> outlining the main features of a
> totally new civilization.

Sentence (3) does not assert that Charles Reich
wrote The Third Wave (although that is false, for
its author was Alvin Toffler--Charles Reich wrote
The Greening of America). Nor is it being asserted
that The Third Wave is concerned with outlining
the main features of a totally new civilization
(although that is true). Again what is being
asserted is a relationship of implication between
antecedent and consequent: if Charles Reich wrote
The Third Wave, then it is concerned with outlining
the main features of a totally new civilization.
The sentence expresses implicative sense.

Consider yet another sentence:
> (4) If Stalin is a Marxist, then he
> would favor capitalism in the
> Ukraine.

Sentence (4) does not assert that Stalin is a
Marxist (although that is true). Nor is it being
asserted that he would favor capitalism in the
Ukraine (although that is false). Again what is

being asserted in this conditional sentence is a relationship between antecedent and consequent: if Stalin is a Marxist, then he would favor capitalism in the Ukraine. The sentence expresses implicative sense.

In all 4 examples above, the conditional sentence expresses implicative sense. This is the case whether or not the antecedent and consequent are both true (as in 1), or both false (as in 2), or whether the antecedent is false and the consequent true (as in 3), or whether the antecedent is true and the consequent false (as in 4). In each case the "if... then..." sentence expresses implicative sense.

In (4), however, note that there is something odd about the alleged implication: if Stalin is a Marxist, then he would favor capitalism in the Ukraine. If what is said in the antecedent is true and if what is said in the consequent is however false, then it is hard to see how the implication itself is true, even though the sentence expresses implicative sense. As the exposition of material implication develops, this point will assume considerable importance in tracking down the meaning of implicative sense. Simply note at this point that it is hard to see how the implication could be true when the antecedent is true, and the consequent false.

All conditional sentences express at least <u>implicative sense</u>. In ordinary language usage, however, conditional sentences normally express <u>more</u> than implicative sense. Consider, for instance, the following sentence:

> If you jump out of the 10th story
> window onto the pavement below, then
> you will kill yourself.

This sentence expresses implicative sense. That is, the person putting forward this sentence is claiming that one's killing oneself follows from one's jumping out of the 10th story window. The sentence also expresses, however, a <u>causal sense</u>: it expresses that jumping out of the 10th story window onto the pavement below will cause that person's

demise. Consider, too, the following sentence:
>   If a marshmallow is toasted gently
>   in the dying embers of a fire, then
>   it is said "to glubbify."

This sentence expresses implicative sense: the
glubbification of the marshmallow is said to follow
from its being toasted in a certain manner. But the
sentence also expresses a definitional sense: it is
offering a definition of what it means for a marshmallow to glubbify. It states the conditions under
which the word 'glubbify' is correctly applied to
marshmallows.

The situation in which conditional sentences express
several different senses at the same time is not unusual. The same situation applied in conjunction
where we noted that sentences containing 'and' often
express causal or contrastive sense in addition to
conjunctive sense. Just as all conjunctions express
conjunctive sense, so, too, all material implications
express implicative sense.

truth table definition of p ⊃ q

In symbolic logic we are concerned with defining
only the implicative sense of conditional sentences,
ignoring the additional senses such sentences may
have. In other words, we're defining only a portion
of the meaning of conditional sentences, just as we
did when we defined conjunction. As it turns out,
however, this is an especially important and useful
part of the meaning of such sentences.

The truth table definition of "p ⊃ q" is as follows:

p	q	p ⊃ q
T	T	T
T	F	F
F	T	T
F	F	T

Why this is so can be understood in either of two
ways: a loose way, and a technical way.

298

Let's start with the loose explanation. It builds upon the notion of deductive validity, already familiar from the last chapter. The notion of implicative sense is very much <u>like</u> the notion of validity. You will recall that va<u>lidity</u> refers to a <u>relationship</u> between the premises and conclusion of a deductive argument. This relationship is <u>like</u> the relationship of implicative sense between the antecedent and consequent of a conditional sentence.

In a deductive argument, we are in effect saying that <u>if</u> these are the premises <u>then</u> this conclusion is alleged to follow from the information contained in them. Notice this "if...then..." structure to deductive arguments. It shows that the premises of such an argument are <u>like</u> the antecedent of a conditional sentence, the conclusion <u>like</u> the consequent of a conditional sentence, and the relation of validity <u>like</u> the relation of implicative sense. In sum, the similarities can be depicted as follows:

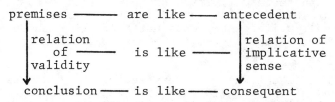

```
premises ──────── are like ──── antecedent

        │relation                    │relation of
        │  of ──────  is like ────   │implicative
        │validity                    │sense
        ▼                            ▼
conclusion ──── is like ──── consequent
```

In fact, as we shall see shortly, we'll use '⊃' in symbolizing deductive arguments. How we'll do that will be explained soon enough. Right now the important point to grasp is that the relation of implicative sense is like the relation of validity.

This similarity is useful in understanding the truth table definition of "p⊃q". You will recall from the last chapter that there can be valid deductive arguments in these three cases:

premises T, conclusion T
premises F, conclusion T
premises F, conclusion F

but <u>not</u> in this case:

premises T, conclusion F

For this would violate the relationship of validity

between premises and conclusion.

This corresponds to the truth table definition of "p⊃q". Bearing in mind that 'p' (the antecedent) is like the premises of a deductive argument and that 'q' (the consequent) is like the conclusion of such an argument, we find that "p⊃q" holds true when

p is T, q is T
p is F, q is T
p is F, q is F

but not when

p is T, q is F

For this would violate the relationship of implicative sense between the antecedent and consequent of a conditional sentence.

The analogy between deductive validity and implicative sense is a helpful, although loose, way of understanding the truth table definition of "p⊃q". The truth table definition of "p⊃q" serves to block the one instance where validity (and, correspondingly, implicative sense) does not hold: when the premises (or antecedent) is T, and the conclusion (or consequent) is F.

That is one way of understanding the truth table definition of material implication. The next explanation is more technical, for, to speak more precisely, "p⊃q" is introduced in symbolic logic as an abbreviation of the expression "∼(p . ∼q)". Why this is so can be seen from the following line of reasoning.

Let us consider the circumstances under which the implicative sense of conditional sentences would be violated (that is, rendered false). This would occur where there is an antecedent and the consequent does not follow from it. In this case, the implicative relationship would be broken, and the whole expression rendered false.

Recall an earlier example in which an oddity was noted, namely, the following conditional sentence:

If Stalin is a Marxist, then he would
favor capitalism in the Ukraine.

(See pages 296, 297 above). Using the letters underlined, we would symbolize this sentence as follows:
$$S \supset f$$
In this sentence, the antecedent (that is, 'S') is
true, the consequent (that is, 'f') is false. The
consequent does not follow from the antecedent. The
implicative sense of the conditional is violated
(that is, rendered false). So
"$S \supset f$" is F when S is T and f is F
To repeat, using more of our symbols:
"$S \supset f$" is F when (S . $\sim$ f)
This indicates the circumstances under which the implicative sense of a conditional sentence "$S \supset f$" is
violated.

Knowing this, it is now possible for us to state
the circumstances under which the implicative sense
of a conditional sentence "$S \supset f$" is not violated
(in other words, is true). Remember what has just
been said:
"$S \supset f$" is F when (S . $\sim$ f)
So (changing the negation around) we get:
"$S \supset f$" is T when it is not the case
that (S . $\sim$ f)
or, in other words (using more of our symbols):
"$S \supset f$" is T when $\sim$(S . $\sim$ f)

The point can now be generalized: for any two informative sentences 'p' and 'q':
the implicative sense of "$p \supset q$" holds
(that is, is true) when $\sim$(p . $\sim$ q).

So, to find the truth table definition of "$p \supset q$",
the truth table definition of "$\sim$(p . $\sim$ q) must first
be found. Once that is obtained, then the truth
table for "$p \supset q$" will be the same. Finding the
truth table definition for "$\sim$(p . $\sim$q)" is not
difficult. It goes as follows:

(1) p	(2) q	(3) $\sim$q	(4) p . $\sim$q	(5) $\sim$(p . $\sim$q)
T	T	F	F	T
T	F	T	T	F
F	T	F	F	T
F	F	T	F	T

301

The truth table definition for the expression
"$\sim$(p . $\sim$q)" is what is contained in column (5). It
was arrived at in the following manner:
  - columns (1) and (2): these set out the
    possible combinations of T's and F's
    for the two sentence letters 'p' and
    'q'.
  - column (3) is the negation of column (2).
    Where q is T, not-q is F, where q is
    F, not-q is T, and so on. This information
    is needed for column (4) which conjoins
    p with not-q.
  - column (4) is the conjunction of p with
    not-q. In filling in this column you need
    to look at column (1) which gives the
    truth values for p and column (3) which
    gives the truth values for not-q and you
    need to remember also the truth table
    definition for conjunction.
  - column (5) is the negation of column (4).

The truth table definition for "p$\supset$q" can now be
given. It is the same as the truth table definition
for "$\sim$(p . $\sim$q)" which has just been given:

p	q	p $\supset$ q
T	T	T
T	F	F
F	T	T
F	F	T

This table is referred to as the truth table definition of material implication. It indicates the
truth table definition of the implicative sense of
conditional sentences. Implicative sense holds in
all but one case: where the antecedent (p) is T
and the consequent (q) is F. It blocks the loss of
truth going from antecedent to consequent.

This now completes the task of defining the 5 basic
symbols used in the language of symbolic logic.
These definitions must be learned. Indeed, as we
come closer to outlining Step #8, they will be
learned by considerable practice.

302

English	symbol-ization	truth table definition		
NOT-p IT IS NOT THE CASE THAT p IT IS FALSE THAT p p IS FALSE (WRONG,UNTRUE)	$\sim$ p	p | $\sim$ p T | F F | T		
p AND q p MOREOVER q p ALSO q p BUT q p HOWEVER q p ALTHOUGH q BOTH p AND q p IN ADDITION q	p $\cdot$ q	p q | p $\cdot$ q T T | T T F | F F T | F F F | F		
p OR q EITHER p OR q p OR ELSE q	p v q	p q | p v q T T | T T F | T F T | T F F | F		
p IS EQUIVALENT TO q p IF AND ONLY IF q	p $\equiv$ q	p q | p $\equiv$ q T T | T T F | F F T | F F F | T		
IF p THEN q IF p, q q, IF p q, PROVIDED THAT p p IMPLIES q q IS IMPLIED BY p q FOLLOWS FROM p	p $\supset$ q	p q | p $\supset$ q T T | T T F | F F T | T F F | T		

Symbolize the following expressions:
(1) Both p and q
(2) Both not p and q
(3) Either p or q
(4) Either not p or not q
(5) not p or q; moreover, not s or t
(6) it is not the case that either p or q
(7) it is not the case that both not p and q
(8) not p if and only if not q
(9) q if and only if p
(10) if q then p
(11) q, if p
(12) if j, k
(13) it is not the case that if not p then not q
(14) either p or q if and only if either not t or z
(15) it is not the case that p and not q
(16) if p then if q, r
(17) if either p or q, then either t or v
(18) either if p and q, then r, or if b, then a or d
(19) r and t; moreover, if r then p
(20) p but also q
(21) if p implies q and q implies r, then p implies r
(22) not p and not q
(23) p and q is equivalent to q and p
(24) b is not equivalent to c
(25) if both d and not e, then c

Exercise #4

Complete the following truth table definitions:

p	q	p . q
T	T	
T	F	
F	T	
F	F	

p	q	p v q
T	T	
T	F	
F	T	
F	F	

p	q	p ⊃ q
T	T	
T	F	
F	T	
F	F	

p	q	p ≡ q
T	T	
T	F	
F	T	
F	F	

p	~ p
T	
F	

Compare your answers here with the summary of truth table definitions on the previous page.

4. Step #8: Truth Table Method

Step #8: One Method

Consider once again this argument:
(a)   If God exists, then there would be no evil
      in the world. There is evil in the world.
      Therefore God does not exist.
The argument is deductive. It is very important for
us to ascertain, then, if the argument is valid or
invalid. We must apply Step #8 (in addition, of
course, to other applicable steps in argument
evaluation, but we're focusing just on Step #8 at
the moment).

If the argument turns out to be valid, then this
indicates that the conclusion follows conclusively
from the information contained in the premises, as
the argument alleges. To indicate that a deductive
argument is valid is to show that it has passed one
of the most severe tests in argument evaluation.
If the deductive argument is valid, then this means
that the premises do support the conclusion in the
manner indicated. The argument may have other flaws
which will show up when other Steps are applied,
but at least it has passed this one important, and
crucial, step.

On the other hand, if the argument turns out to be
invalid, then the conclusion does not in fact
follow conclusively from the information contained
in the premises. It should be obvious from this
that for a deductive argument to be invalid represents an extremely serious defect. It points out
that the premises do not support the conclusion
in the manner indicated. And for premises to fail
to support the conclusion represents just about
the most serious flaw any argument can have.

One method for finding out the validity or invalidity of a deductive argument is called "the
truth table method." This method builds upon the
symbols and the definitions of the symbols already
learned.

In a deductive argument, determine if
the argument is valid or invalid
(a) by truth table method.

In this section, the main steps of this method will
be outlined and applied to a number of deductive
arguments. In the next chapter an additional method
will be discussed.

Truth Table Method

There are 4 steps to this method.

The first step is to symbolize the argument, setting
it out in the standard format for identifying and
evaluating arguments. So: the argument in (a) would
be displayed as follows (using the sentence letters
underlined):

support space	main argument space	evaluation space
	1. G ⊃ ~ e	
	2. e	
	∴ ~ G	

As we have already had occasion to note, in any
argument, what is actually being said has an "if...
then..." structure. The form that an argument takes
is that if the premises are true, then the conclusion
follows. In the case of argument (a) above, what is
being said is that if premise 1 and premise 2 are
true, then the conclusion follows. Arguments generally have the following form:
        if (the premises), then (the conclusion)
This simply repeats the point already made that
there are similarities between deductive validity
and implicative sense. The premises of an argument
are like the antecedent of a conditional sentence;
the conclusion, like the consequent of a conditional
sentence. The "if...then..." structure of arguments
allows deductive arguments to be re-written as a
material implication.

The second step, then, is to write the argument horizontally as a material implication. The premises of the argument will be the antecedent, the conclusion will be its consequent. In argument (a) what is being said is:

if [(premise 1) and (premise 2)] then (conclusion)

Using symbolic language, argument (a) is re-written horizontally as a material implication as follows:

$$[(G \supset \sim e) \cdot (e)] \supset \sim G$$

      premises   conclusion

Re-writing the argument as a material implication is best placed under the argument as reconstructed in standard format (There usually isn't sufficient space in evaluation space). Note that the premises are joined together by 'and'.

The third step consists of constructing a truth table chart in order to ascertain the truth value of the whole argument expressed as a material implication. The truth table chart, then, is set up in order to ascertain the truth value of the following whole expression:

$$[(G \supset \sim e) \cdot (e)] \supset \sim G$$

The truth table chart (see the chart below) is set up as follows:

- first the possible combinations of T's and F's for the two sentence letters 'G' and 'e' are set up. This is done in columns (1) and (2) below.
- then the truth value of the first premise is found, although, noting that it contains a '$\sim$e', column (3) is devoted to finding out the truth value of '$\sim$e'. This is easily done: column (3) is simply the negation of column (2). Now we are ready to find out the truth value of the first premise. This is done in column (4), looking at the truth values for 'G' in column (1) and for '$\sim$e' in column (3) and remembering the truth table definition of '$\supset$'. So: column (4) gives the truth value of the first premise.
- next consider the second premise: in column (5) state its truth value. It's the same as

307

column (2). So: at this point, the truth
values of the two premises are known.
- now consider the truth value of the two
  premises taken together, that is, consider
  the truth value of the expression (G⊃~ e).(e).
  This is accomplished in column (6). Column (6)
  is the conjunction of the truth values expressed in columns (4) and (5).
- next find the truth value of the conclusion,
  ~G. This is done in column (7): it simply
  is the negation of the truth values expressed
  in column (1).
- finally: find the truth value of the whole
  expression. The truth value of the premises
  taken together is found in column (6); the
  truth value of the conclusion is stated in
  column (7). So, in column (8), the whole
  material implication is considered.

(1)	(2)	(3)	(4)	(5)	(6)	(7)	(8)
G	e	~e	G⊃~e	e	(G⊃~e).(e)	~G	[(G⊃~e).(e)]⊃~G
T	T	F	F	T	F	F	T
T	F	T	T	F	F	F	T
F	T	F	T	T	T	T	T
F	F	T	T	F	F	T	T

In column (8) is expressed the truth value for the
whole argument under consideration written out as a
material implication.

The fourth step consists of interpreting the result
obtained in the last column of the truth table chart
for the whole argument written as a material implication. If all T's are found, then the argument is
valid. The reason for this interpretation is that
the conclusion follows, no matter what the truth
values are of the individual component sentence
letters. It indicates that the conclusion follows
conclusively from the information contained in the
premises. If the last column of the truth table
chart for the whole argument written as a material
implication contains a mixture of T's and F's, or
all F's, then the argument is invalid. This indicates that the conclusion does not follow regardless

308

of the truth values of the individual component
sentence letters.

In argument (a), all T's are found in the last
column, namely, column (8). The argument is valid.

```
┌──────────────────────────────────────────────┐
│ summary of truth table method                 │
│   (1) symbolize the argument                   │
│   (2) write argument horizontally as a         │
│       material implication                     │
│   (3) construct a truth table chart for        │
│       the whole expression                     │
│       - find truth values of individual        │
│         premises                               │
│       - find truth value of the premises       │
│         taken together                         │
│       - find truth value of the conclusion     │
│       - find truth value of whole              │
│         expression.                            │
│   (4) interpret the result in the last         │
│       column                                   │
└──────────────────────────────────────────────┘
```

So, in applying Step #8 to argument (a), our evaluation of it (simply with respect to Step #8) would
appear as follows:

support space   main argument space   evaluation space

            1. G ⊃ ~e
            2. e   This is a deductive
          ∴ ~G   argument: it is
                                           valid (see below)

        [(G ⊃ ~e) . (e)] ⊃ ~G

   (and here we would place the truth table chart
   worked out on the previous page)

Step #8 has been applied to argument (a). It is
valid. All this means is that, as alleged, the conclusion follows conclusively from the information
contained in the premises. This, of course, does not
mean that the argument is flawless, for other Steps
need to be considered. But it does mean that the
argument has passed a major and important consideration
in argument evaluation. Whatever defects it may con-

309

tain, at least the premises do support the conclusion in the manner indicated.

some further examples

Consider next this argument:
(b)   If you smoke three packs of cigarettes
       a day, then you'll get lung cancer.
       Well, you do smoke three packs of cig-
       arettes a day. So: you'll get lung
       cancer.
This is a deductive argument: the conclusion, as
put forward by the arguer, purports to follow conclusively from the information contained in the
premises. Since it is a deductive argument, Step #8
applies. Using truth table method, our work appears
as follows:

support space   main argument space   evaluation space

                1. s ⊃ c

                2. s   This is a deductive
                _____   argument. It is
                ∴ c   valid (see below).

$$[(s \supset c) \cdot (s)] \supset c$$

| (1) | (2) | (3) | (4) | (5) | (6) | (7) |
s	c	s⊃c	s	[(s⊃c).(s)]	c	[(s⊃c).(s)]⊃c
T	T	T	T	T	T	T
T	F	F	T	F	F	T
F	T	T	F	F	T	T
F	F	T	F	F	F	T
						(valid)

Step #8 has been applied to argument (b). The argument is, first of all, symbolized. Then it is
written as a material implication: if (premise 1)
and (premise 2), then (the conclusion). This is
done beneath the argument where there is more
space. Next a truth table chart is constructed.
        - columns (1) and (2): these set out the
          possible combinations of T's and F's for
          the two sentence letters 's' and 'c'.

310

- column (3): this is the truth value of
  premise 1. It is found by looking at the
  truth values in columns (1) and (2) and by
  remembering the truth table definition of
  '⊃'.
- column (4): this is the truth value of
  premise 2. It is the same as column (1).
- column (5): this is the truth value of the
  two premises taken together. It is obtained
  by looking at the truth values in columns
  (3) and (4) and by remembering the truth
  table definition of '.'.
- column (6): this is the truth value of the
  conclusion. It is the same as column (2).
- column (7): the grand finale! This is the
  truth value of the whole expression, found
  by looking at the truth values in columns
  (5) and (6) and by remembering the truth
  table definition of '⊃'.

Finally, the results in the last column are interpreted: the whole column is composed of T's, indicating that the argument is valid. The implication holds regardless of the truth or falsity
of the component sentences.

This completes our application of Step #8 to argument (b). In a complete evaluation of the argument,
of course, other pertinent steps would need to be
applied.

Consider next argument (c) which bears a superficial
resemblance to argument (b):
(c) If you smoke three packs of cigarettes
     a day, then you'll get lung cancer. Well,
     you've got lung cancer. Therefore you
     smoke three packs of cigarettes a day.
The argument is deductive: the conclusion purports
to follow conclusively from the information contained in the premises. Since it is a deductive
argument, Step #8 applies. Using the truth table
method, our work appears as follows:

support space	main argument space	evaluation space
	1. s ⊃ c	
	2. c	This argument is
	∴ s	deductive. It is

311

invalid (see below)

$$[(s \supset c) \cdot (c)] \supset s$$

(1) s	(2) c	(3) s⊃c	(4) c	(5) [(s⊃c).(c)]	(6) s	(7) [(s⊃c).(c)]⊃s
T	T	T	T	T	T	T
T	F	F	F	F	T	T
F	T	T	T	T	F	F
F	F	T	F	F	F	T

(invalid)

Step #8 has been applied to argument (c). The argument has been symbolized, written horizontally as a material implication, had a truth table chart constructed, and has had the results obtained in the last column interpreted. A few notes on the truth table chart:
- columns (1) and (2): set out the possible combinations of T's and F's for the two sentence letters.
- columns (3) and (4): set out the truth values for the two premises
- column (5): sets out the truth values for the two premises taken together (found by conjoining the truth values in column (3) with those in column (4)).
- column (6): sets out the truth value for the conclusion
- column (7): sets out the truth value of the whole expression. (This is found by looking at columns (5) and (6) and by remembering the truth table definition of '⊃'.

Regardless of what other sorts of flaws this argument may exhibit, detection of it as an invalid argument represents a major indictment of it as an argument. To repeat, it indicates that the conclusion does not follow conclusively from the information contained in the premises. Notice, in passing, how argument (c) differs from argument (b) which was valid.

a brief pause

Take a moment to check your comprehension.

Questions

(1) Write out the truth table definitions of negation, conjunction, disjunction, material equivalence, material implication.

(2) What is Step#8?

(3) What are the individual steps to the truth table method?

(4) Apply Step #8 to the following arguments (using the sentence letters underlined):

   (a) If I go to the sunny south for my holidays, then I'll take my camera. I do go to the sunny south for my holidays. Thus I'll take my camera.

   (b) If I become senile, then I'll do crazy things. I do crazy things. Thus I'm senile.

Answers

(1) See summary on p.303.
(2) See p.306
(3) See p.309 (also review example, pp.306-309)
(4) (a) This is the same sort of argument as argument (b) on p.310. See discussion and truth table chart there.

   (b) This is the same sort of argument as argument (c) on p.311. See discussion and truth table chart there.

Diagnosis

If you had any trouble with this brief pause, note where your difficulties occur:
(1) in the truth table definitions, namely...
(2) in knowing Step #8
(3) in knowing the steps of truth table method.
(4) in applying Step #8
   - symbolizing the argument
   - writing it horizontally as a material implication

- constructing a truth table chart
  - setting up the combinations for the sentence letters
  - each premise
  - premises taken together
  - conclusion
  - whole expression

more examples

So far only deductive arguments with two sentence letters have been considered. Note the following selection, however:

(d) If Oswald alone killed Kennedy, then there were no shots fired from in front of the motorcade and there were no shots fired from behind the picket fence in the grassy knoll area. There were, however, shots fired from in front of the motorcade, and there were shots fired from behind the picket fence in the grassy knoll area. Consequently, Oswald alone did not kill Kennedy.

The argument is deductive. Therefore Step #8 applies. As symbolized, the argument would appear as follows:

support space	main argument space	evaluation space

1. $k \supset (\sim f \, . \sim b)$

2. $f \, . \, b$

This is a deductive argument. It is ?

$\therefore \sim k$

Set out as a material implication, the argument appears as follows:

$$\{[k \supset (\sim f \, . \sim b)] \, . \, (f \, . \, b)\} \supset \sim k$$

Notice that there are three sentence letters: 'k', 'f', and 'b'. In terms of possible combinations of T's and F's for 3 sentence letters, there are 8 arrangements. The formula for finding out the number of possible truth functional arrangements is 2^n, where 'n' is the number of sentence letters. Thus an argument of 4 different sentence letters would have 2^4 (that is, 2x2x2x2) or 16 possible

arrangements; and argument of 5 different sentence
letters would have 2^5 (that is, 2x2x2x2x2) or 32
possible arrangements, and so on.

In setting out the truth table chart for the whole
expression, the procedure is the same as it has been
in previous examples: do the initial set up for the
various sentence letters; find out the truth value
of each premise; then the premises taken together;
then the conclusion; and finally the whole expression.

The argument is:

$\{[k \supset (\sim f \cdot \sim b)] \cdot (f \cdot b)\} \supset \sim k$

(1) k	(2) f	(3) b	(4) ~f	(5) ~b	(6) ~f.~b	(7) k⊃(~f.~b)	(8) (f.b)	(9) * 7.8	(10) ~k	(11) # 9⊃10
T	T	T	F	F	F	F	T	F	F	T
T	T	F	F	T	F	F	F	F	F	T
T	F	T	T	F	F	F	F	F	F	T
T	F	F	T	T	T	T	F	F	F	T
F	T	T	F	F	F	T	T	T	T	T
F	T	F	F	T	F	T	F	F	T	T
F	F	T	T	F	F	T	F	F	T	T
F	F	F	T	T	T	T	F	F	T	T

(valid)

Note:
* This shorthand device used to save space simply
indicates the conjunction of the expression mentioned
in column (7) with that in (8), namely $[k \supset (\sim f \cdot \sim b)]$.
(f.b).
This shorthand device simply indicates the mater-
ial implication of the expression in column (9) with
that in column (10)--in other words, the whole
expression under consideration.

A few observations on the truth table chart:
- columns (1), (2) and (3): set out the 8
  possible combinations for the 3 sentence
  letters.
- column (7): sets out the truth value for
  the first premise. To ascertain this
  requires setting up columns (4),(5) and
  (6) first to find out the truth values
  of the component expressions.

- column (8): sets out the truth values of
  the second premise.
- column (9): sets out the truth values of
  the 2 premises taken together.
- column (10): sets out the truth value of
  the conclusion.
- column (11): the truth value of the whole
  expression.

Interpreting the results obtained in the last column, we find the argument is valid.

Consider this argument. For practice, try working out the truth table on your own first, and then compare with the work below.

(e) Israel has 3 current options: to defeat
  the Arab states, or to surrender to them,
  or to negotiate a secure peace with them.
  Israel won't defeat the Arab states.
  Israel won't surrender to them. Thus Israel
  will negotiate a secure peace with them.

This is a deductive argument. Step #8 applies.

support space main argument space evaluation space

1. d v s v n

2. ~d

3. ~s
———————

∴ n

This is a deductive
argument. It is
valid (see below)

$[(d \vee s \vee n) \cdot (\sim d) \cdot (\sim s)] \supset n$

| (1) | (2) | (3) | (4) | (5) | (6) | (7) | (8) | (9) |
d	s	n	d v s v n	~d	~s	4.5.6	n	7 ⊃ 8
T	T	T	T	F	F	F	T	T
T	T	F	T	F	F	F	F	T
T	F	T	T	F	T	F	T	T
T	F	F	T	F	T	F	F	T
F	T	T	T	T	F	F	T	T
F	T	F	T	T	F	F	F	T
F	F	T	T	T	T	T	T	T
F	F	F	F	T	T	F	F	T

(valid)

A few notes on the truth table chart above:
- columns (1),(2),(3): the 8 possible arrange-

for 3 sentence letters.
- column (4): truth value of premise 1 (remember truth table definition for 'v' where the whole expression is F when all disjuncts are F.)
- column (5): truth value of premise 2.
- column (6): truth value of premise 3.
- column (7): truth value of the 3 premises taken together. Remember that a conjunction is T when all conjuncts are T; otherwise F. (The shorthand devise of 4.5.6 simply refers to the expressions in columns (4) and (5) and (6).)
- column (8): truth value of conclusion
- column (9): the whole expression.

The results in the final column of the truth table chart are then interpreted: argument (e) is valid.

a final note

It should be remembered that Step #8 is only one step in argument evaluation. It is, however, for deductive arguments, a tremendously important step. In a complete evaluation of a deductive argument, we would, of course, apply not only Step #8 but also other Steps in argument evaluation.

Recall Quiz

(1) What 2 sorts of symbols are used in the symbolic language discussed in this chapter?

(2) How are informative sentences symbolized?

(3) How are the following expressions symbolized: not-p; p and q; p or q; if p then q; p is equivalent to q.

(4) When applied to arguments, what do these symbols help us do?

(5) What are the truth table definitions of the following: negation, conjunction, disjunction, material equivalence, material implication.

(6) How are the following expressions symbolized: not p or q; it is not the case that p or q; p is not equivalent to q; q, if p.

317

(7) What are "conjuncts"? "disjuncts"? "an ante-cedent"? "a consequent"?

(8) In what ways are deductive validity and impli-cative sense similar?

(9) What is Step #8 of argument evaluation?

(10) What are the individual steps to truth table method?

(11) Why is it important to apply Step #8 when an argument is deductive? What does labelling a deductive argument "valid" indicate? What does labelling it "invalid" indicate?

(12) Is Step #8 the only step applied to deductive arguments?

Exercise #5

Using standard format, identify the arguments con-tained in the following selections. Then apply Step #8, using truth table method and the sentence letters underlined.

(1) If you lose weight, then you'll become a sex symbol. You have, by golly, lost weight. Thus you'll become a sex symbol.

(2) If you lose weight, then you'll become a sex symbol. Well, you have become a sex symbol. Therefore you've lost weight.

(3) If you don't lose weight, then you'll have a heart attack. You haven't had a heart attack. Hence you've lost weight.

(4) If God does not exist, then matter is eternal. Matter, however, is not eternal. Thus God exists.

(5) Do you notice anything the same in selections (3) and (4) above? If so, what?

(6) If you smoke pot and pot is not legalized, then you will receive a $500 fine. You smoke pot. Pot is not legalized. Consequently you'll receive a $500 fine.

318

(7)   Indians in North America today have two options:
      either to become assimilated and lose their id-
      entity or else to retain their own culture. They
      can't retain their own culture. Thus Indians
      will become assimilated and lose their identity.

(8)   If I make more money, then I'll move up two
      income tax brackets. If I move up two income
      tax brackets, then I'll pay more income tax to
      the government. Thus, if I make more money,
      I'll pay more income tax to the government.

(9)   If people favor capital punishment, then a law
      will be passed. People do favor capital punish-
      ment (recent public opinion polls indicate
      this). Therefore a law will be passed.

(10) What previous argument in this exercise ex-
      hibits the same pattern as the argument con-
      tained in selection (9)?

(11) If I'm to get into law school, then I'll have
      to excel in logic and I'll have to do well in
      economics. I don't excel in logic. Moreover,
      I don't do well in economics. As a result, I'm
      not going to get into law school.

(12) I'll have to fire Harry if I adopt this policy.
      I'll cost the company money if I don't adopt
      this policy. I'll not cost the company money.
      Therefore I'll adopt this policy.

(13) If a science of human behavior is possible,
      then man is not free. A science of human
      behavior, however, is possible. After all,
      B.F. Skinner showed that it's possible in
      his two books entitled Walden Two and Beyond
      Freedom and Dignity. Thus man is not free.

(14) I'll have scars, if I try heroin. If I have
      scars, then I'll risk losing my sex appeal
      in my bikini. I'll not risk losing my sex
      appeal in my bikini. Consequently I'll not
      try heroin.

(15) If ancient astronauts visited the earth, then
      the god-hypothesis is not correct. Thus, if
      the god-hypothesis is correct, then ancient
      astronauts did not visit the earth.

319

(16) If I play around with John, then if my husband finds out he'll be mad. My husband won't find out. Therefore I'll play around with John.

(17) If you take 500mg of vitamin C, then if you get a cold it won't be so severe. Study after study confirms this finding, one of them having been done right here in our famed City Hospital. Well, judging from what you've told me, you do take 500mg of vitamin C daily. Thus, if you get a cold, it won't be so severe.

(18)   There are three ways of accounting for the giant statues on Easter Island: either the ancient people of Easter Island built them, or they were naturally fashioned by unseasonable weather, or else ancient astronauts built them with space age technology.
    The second alternative should be rejected [that is, negated]. For, after all, it is simply too preposterous for serious discussion.
    Likewise the first alternative should also be rejected [that is, negated], for the following reasons: (1) if the ancient people of Easter Island built them, then they must have had a far more advanced technology than we have so far supposed, and (2) there is no reason to suppose that they did have such an advanced technology (no tools have been found, after all, and no writing, no other evidence of alleged technological sophistication). Thus, as I have already mentioned, the first alternative should be rejected.
    The conclusion is obvious.

Exercise #6

(1) You are involved in a public debate. Your opponent has introduced many considerations and an impressive number of statistics. But basically what he has said boils down to the following main argument.
    1. If the government builds more nuclear generating stations, then energy will be plentiful in the future.

2. If energy is plentiful in the future, then people will be happy.

∴ If the government builds more nuclear generating stations, then people will be happy.

(a) Has your opponent presented a valid argument? (use truth table method and the sentence letters underlined).

(b) Can you respond validly to his argument by arguing the following (use truth table method and the sentence letters underlined):
    1. If the government builds more nuclear generating stations, then people will run the risk of a serious nuclear disaster.
    2. If people run the risk of a serious nuclear disaster, then they will not be happy.

    ∴ If the government builds more nuclear generating stations, then people will not be happy.

(c) Could you also respond validly to his argument by arguing the following (use truth table method and sentence letters underlined):
    1. If the government builds more nuclear generating stations, then people will run the risk of a serious nuclear disaster.
    2. People will not run this risk (of having a serious nuclear disaster).

    ∴ The government won't build more nuclear generating stations.

(2) You are involved in another debate. In his presentation, your opponent has essentially made the following main argument:
    1. This is a scientific world.
    2. If this is a scientific world, then it is important that people learn

scientific method and that they understand the basic concepts of science.

∴ It is important that people learn
scientific method and that they understand the basic concepts of science.

(a) Has your opponent presented a valid argument? (use truth table method and the
sentence letters underlined)

(b) Suppose you present the following argument in reply: do you argue validly?
1. If this is a scientific world, then
it is important that people learn
scientific method and that they understand the basic concepts of science.
2. This is not a scientific world.

∴ It is not the case that it is important that people learn scientific
method and that they understand the
basic concepts of science.

(3) Here are two bits of information:
r = you plan to serve red wine with fish
b = you are a boor
Using these two bits of information, construct
a valid argument that has as its conclusion
∴ you'll not plan to serve red wine
with fish.

(4) You are involved in a debate. Your opponent
has cited many facts, statistics, and examples,
but basically what he has said comes down to
the following main argument:
1. If the government legalizes marijuana,
then the way will be paved for many
abuses.
2. If the way is paved for many abuses,
then people will run the risk of
hurting themselves.
3. People will not run the risk of
hurting themselves.
4. The government has the obligation
to protect people.

322

∴. The government won't legalize marijuana.

(a) Has your opponent presented a valid argument? (use truth table method and sentence letters underlined)

(b) Ignore premise 4 temporarily. Without premise 4 does your opponent have a valid argument? (use truth table method)

(c) Ignore premise 3 temporarily. Without premise 3 does your opponent have a valid argument? (use truth table method)

(d) From the point of view of validity, which premise (3? 4?) is most essential to your opponent's argument? Why?

(e) From the point of view of validity, on what premise should your counterattack be placed? Why?

(f) Knowing now the status of your opponent's argument as to validity, you quickly move to the counterattack. You consider the following possible move. You zero in on your opponent's second premise. You want to show that it is not the case. Can you argue validly for this conclusion on the basis of the following premises:
   1. If the way is paved for many abuses, then people will grow in mature decision-making.
   2. If people grow in mature decision-making, then they won't run the risk of hurting themselves.

(g) On the basis of your experience in (f) you quickly consider another approach. If you presented the following argument, you wonder, would it be valid? (use truth table method)
   1. If people do not run the risk of hurting themselves, then the government will legalize marijuana.

2. People do not run the risk of
   <u>hurting themselves.</u>

.·. The government will <u>l</u>egalize
    marijuana.

(5) In Josephine Tey's novel, <u>The Daughter of Time</u>
     (Penguin books, 1973), the following argument
     is presented (supported by many, many mini-
     premises):
     1. Either Richard III killed the two
        princes in the Tower of London in
        1485 or else Henry VII killed them.
     2. Richard III dIdn't.

.·. <u>H</u>enry VII did.

Using standard format, identify this argument.
Then apply Step #8.

(6) In D.L. Rosenhan's article entitled "On Being
     Sane in Insane Places," (<u>Science</u> 179, Jan.19,
     1973, pp.250-258) is presented the following
     argument, supported by many mini-premises:
     1. There are two options concerning where
        the salient characteristics that lead
        to diagnoses of insanity reside: either
        in the <u>p</u>atient or in the <u>e</u>nvironment.
     2. They don't reside in the <u>p</u>atient.

.·. The reside in the <u>e</u>nvironment.

Using standard format, identify this argument.
Then apply Step #8.

(7) What do the arguments in (5) and (6) have in
     common?

CHAPTER TEN

ARGUMENT EVALUATION: DEDUCTIVE ARGUMENT II

In Chapter Nine we presented the truth table method
for finding out the validity or invalidity of deductive arguments. In this chapter an additional
method will be discussed. It consists of using
common patterns of reasoning to spot valid or invalid deductive arguments.

Before we examine these common patterns, however,
there is another use to which truth table method
may be put that has a bearing upon the study of
argument. Truth table method can be used to find
out what expressions are equivalent, a useful tool,
on occasion, for detecting misrepresentation or
distortion. We'll examine this use first and then
take a look at some common patterns.

1. Equivalent Expressions

the method

Consider the following situation:
(a)   Suppose arguer A has presented an argu-
      ment which contains the following sentence
      as a premise:
          If I take Suzanne to the party,
          then I'll have a good time.
      Suppose, furthermore, that arguer B, in
      replying to arguer A, reports what arguer
      A has said as follows:
          If I don't take Suzanne to the
          party, then I won't have a good
          time.
      Has arguer B misrepresented what arguer
      A has said?

In considering this question, it is helpful to have
a method of finding out whether or not two expressions

325

are equivalent. For, if the two expressions are equivalent, then no misrepresentation has occurred. If, on the other hand, the two expressions are not equivalent, then arguer B has indeed misrepresented what arguer A has said.

We can use truth table method as follows to ascertain if these expressions are equivalent.

step 1: Symbolize the expression in question.

Using the sentence letters underlined in the expressions in example (a) above, we find that

arguer A has said:	arguer B has stated that arguer A has said:
$t \supset h$	$\sim t \supset \sim h$

The question is: is what B has said equivalent to what A actually said?

step 2: State the purported equivalence.

In terms of example (a), the purported equivalence is:

$$(\sim t \supset \sim h) \equiv (t \supset h)$$

(note: as we shall see, it does not matter which expression is placed on the left or right side of the purported equivalence)

step 3: Set up a truth table chart to see if the two expressions are equivalent.

Two expressions are equivalent, you will remember, when they have the same truth values. So, in setting out the truth table chart, the general procedure is as follows:
- find out the truth value of the first expression
- find out the truth value of the second expression
- finally, compare their respective truth values to see if they are equivalent (that is, the same)

The truth table chart for the purported equivalence in example (a) is constructed as follows:

| (1) | (2) | (3) | (4) | (5) | (6) | (7) |
t	h	~t	~h	~t ⊃ ~h	t ⊃ h	(5)≣(6)
T	T	F	F	T	T	T
T	F	F	T	T	F	F
F	T	T	F	F	T	F
F	F	T	T	T	T	T

In the above,
- column (5): truth value of first expression
- column (6): truth value of second expression
- column (7): compares the truth values in column (5) with those in column (6). Note that the sign is '≣'. The two expressions do not have the same truth values

step 4: Interpret the result obtained in the last column.

If there are all T's in the last column, then the two expressions are equivalent. Having all T's in the last column would indicate that the truth values of the two expressions are the same. If there are all F's in the last column, or a mixture of T's and F's, then this indicates that the two expressions do not have the same truth values and are therefore not equivalent.

In (a) above, then, the two expressions are not equivalent. What arguer B has reported A as saying is not equivalent to what A actually said. Arguer B has therefore misrepresented or distorted what arguer A said. The result is, of course, not unexpected: just because t implies h is no reason to suppose that not-t implies not-h.

The point can be generalized:
(~ p ⊃ ~q) is not equivalent to (p ⊃ q)
And the method can be summarized as follows:

summary of method for showing equivalences:
(1) symbolize the expressions in question.
(2) state the purported equivalence
(3) set up a truth table chart to find out if the two expressions are equivalent
(4) interpret the result obtained in the last column

327

some further examples

(b) Suppose a politician has just made a speech in which he has maintained that if you vote for Smith, then you're a racist (in other words, v ⊃ r). Is this the same as saying: if you are not a racist, then you will not vote for Smith (in other words, ~r⊃~v)?

The purported equivalence is:

$$(\sim r \supset \sim v) \equiv (v \supset r)$$

The truth table chart is as follows:

(1) r	(2) v	(3) ~r	(4) ~v	(5) ~r⊃~v	(6) v⊃r	(7) (5)≣(6)
T	T	F	F	T	T	T
T	F	F	T	T	T	T
F	T	T	F	F	F	T
F	F	T	T	T	T	T

In the above,
- column (5): truth value of 1st expression
- column (6): truth value of 2nd expression
- column (7): compares the truth values of the expressions in columns (5) and (6)

Interpreting the result obtained in the last column, we find that the two expressions do have the same truth values. Thus they are equivalent. In other words, saying "if you are not a racist, then you will not vote for Smith" is the same as saying "if you vote for Smith, then you're a racist."

The point can be generalized:

$(\sim q \supset \sim p)$ is equivalent to $(p \supset q)$

Compare these results with those obtained in example (a) above.

(c) In example (b) above, the purported equivalence was written:

$$(\sim r \supset \sim v) \equiv (v \supset r)$$

Would it have been all right to have written it in reverse order, as follows:

$$(v \supset r) \equiv (\sim r \supset \sim v)$$

328

It would be all right to write this equivalence in
reverse order if the latter expression
$$(v \supset r) \equiv (\sim r \supset \sim v)$$
were equivalent to the former expression
$$(\sim r \supset \sim v) \equiv (v \supset r)$$
In other words, to answer the question posed in (c)
we must ascertain if the following two expressions
are equivalent:

$$[(v \supset r) \equiv (\sim r \supset \sim v)] \equiv [(\sim r \supset \sim v) \equiv (v \supset r)]$$

The truth table chart appears as follows:

(1)	(2)	(3)	(4)	(5)	(6)	(7)	(8)	(9)
v	r	$v \supset r$	$\sim r$	$\sim v$	$\sim r \supset \sim v$	(3)≡(6)	(6)≡(3)	(7)≡(8)
T	T	T	F	F	T	T	T	T
T	F	F	T	F	F	T	T	T
F	T	T	F	T	T	T	T	T
F	F	T	T	T	T	T	T	T

In the above,
- column (7): indicates truth value of first
             expression
- column (8): truth value of 2nd expression
- column (9): compares truth values in (7) with
             those in (8).

Interpreting the result obtained in column (9), we
find that the two expressions are equivalent. So it
is perfectly fine to write the purported equivalence
in reverse order as asked by example (c).

Consider another purported equivalence:
(d) Is the expression
       $\sim(p \cdot q)$
     equivalent to the following expression:
       $\sim p \cdot \sim q$

In other words, the purported equivalence in (d)
is:
$$\sim(p \cdot q) \equiv (\sim p \cdot \sim q)$$

Simply by noting what these two expressions say, it
should be fairly obvious to us that the two expressions are not equivalent. The expression on
the left side of the purported equivalence states

329

that it is not the case that p is conjoined with
q. The expression on the right side of the purported equivalence makes a much stronger claim:
it says that not-p is conjoined with not-q. Using
the truth table method, the two expressions are
shown not to be equivalent:

(1)	(2)	(3)	(4)	(5)	(6)	(7)	(8)
p	q	(p . q)	~(p . q)	~p	~q	~p.~q	(4)≣(7)
T	T	T	F	F	F	F	T
T	F	F	T	F	T	F	F
F	T	F	T	T	F	F	F
F	F	F	T	T	T	T	T

In the above,
- column (4): truth value of 1st expression
- column (7): truth value of 2nd expression
- column (8): compares the truth values for
  the expressions in columns (4) and (7).
Interpreting the result obtained in the last column,
we find that the two expressions do not have the
same truth values. Thus they are not equivalent.
This confirms our initial intuitions: the two
expressions say quite different things.

Consider one further example:
(e) Is a doubly negated expression equivalent
to the original unnegated expression?
In other words, is
$$\sim\sim p$$
equivalent to
$$p$$

Simply by reflecting on what the two expressions
indicate, it would seem fairly obvious to us that
the two expressions are indeed equivalent. After
all, not-p is the negation of p, and not-not-p is
the negation of not-p, and the negation of not-p
would be the same as p itself. Using truth table
method to illustrate this, the purported equivalence
is tested as follows:

(1)	(2)	(3)	(4)
p	~p	~~p	~~p $\equiv$ p
T	F	T	T
F	T	F	T

In the above,
- column (1): the 2 possible truth values for p
- column (2): the negation of p
- column (3): the negation of not-p
- column (4): compares the truth value for not-not-p in column (3) with the truth value for p in column (1).

Interpreting the results obtained in the last column, we see that the two expressions have the same truth value. They are equivalent.

in sum

In applying the truth table method to the purported equivalences in the examples above, the following general results concerning equivalences have been found:

(a) (~p $\supset$ ~q) is not equivalent to (p $\supset$ q)

(b) (~q $\supset$ ~p) is equivalent to (p $\supset$ q)

(c) If one expression is equivalent to another, then the order in which the equivalence is written does not matter.

(d) ~(p . q) is not equivalent to ~p . ~q

(e) ~~p is equivalent to p

Exercise #1

In the following, show whether or not the two expressions are equivalent using truth table method and the letters underlined.

(1) Arguer A has just contended that if a person favors abortion, then he favors euthanasia as well. Arguer B, however, reports that his opponent has maintained that if a person does not favor euthanasia, then he does not favor

abortion. Is what arguer B reports equivalent to what arguer A has actually said?

(2) Arguer A has just maintained that if a person favors abortion, then he favors euthanasia as well. Arguer B, however, reports that his opponent has contended that if a person does not favor abortion, then he does not favor euthanasia. Is what arguer B reports equivalent to what arguer A actually said?

(3) According to a popular slogan, if you're not part of the solution, then you're part of the problem. Is this the same as saying, if you're part of the solution, then you're not part of the problem?

(4) Ross: If you do not favor affirmative action legislation, then you're a male chauvinist pig.
    John: Oh, I know what you're saying. You're saying, in other words, that if you're not a male chauvinist pig, then you favor affirmative action legislation.
    Is what John says Ross says equivalent to what Ross actually said?

(5) Arguer A has said: if you believe in life after death, then if you are a Christian then you believe in heaven. Arguer B, however, in replying to arguer A, states that A said: if you believe in life after death and you're a Christian, then you believe in heaven. Has arguer B misrepresented what arguer A has actually said?

(6) Is (p v q) equivalent to (q v p)?

(7) Is (p . q) equivalent to (q . p)?

(8) Joan: If prison reform is doomed to failure, then increased capital punishment is the only solution.
    Lou: What's that? Are you saying: if increased capital punishment is the only solution, then prison reform is doomed to failure?
    Is what Lou says Joan said equivalent to what

332

Joan actually said?

(9)   As has already been made obvious, one useful
       purpose to which this method of showing equi-
       valences can be put is to assist us in detect-
       ing when misrepresentation or distortion has
       occurred. This technique therefore serves as
       a useful tool in what specific step in argu-
       ment evaluation?

2. Patterns of Deductive Argument

Step #8

A second important method for finding out the
validity or invalidity of deductive arguments is
to recognize common patterns of deductive reasoning.

Step #8

In a deductive argument, determine if
the argument is valid or invalid:
(a) by truth table method
(b) by detecting common patterns
    of deductive argument.

In this text we will study 6 important patterns of
deductive argument.

Pattern #1: Modus Ponens (MP)

Consider the following argument:
(f)   If there are bees buzzing, then there is
       honey in the tree. There are bees buzzing.
       Therefore there is honey in the tree.
In looking over this argument critically, we should
first of all note that it's a deductive one. So:
Step #8 applies. Applying method (a) of Step #8,
our work would appear as follows:

support space	main argument space	evaluation space
	1. b ⊃ h	
	2. b	This is a deductive
	———	argument. It is
	∴ h	valid (see below).

333

$$[(b \supset h) \cdot (b)] \supset h$$

(1)	(2)	(3)	(4)	(5)
b	h	b⊃h	(3).(1)	4)⊃(2)
T	T	T	T	T
T	F	F	F	T
F	T	T	F	T
F	F	T	F	T	(valid)

Consider next this argument:
(g) If it rains, then I'll watch TV. It is
     raining. Therefore I'll watch TV.
Again this is a deductive argument. So: Step #8
applies. Proceeding with this, our work would begin
to take shape as follows:

support space	main argument space	evaluation space
	1. r ⊃ w	
	2. r	This is a deductive
	⎯⎯⎯⎯⎯⎯⎯⎯	argument. It is ___?___ .
	∴ w	

We could go on to complete our work by applying
method (a) of Step #8, that is, by constructing a
truth table chart. But before we do this, however,
there is something the wary argument analyst would
notice. We should notice that the pattern of argument exhibited in (g) is the same as the pattern
of argument exhibited in (f). We've already shown
that the argument in (f) is valid. It would be
helpful, therefore, if we could simply label (g)
valid, and, indeed, all future arguments we might
meet that have the same pattern as in (f).

This brings us to the second method in Step #8:
showing validity or invalidity by detecting common
patterns of deductive argument. The pattern exhibited by the arguments in (f) and (g) is a common
one, and it has the name "modus ponens," a name
going back to the Middle Ages.

Using 'p' and 'q' to stand for any informative

sentences whatsoever, the general pattern of modus ponens is as follows:

modus ponens (MP)

1. $p \supset q$
2. p

———————

$\therefore q$ (valid)

Notice the construction of this pattern of argument. First of all, it contains a premise which expresses an implication: $(p \supset q)$. Then it contains another premise which affirms the antecedent of this implication: namely, p. Finally, it contains a conclusion which affirms the consequent of the initial implication: namely, q. It represents a valid pattern of deductive argument.

This is the first of the 6 patterns of deductive argument of which we'll make use in this text. If we should detect its presence in an argument, then in evaluation space of the standard format, we'll simply write: This is a deductive argument. It is valid (modus ponens). Let us return, then, to argument (g) and apply method (b) of Step #8.

support space	main argument space	evaluation space
	1. $r \supset w$ 2. r ——————— $\therefore w$	This is a deductive argument. It is valid (modus ponens).

Method (b) of Step #8 is particularly useful, for it saves us considerable time and trouble having to construct a truth table chart. Building up a repertoire of common patterns of deductive argument cuts down considerably on the time needed to evaluate this kind of argument.

Not only main arguments, but also mini-arguments may be deductive. The same considerations and annotation applies. For example:

335

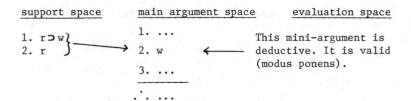

1. r ⊃ w ⎫
2. r   ⎬ ⟶   2. w ⟵   This mini-argument is
            1. ...   deductive. It is valid
            2. w   (modus ponens).
            3. ...
            ____
            · · ...

Before leaving modus ponens for other common
patterns, there are some other features about this
pattern of which you ought to become aware. For one
thing, the order in which the premises occur makes
no difference. The following argument is also modus
ponens:

> 1. p
>
> 2. p ⊃ q
> _____
> ∴ q

The order in which the premises occur is purely
stylistic. The pattern of reasoning is the same:
it contains one premise which states an implication,
another premise which affirms the antecedent of the
implication, and a conclusion which affirms the consequent of the initial implication.

The following are also examples of arguments which
exhibit the modus ponens pattern. Note these
carefully.

1. p ⊃ ~q	1. ~p ⊃ ~q	1. ~p ⊃ q
2. p	2. ~p	2. ~p
∴ ~q	∴ ~q	∴ q

The negations here should not throw us off if we
understand the moves made within the basic pattern
of modus ponens reasoning. In all these instances,
the pattern is the same. An initial implication is
expressed in one premise, the antecedent is affirmed
in another, and the consequent expressed in the
conclusion. They are each instances of modus
ponens reasoning. Each is valid.

336

The following, too, are examples of modus ponens reasoning. Think about them carefully.

1. p⊃(q v r)	1. (p . q)⊃(m⊃r)	1. (x . t)⊃1
2. p	2. (p . q)	2. (x . t)
∴ (q v r)	∴ (m⊃r)	∴ 1

The number of sentence letters here should not throw us off, if we focus on the pattern exhibited by each argument and we understand the moves made within modus ponens reasoning. In each of these instances, the pattern is the same. First of all, an implication is expressed. Then, in the second premise, the antecedent of the implication is affirmed. Finally, in the conclusion, the consequent of the initial implication is expressed. This is what occurs in modus ponens reasoning. They are each instances of this pattern. They are each valid.

As you can readily see from the example above which contain 4 sentence letters, being able to spot common patterns of deductive reasoning can save us considerable time in not having to write out a lengthy truth table chart!

Pattern #2: Modus Tollens (MT)

Consider next this argument:
(h) If the world is flat, then it would have an edge. The world does not have an edge. Therefore the world is not flat.

Argument (h) is deductive. Applying method (a) of Step #8, we arrive at the following:

support space	main argument space	evaluation space
⟨the world is finite⟩	1. f ⊃ e	
	2. ~e	This is a deductive argument. It is
	∴ ~f	valid (see below).

337

$$[(f \supset e) \ . \ (\sim e)] \ \supset \sim f$$

(1) f	(2) e	(3) f⊃e	(4) ~e	(5) (3).(4)	(6) ~f	(7) (5)⊃(6)
T	T	T	F	F	F	T
T	F	F	T	F	F	T
F	T	T	F	F	T	T
F	F	T	T	T	T	T (valid)

Notice the pattern exhibited by this argument. It differs somewhat from modus ponens. In the first premise, an implication is stated. But then, in the second premise, the consequent of the initial implication is negated. And then, in the conclusion, the antecedent of the initial implication is negated.

The pattern is a common one in deductive reasoning. It is called "modus tollens," and it is a valid pattern of reasoning. The basic pattern is as follows:

<u>modus tollens (MT)</u>

1. p ⊃ q

2. ~ q
_____

∴ ~ p

When we come across arguments which exhibit this particular pattern, we can simply state, in evaluation space, this is a deductive argument. It is valid (modus tollens).

Notice how this pattern is exhibited in the following argument.
(i) If one ounce of this chemical is harmful, then it would cause mice to die. But it does not cause mice to die. Thus one ounce of this chemical is not harmful.

support space	main argument space	evaluation space
	1. h ⊃ d	
	2. ~ d	This is a deductive argu-
	_____	ment. It is valid (modus
	∴ ~ h	tollens).

Before we move on to yet another pattern, there are some further matters you should recognize about modus tollens. For one thing, the order in which the premises are written does not matter, being purely stylistic. The following argument also portrays modus tollens reasoning.

$$1. \sim q$$

$$2. \ p \supset q$$

$$\therefore \sim p$$

The reason for this is obvious: one premise states an implication (the second premise here), another premise states the negation of the consequent in that implication (the first premise here), and the conclusion states the negation of the antecedent in that implication. This is the move made in modus tollens reasoning, and the argument exhibits it.

Similarly, we should not be thrown off by the presence of negations in the argument. Note the pattern exhibited by the following arguments carefully, bearing in mind that the negation of not-p is not-not-p (or simply p itself).

1. $p \supset \sim q$	1. $\sim p \supset \sim q$	1. $\sim p \supset q$
2. q	2. q	2. $\sim q$
$\therefore \sim p$	$\therefore p$	$\therefore p$

In each of these instances, an initial implication is expressed: then, in the second premise, the consequent of the initial implication is negated; finally, in the conclusion, the antecedent of the initial implication is negated. Each of these arguments exhibits the same pattern, namely, the pattern called "modus tollens," and each is valid.

Finally, the following are also examples of modus tollens reasoning. Note carefully the pattern portrayed in the two examples below. Do not let the number of sentence letters deter you from seeing the basic pattern.

1. $(1 \lor m) \supset s$	1. $[j \supset (k \cdot t)] \supset [(t \lor r) \cdot x]$
2. $\sim s$	2. $\sim [(t \lor r) \cdot x]$
$\therefore \sim (1 \lor m)$	$\therefore \sim [j \supset (k \cdot t)]$

Again the pattern is a familiar one. An initial implication is stated. Then, in the second premise, the consequent of the initial implication is negated. Finally, in the conclusion, the antecedent of the initial implication is negated. This is modus tollens reasoning. Again, recognition of this pattern is extremely useful in saving us considerable time constructing a complex truth table chart.

So far two common patterns have been discussed: modus tollens and modus ponens. Note carefully how they differ. And note also the moves characteristic of each pattern of deductive reasoning. The next two patterns of reasoning bear a superficial resemblance to these two valid patterns, but they differ significantly.

Pattern #3
Fallacy of Denying the Antecedent (FDA)

Consider this argument:
(j) If this letter is typed on an IBM Selectric typewriter, then it'll have a professional appearance. This letter isn't typed on an IBM Selectric typewriter. Consequently it hasn't a professional appearance.

This deductive argument looks suspiciously like modus ponens, but it isn't. Note the second premise: here the antecedent of the initial implication is denied, not affirmed as in modus ponens. Applying method (a) of Step #8 we find the following inter- esting result:

support space	main argument space	evaluation space
	1. $t \supset h$	
	2. $\sim t$	This is a deductive argument. It is in-
	$\therefore \sim h$	valid (see below).

340

$[(t \supset h) \cdot (\sim t)] \supset \sim h$

(1) t	(2) h	(3) t⊃h	(4) ∼t	(5) (3).(4)	(6) ∼h	(7) (5)⊃(6)
T	T	T	F	F	F	T
T	F	F	F	F	T	T
F	T	T	T	T	F	F
F	F	T	T	T	T	T (invalid)

Notice carefully the pattern of reasoning exhibited by this particular argument. First of all, an implication is stated. Then, in another premise, the antecedent of this initial implication is negated. Finally, in the conclusion, the consequent of this initial implication is negated.

The pattern represented here is known as the "fallacy of denying the antecedent," taking its name from what occurs in the second premise (where the antecedent of the initial implication is negated). It represents an invalid pattern of deductive reasoning. The general pattern is as follows:

fallacy of denying the antecedent (FDA)

1. $p \supset q$

2. $\sim p$

$\therefore \sim q$

As with other patterns of deductive reasoning, we can put this information to good use in argument evaluation. Note carefully the following argument:
(k)   If John advocates abortion, then he favors euthanasia as well. John does not advocate abortion. Therefore he does not favor euthanasia as well

Applying method (b) of Step #8 to this deductive argument, we obtain the following:

support space	main argument space	evaluation space
	1. $a \supset e$	This is a deductive
	2. $\sim a$	argument. It is
	$\therefore \sim e$	invalid (FDA).

As with modus ponens and modus tollens, the order in which the premises occur does not matter, so long as the moves exhibited by the fallacy of denying the antecedent are present. Similarly, too, the following arguments exhibit FDA kind of reasoning. (Remember that $\sim\sim p \equiv p$)

1. $p \supset \sim q$	1. $\sim p \supset \sim q$	1. $\sim p \supset q$
2. $\sim p$	2. p	2. p
$\therefore$ q	$\therefore$ q	$\therefore \sim q$

Each of these instances exhibits the pattern of reasoning called "fallacy of denying the antecedent." In each instance, an implication is initially stated. Then, in the second premise, the antecedent of the implication initially stated is denied. Then finally, in the conclusion, the negation of the consequent of the initial implication is expressed.

As with all patterns of reasoning, it is important for us to bear in mind the moves that are being made within the argument. As long as these are clearly recognized, then we won't be thrown off by negations and double negations.

Just note in passing how FDA differs from the following valid MP argument:

1. $\sim p \supset \sim q$
2. $\sim p$
$\therefore \sim q$

Note that in premise 2 of this argument, the antecedent of the initial implication stated in premise 1 is not negated: the antecedent, not-p, is simply affirmed.

Pattern #4
Fallacy of Affirming the Consequent (FAC)

Consider this argument:
(1) If I'm a truly liberated <u>w</u>oman, then I

favor abortion as a matter between doctor
and patient. I do favor abortion as a
matter between doctor and patient. Thus
I'm a truly liberated woman.

As it turns out, applying method (a) of Step #8,
this deductive argument is invalid.

support space	main argument space	evaluation space
	1. w ⊃ a	
	2. a	This is a deductive
	―――――	argument. It is in-
	∴ w	valid (see below).

$$[(w \supset a) \, . \, (a)] \supset w$$

(1) w	(2) a	(3) w⊃a	(4) (3).(2)	(5) (4)⊃(1)	
T	T	T	T	T	
T	F	F	F	T	
F	T	T	T	F	
F	F	T	F	T	(invalid)

Notice carefully the construction of this pattern
of argument. First of all, an initial implication
is stated. Then, in another premise, the consequent
of the initial implication is affirmed. Finally,
in the conclusion, the antecedent of the initial
implication is stated.

The pattern exhibited here is known as "the fallacy of affirming the consequent," deriving its
name from what occurs in the second premise (where
the consequent of the initial implication is
affirmed). It represents an invalid pattern of
deductive reasoning. The general pattern is as
follows:

<u>fallacy of affirming the consequent (FAC)</u>

1. p ⊃ q

2. q

―――――

∴ p

(Note, in passing, how this pattern of reasoning
differs from the valid reasoning of modus tollens)

Examine the following argument closely to see if it contains a familiar pattern of deductive reasoning.

(m)   If you use Brand X in your dishwater, then your dishes will be spotless. Your dishes are spotless. Hence you use Brand X in your dishwater.

support space	main argument space	evaluation space
	1. B ⊃ s	
	2. s	This is a deductive
	———	argument. It is
	∴ B	invalid (FAC).

As in previous patterns, the order in which the premises are written makes no difference. The following argument also exhibits FAC kind of reasoning:

1. q

2. p ⊃ q
———
∴ p

The pattern is that of FAC: in one premise, an implication is stated; in another premise, the consequent of that implication is affirmed; and, finally, in the conclusion, the antecedent of that implication is expressed.

The following arguments also exhibit the same pattern of deductive reasoning:

1. p ⊃ ~q	1. ~p ⊃ ~q	1. ~p ⊃ q
2. ~q	2. ~q	2. q
———	———	———
∴ p	∴ ~p	∴ ~p

In each of these instances, an initial implication is stated. Then, in the next premise, the consequent of that initial implication is affirmed. And, finally, in the conclusion, the antecedent of the initial implication is affirmed. The pattern is that of FAC.

Pattern #5: Disjunctive Syllogism (DS)

Not all common patterns of deductive reasoning contain premises which state implications. Consider,
for example, the following argument:
(n)   This afternoon either I'll go shopping or
      I'll have my hair cut. I won't go shopping.
      Consequently I'll have my hair cut.

Using method (a) of Step #8 we quickly find that
this argument is valid.

support space	main argument space	evaluation space
	1. s v h	
	2. ~ s	This is a deductive argument. It is valid (see below).
	—————	
	∴ h	

$$[(s \lor h) \cdot (\sim s)] \supset h$$

(1)	(2)	(3)	(4)	(5)	(6)
s	h	s v h	~s	(3).(4)	(5)⊃(2)
T	T	T	F	F	T
T	F	T	F	F	T
F	T	T	T	T	T
F	F	F	T	F	T (valid)

Note the pattern exhibited by this particular deductive argument. First of all, in one premise, a
disjunction is expressed (one option or some other
option). Then, in another premise, one of these
options is negated. Finally, in the conclusion,
the other option stated initially--the one that
hasn't been negated--is affirmed.

This pattern is called "disjunctive syllogism" (DS),
and it is valid. Its general pattern can be represented as follows:

disjunctive syllogism (DS)

1. p v q

2. ~ p
—————
∴ q

It does not matter which of the two initial alternatives is negated in the second premise. The following argument is equally disjunctive syllogism:

1. p v q

2. ~q
_____

∴ p

As with previous patterns, it can be put to good
use by us in evaluating arguments. Consider, for
instance, this argument:

(o)   Northern Ireland is faced with two alternatives:
      to ruin its economy by continued civil strife
      or to work out a new social order that's fair
      to all factions. It won't ruin its economy by
      continued civil strife. Therefore it will
      work out a new social order that's fair to
      all factions.

support space	main argument space	evaluation space
	1. r v w	
	2. ~r	This is a deductive
	_____	argument. It is
	∴ w	valid (DS).

Just in passing, you should note that in examples
(n) and (o), as with other examples in this chapter,
we are just considering Step #8. In any full-scale
evaluation, other steps would have to be brought
into play. With respect to the arguments contained
in (n) and (o) care would have to be taken, of
course, that premise 1 in each case does not involve a false dilemma. The premises, moreover,
would need support, and in (o) some of the key
basic terms (e.g. "ruin its economy," "a new
social order that's fair...") would have to be
clarified.

Consider also these arguments, noting their
pattern carefully:

346

1. ~p v q	1. ~p v ~q	1. p v ~q	1. p v ~q
2. ~q	2. p	2. q	2. ~p
∴ ~p	∴ ~q	∴ p	∴ ~q

In each instance, the following happens. First, a disjunction is stated. Then, in the second premise, one of these disjuncts is negated. Finally, in the conclusion, the other disjunct (the one not negated in the second premise) is expressed. In each instance, in other words, the pattern of reasoning exhibited is that of disjunctive syllogism.

Pattern #6: Hypothetical Syllogism (HS)

One final pattern, this one containing statements all of which express implication, remains to be considered. Examine the following argument:

(p) If society allows abortion on demand, then any unwanted life can be terminated. If any unwanted life can be terminated, then this paves the way for society to allow whole-sale killing of unwanted old people. Hence, if society allows abortion on demand, then the way is paved for society to allow the wholesale killing of unwanted old people.

Applying method (a) of Step #8 we quickly discover that this is a valid deductive argument.

support space	main argument space	evaluation space
	1. a ⊃ l	
	2. l ⊃ o	This is a deductive argument. It is valid (see below).
	∴ a ⊃ o	

$$[(a \supset l) . (l \supset o)] \supset (a \supset o)$$

347

(1)	(2)	(3)	(4)	(5)	(6)	(7)	(8)
a	1	o	a⊃1	1⊃o	(4).(5)	a⊃o	(6)⊃(7)
T	T	T	T	T	T	T	T
T	T	F	T	F	F	F	T
T	F	T	F	T	F	T	T
T	F	F	F	T	F	F	T
F	T	T	T	T	T	T	T
F	T	F	T	F	F	T	T
F	F	T	T	T	T	T	T
F	F	F	T	T	T	T	T

Note the pattern exhibited by this particular argument. At the outset, an implication is expressed.
Then, in another premise, another implication is
stated, containing as its antecedent the consequent
of the previous implication. Then, finally, in the
conclusion, another implication is stated, this
one containing as its antecedent the antecedent
of the first implication and as its consequent
the consequent in the second implication.

This pattern is called "hypothetical syllogism"
(HS), and it represents a valid pattern of deductive
reasoning. Its basic form can be depicted as
follows:

<u>hypothetical syllogism (HS)</u>

1. p ⊃ q
2. q ⊃ r

∴ p ⊃ r

Consider next this argument:
(q) If I want to become a millionaire, then I
should invest in the stock market. If I
invest in the stock market, then I'll have
to participate at least indirectly in
dubious corporate doings. Therefore, if I
want to become a millionaire, then I'll
have to participate at least indirectly
in dubious corporate doings.

348

support space	main argument space	evaluation space
	1. m ⊃ s	
	2. s ⊃ p	This is a deductive
	_____	argument. It is
	∴ m ⊃ p	valid (HS).

The following are also examples of the same pattern
of deductive reasoning:

1. p ⊃ ~q	1. ~p ⊃ q	1. p ⊃ q
2. ~q ⊃ r	2. q ⊃ ~r	2. q ⊃ ~r
_____	_____	_____
∴ p ⊃ r	∴ ~p ⊃ ~r	∴ p ⊃ ~r

This completes the patterns of deductive argument
we will study in this text.

summary

six basic patterns			
#1	modus ponens (MP)	1. p ⊃ q 2. p ∴ q	valid
#2	modus tollens (MT)	1. p ⊃ q 2. ~q ∴ ~p	valid
#3	fallacy of denying the antecedent (FDA)	1. p ⊃ q 2. ~p ∴ ~q	invalid
#4	fallacy of affirming the consequent (FAC)	1. p ⊃ q 2. q ∴ p	invalid
#5	disjunctive syllogism (DS)	1. p v q 2. ~p ∴ q	valid
#6	hypothetical syllogism (HS)	1. p ⊃ q 2. q ⊃ r ∴ p ⊃ r	valid

349

three final reminders

(1) While we have described two main methods for finding out the validity or invalidity of deductive arguments, these do not exhaust the possible methods nor do they suffice to cover the evaluation of all deductive arguments. For example, the methods we've described won't cover deductive reasoning involving "all" and "some" statements. Neither of our two methods will help us evaluate the following sort of deductive argument, for instance:

      1. All mathematicians are philosophers.
      <u>2. Some scientists are mathematicians.</u>

    .˙. Some scientists are philosophers.

Statements containing "all" and "some" in this fashion are said to be "quantified". A further step in the study of deductive argument would be to learn more of the symbolic language and more techniques so as to evaluate arguments containing quantified expressions. This matter, however, is beyond the scope of this text. For more advanced work in the area of deductive argument, consult the books suggested in the "For Further Reading" section at the back of this text.

(2) Although, for the sake of ease of exposition, we've examined deductive arguments as main arguments, it should not be overlooked that mini-arguments may be deductive in nature and that Step #8 should be applied to these as well. For example, we may come across an argument which has the following structure and we would therefore place the following comment in evaluation space.

support space	main argument space	evaluation space
	1. ...	
1. m v z	2. ...	
2. ~z	3. m	← This mini-argument
	4. ...	is deductive. It
	————	is valid (DS).
	.	
	. . ...	

or we may encounter the following sort of situation in which both the main argument and the two mini-

350

arguments are deductive:

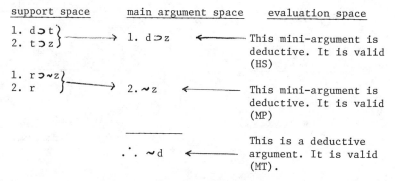

support space   main argument space   evaluation space

1. d⊃t ⎫
2. t⊃z ⎭ ——————→ 1. d⊃z ⟵————— This mini-argument is deductive. It is valid (HS)

1. r⊃~z ⎫
2. r   ⎭ ——————→ 2. ~z ⟵————— This mini-argument is deductive. It is valid (MP)

∴ ~d ⟵————— This is a deductive argument. It is valid (MT).

(3) Throughout this chapter, and the previous one, we have focused exclusively on the application of Step #8. This was done solely for the purposes of clear exposition. It should not be forgotten, however, that full-scale critical evaluation of any deductive argument includes not only Step #8 (which is essential) but other relevant steps in argument evaluation.

Exercise #2

Let us suppose that we have come across the following arguments which we have symbolized as follows. Look closely at their respective patterns. In each case (1) state what pattern of deductive argument it exhibits, and (2) state whether or not the argument is valid.

(1) 1. z⊃c
    2. c⊃l
   ∴ z⊃l

(2) 1. p v m
    2. ~m
   ∴ p

(3) 1. z⊃j
    2. ~z
   ∴ ~j

(4) 1. d⊃f
    2. ~f
   ∴ ~d

(5) 1. k⊃(l . m)
    2. (l . m)
   ∴ k

(6) 1. y
    2. y⊃z
   ∴ z

351

(7) 1. (j v n) ⊃ i   (8) 1. ~r   (9) 1. z v (t . s)
    2. i   2. r v v   2. ~(t . s)
∴ (j v n)   ∴ v   ∴ z

(10) 1. (p ⊃ r) ⊃ t   (11) 1. d ⊃ (1 . m)
     2. t ⊃ (a v b)   2. ~(1 . m)
∴ (p ⊃ r) ⊃ (a v b)   ∴ ~d

(12)   1. ...   (13)
  1. d v m ⎫ 2. ...   1. ...
  2. ~d   ⎬→3. m   1. p ⊃ z ⎫→2. ~p
           4. ...   2. ~z   ⎬ 3. ...
         ∴ ...   ∴ ...

(14) 1. a ⊃ 1   (15) 1. p ⊃ ~q
    2. a   2. ~q ⊃ b
∴ 1   ∴ p ⊃ b

(16) 1. a ⊃ ~b   (17) 1. z ⊃ ~1
    2. a   2. ~1
∴ ~b   ∴ z

(18) 1. ~z v d   (19) 1. ~r ⊃ ~s
    2. ~d   2. s
∴ ~z   ∴ r

(20) 1. ~p v ~q   (21) 1. ~n ⊃ ~m
    2. q   2. ~m ⊃ ~o
∴ ~p   ∴ ~n ⊃ ~o

(22)   1. ...
  1. r v ~s ⎫ 2. ...
  2. ~r   ⎬→3. ~s
         ∴ ...

Exercise #3
As assigned by the course director, re-examine the
following arguments mentioned in this text. Then
(1) state what pattern of deductive argument each
exhibits, and (2) state whether or not the argument
is valid.

CHAPTER ELEVEN

ARGUMENT EVALUATION: INDUCTIVE ARGUMENT

1. About Inductive Arguments

recognizing inductive arguments

Compare the kinds of arguments in the following two groups:

group A

(a) 1. All people who live in suburbia have a sense of isolation and do not know their neighbors.
  2. Jones lives in suburbia.

  ∴. Jones has a sense of isolation and does not know his neighbors.

(b) 1. Either we go to Tampa for Christmas or else we'll go to Cincinnati.
  2. We won't go to Cincinnati.

  ∴. We'll go to Tampa for Christmas.

(c) 1. If wind power proves economical and practical, then there is no need to build more nuclear generating stations.
  2. Wind power proves economical and practical.

  ∴. There is no need to build more nuclear generating stations.

group B

(a) 1. Over the past 85 years of recorded history, whenever solar flares and sunspots occur, the earth experiences more than its usual share of earthquakes, tornados, volcanic activity, and the

353

_____like._____

.˙. It is likely that during the next bout of solar flares and sunspots, the earth will undergo the same sort of upheaval.

(b) 1. The last 3 batches of wine I've made from Tastee Grape Concentrate have turned to _____sour vinegar._____

.˙. Tastee Grape Concentrate is an inferior product.

(c) 1. According to many studies done by Dr. G. Smack at the Marijuana Research Clinic in Sacramento, daily smoking of pot by males aged 18-28 significantly reduces the sperm _____count._____

.˙. Smoking pot greatly reduces the male sex drive.

The arguments in group A are deductive; those in group B, inductive.

We have devoted the last two chapters to the study of deductive arguments. While important, deductive arguments are not the only kind of argument. Inductive arguments frequently occur in reasoning about points of view and we need to be sensitive to their particular characteristics and to their appropriate criteria of evaluation.

There are considerable differences between deductive and inductive arguments. [Here you may want to refresh your memory on these differences. See pages 252-259 above.] Inductive arguments are those in which the premises provide some support for the conclusion and where the conclusion does not follow conclusively from the information contained in the premises. The conclusion in an inductive argument goes beyond the evidence cited in the premises, and, in so doing, gives us new information.

We find inductive arguments in many different contexts. For example:
- in some scientific contexts: e.g. what

studies on several generations of fruit
flies probably shows, studies on what
chemicals are probable carcinogens, etc.
- in some legal arguments: e.g. whether there
is reasonable doubt that the accused committed the crime, etc.
- in some historical arguments concerning what
probably happened in the past: e.g. whether
Oswald probably killed Kennedy, whether
Martin Luther King's assassination was perhaps the result of a conspiracy, etc.
- in some arguments from personal experience:
e.g. those in which we try to convince others
what to do, what to avoid, how to handle life
crises, etc.
- in some speculative arguments: e.g. if Japan
had not bombed Pearl Harbor, would the USA
have entered World War II; was there a continent called Atlantis, and when and how was
it destroyed; do UFOs represent visits by
alien life-forms: etc.

And so on.

identifying inductive arguments

There are no particular problems in identifying inductive arguments using standard format. You have
encountered and identified many such arguments,
although you may not have explicitly recognized
their inductive nature. Two things should be
remembered, however.

First of all, many inductive arguments refer to a
study (or experiment), or a series of studies (experiments), to back up a more general point. As has
already been pointed out (see pages 99 and following
above), it is important in identifying such arguments that you become clear about the following:
- the number of studies
- the details of the studies
- the finding(s) of the studies
- the general over-all point

Secondly, you should recall that whereas the main

argument may be of one sort (deductive or inductive), each mini-argument may be of the same or another sort (inductive or deductive). So we should expect to find inductive main arguments, and inductive mini-arguments

the inductive base

In an inductive argument, what an arguer is arguing from (i.e. his reasons, premises) is often referred to as the inductive base and what he is arguing for (i.e. his conclusion) is often spoken of as the inductive generalization.

In inductive reasoning, the flow of thought should move clearly from the inductive base to the inductive generalization. As with all arguments, one ought to be able to distinguish clearly between the from what and the to what the arguer is arguing. In other words the inductive base should be clear.

There are several different sorts of inductive bases. Three are of particular importance and they have already been mentioned as reasoning that is characteristically inductive (see pages 252-259 above)

	inductive base	inductive generalization
(1)	moving from a statement in the premises concerning what has been the case in the past	to a statement in the conclusion concerning what is likely to happen in the future
(2)	moving from selected examples of a particular phenomenon (in the premises)	to a generalization about the phenomenon in question (in the conclusion)
(3)	moving from what was found to be the case in one or more studies (in the premises)	to a statement concerning what is generally the case (in the conclusion)

Examples of arguments which illustrate each of these different kinds of inductive base have been provided in Chapter Eight.

evaluating inductive arguments

In an inductive argument, the premises support the conclusion, at least to some extent. The relationship between premises and conclusion in an inductive argument is referred to as <u>inductive strength</u>. It is this relationship that becomes the focus of our critical assessment of inductive arguments in Step #9.

Evaluating the inductive strength of an inductive argument, however, is quite a different matter than evaluating the comparable facet of deductive arguments, namely deductive validity. These differences should be carefully noted.

For one thing, determining the <u>degree</u> of inductive strength in an inductive argument is much less exact than ascertaining the deductive validity of deductive arguments. Deductive arguments were very clear-cut in this respect: they were either valid or invalid (but not both). Deductive validity is very much like being pregnant--you're either pregnant or not pregnant, but not both.

This clear-cut situation is not the same, however, for inductive arguments. The labels used to describe inductive strength--words like "very weak," "weak," "moderate," "strong," "very strong," etc.--indicate degrees of support but not in any precise measurable sense. Rather these terms serve to provide looser, less exact, rougher categories of assessment than was the case for deductive validity. In this respect inductive strength is very much like having a serious relationship with someone: ascertaining how seriously one is involved admits only of imperfect approximations, not precisely measurable quantities.

Because the degree of inductive strength cannot be precisely measured but only graded in an approximate manner, it should come as no surprise to us that there are bound to be disputes when the <u>amount</u> of inductive strength is made the object of <u>critical</u> assessment. This is indeed the case. If we focus simply on the <u>amount</u> of inductive strength the premises provide the conclusion, we are apt to run into the following kinds of controversies:

(1) what precise label or grade (e.g. very weak, weak, moderate, strong, very strong) should be attached to this particular inductive argument?

(2) how much evidence is needed to establish the conclusion of this particular inductive argument?

(3) how much evidence is, in general, strong evidence?

These questions admit of no hard-and-fast rules. It would be very difficult, for instance, to come up with an informative general answer to question (3). Questions (2) and (1), moreover, depend very much on the particular circumstances in which the inductive argument is presented. These circumstances include at least the following:

- the information available to the arguer (e.g. how much research is available, how much research the arguer is willing to do, how much he can remember, etc.)

- the purposes of the arguer (e.g. to what extent he wants to convince us, how crucial he estimates the particular argument is to his over-all case, etc.)

- audience expectations and standards of argument judgment (it is one thing to present an inductive argument in a scientific journal, quite another matter in such instances as: a governmental committee, a newspaper article, an open-line radio show, in conversation with friend, etc.)

- time constraints on developing the argument.

And so on. Judging the worth and strength of a particular inductive argument involves detailed consideration of the context in which it occurs.

If we try to assess the amount of inductive strength as if our task were to try to pin a label or grade on an inductive argument, then we should be prepared for considerable controversy. We should be prepared, that is, to back up our evaluation of the argument with an evaluative argument of our own, indicating why we have assessed it the way we have. As we shall see, however, in Step #9 we won't focus specifically on the amount

358

of inductive strength. That is, we won't make as the focus of our evaluative effort to gauge precisely which label, and only which label, applies to the particular inductive argument. Our emphasis in Step #9 will be placed on a different aspect of inductive strength.

The inexact nature of the degree of inductive strength is one way in which the study of inductive arguments differs from the study of deductive arguments where deductive validity is relatively clear-cut. There is, however, another important difference.

There are no black-and-white, rigorous, mechanical methods for finding out if an inductive argument is strong or weak. There were such methods for deductive validity (we studied two of them: truth table method and the method of detecting common patterns). That is not the case in evaluating inductive strength. There is no "method" to be learned and applied by rote. Because the categories of evaluation (from "very weak" to "very strong") are much less exact than the comparable categories for deductive arguments ("valid," "invalid"), the critical assessment of inductive arguments requires a different sort of approach: the careful, thoughtful, argument by argument consideration of a number of aspects that tend either to reduce or increase its inductive strength. In other words, in evaluating inductive arguments we consult a number of guidelines, and discuss the merits of individual inductive arguments in relation to these. We do not apply strict procedural rules.

In sum, the study of inductive strength differs from the logic of deductive validity in two main ways:
    (1) its categories of evaluation are less exact, and
    (2) it lacks a comparable mechanical method for determining the degree of inductive strength.
We are dealing, then, with a very different kind of argument. It is important to recognize this at the outset so that we do not transport expectations or criteria appropriate to the study of deductive argument into our study of this kind of reasoning.

As with our study of deductive arguments, we will
only examine a portion of the study of inductive
reasoning. We will not consider, for example, such
matters as theory of probability, statistics, or
the general nature of scientific method. There are
several books listed in the "For Further Reading"
bibliography at the end of this text which focus
on these matters. Rather we will concentrate here
on providing a "checklist" of various important
aspects of inductive arguments which should be
taken into account when evaluating arguments of
this sort.

2. Step #9

Step #9
In an inductive argument, by considering
the following ... , draw attention to
those features of the argument which
serve to diminish its inductive strength.

Note that this step does not focus on the precise
amount of inductive strength, as if our task were
primarily to settle upon a particular label ("very
weak" to "very strong") for a specific inductive
argument's worth. That is not our basic job, for
reasons already given. Rather the focus is placed
here on a number of important features of inductive
reasoning that affect the inductive strength the
premises provide the conclusion. Step #9 provides,
in other words, a list of guidelines that should
be taken into account in discussing the merits or
defects of an inductive argument.

In an inductive argument, focus specifically on the
following matters:

(a) clear key expressions

It is very important in inductive reasoning that the
key words and expressions needed to understand the
argument be clear and free from vagueness.(This, of
course, overlaps in part Step #2) Suppose, for instance, we come across the following argument:

(a) The Stewart Report of 1979, based on hundreds
     of personal interviews, found that in 10 major
     cities having populations in excess of 500,000,
     28.9% of the people live at or below the poverty
     level. It also found that poverty is increasing
     at an alarming rate. Thus we can see that every-
     where urban poverty is rampant.

This is an inductive argument. It contains two main
premises (the two findings of the Stewart Report of
1979) and a conclusion. The argument concerns poverty,
yet nowhere is this key concept made clear. What is
"urban poverty"? What is "the poverty level"? Perhaps
the Stewart Report made this clear (hopefully it did,
otherwise it would be impossible to know what it
was measuring with such finesse). Until this matter
is cleared up, however, it is very difficult to know
what to make of this inductive argument. It lacks
specificity, definition, and clarity of thought.

Note, too, that the second premise is also vague--
what does "is increasing at an alarming rate"
indicate? By how much is it increasing (1% over 10
years, 25% over 1 year, or ?)? And what is alarming?

Before we can do much with this argument, these
crucial phrases need to be made clear. We would
evaluate it as follows, looking, for the moment,
just at its lack of clarity:

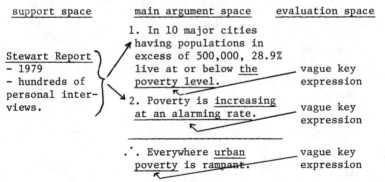

support space	main argument space	evaluation space

Stewart Report
- 1979
- hundreds of
personal inter-
views.

1. In 10 major cities
having populations in
excess of 500,000, 28.9%
live at or below the
poverty level.   vague key
                                  expression

2. Poverty is increasing
at an alarming rate.   vague key
                                  expression

.˙. Everywhere urban
poverty is rampant.   vague key
                                  expression

Consider another argument, one with which the chapter
began:

361

(b)   According to many studies done by Dr. G. Smack
      at the Marijuana Research Clinic in Sacramento,
      daily smoking of pot by males aged 18-28 signifi-
      cantly reduces the sperm count. As we can readily
      see, then, smoking pot greatly reduces the male
      sex drive.

The argument is inductive, containing one premise
(supported by the many studies carried out by Dr.
G. Smack) and a conclusion. Note the phrase "significantly reduces" in the premise. How much reduction is
"significant"? (Here some figures might help clarify
the situation for us: e.g. the average sperm count
before smoking pot compared with the average sperm
count afterwards; or the percentage drop, etc.) The
phrase is, of course, a key one, for if the studies
do not show much of a change in sperm count, the
argument would lose considerable force.

Note, too, a similar vagueness in the conclusion:
"greatly reduces."

Focusing simply on clarity of language, we would
comment critically on this argument as follows:

support space	main argument space	evaluation space
Dr.G. Smack - many studies - M.R.C. in Sacramento - daily smoking of pot - males 18-28 yrs old.	1. Daily smoking of pot by males aged 18-28 significantly reduces the sperm count. ∴ Smoking pot greatly reduces the male sex drive.	vague key expression vague key expression

(Note, too, that this argument lacks a premise that
would connect reduced sperm count with reduced sex
drive)

Similarly, if in the course of making an inductive
argument, we talk about the beneficial effects of
product X, we should specify where and how product X
produces such effects. Or if we claim that crime is

rapidly on the increase, we should make sure to show (i) that it is increasing (e.g. by how much, over what period, etc.), and (ii) that it is doing so "rapidly" (e.g. by showing an accelerated rate of increase, by drawing attention to a marked jump in the number of crimes, etc.). And so on.

Lack of clarity is especially important in inductive reasoning, for it affects inductive strength. If the key expressions are not clearly discussed, then the arguer runs the serious risk of our not being able to comprehend what he is talking about, let alone to evaluate the support he provides his conclusion. It's a defect that can vitiate understanding. It is also a defect that can be overcome by clarification of what the key expressions singled out as "vague" mean.

(b) supported premises

As with all arguments, the premises of an inductive argument need support--at least the primary premises needed to establish the conclusion do. This takes us back, of course, to Step #1, but it is well worth repeating here. Absence of such support diminishes the inductive strength of the argument.

Consider, for instance, the argument contained in the following selection:
(c)   Although men as well as women struggle with extra pounds, in our culture fat seems to be particularly a woman's problem. I do not know whether there are more fat women than fat men, although women's bodies do contain a higher proportion of fat. But women far outnumber men in organizations like Weight Watchers or Overeaters Anonymous. Almost every issue of most women's magazines announces the newest diet; not so magazines for men. Whether or not women are fatter than men, they worry about it more.
(Elsa Dixler, "Fat Liberation," Psychology Today, May 1980, p. 110)

The conclusion, stated in the first sentence, is

that "in our culture fat seems to be particularly a
woman's problem." This is supported by 4 main premises,
each of which is unsupported. Yet they each need some
support and discussion. Do women's bodies contain a
greater proportion of fat than do men's? What does
"far outnumber" indicate in the second premise? As
it stands, it is pretty impressionistic. Do women
worry more than men about fat? And so on.

We would comment on this argument as follows:

support space	main argument space	evaluation space

1. Women's bodies do contain ← support needed
   a higher proportion of
   fat (than do men's)

2. Women far outnumber men in ← support
   organizations like WW or   needed
   OA.

3. Almost every issue of most ← support
   women's magazines announces   needed
   the newest diet; not so
   magazines for men.

4. Whether or not women are ← support
   fatter than men, they worry   needed
   about it more.

∴ In our culture fat seems to
   be particularly a woman's
   problem.

Consider next this argument:
(d) Perhaps the most fascinating of all theories
   [of why the dinosaurs died] is that the dinosaurs simply died of "group old age." Every
   animal has an established life-span. There
   is considerable evidence that a species itself may well grow old and die just as do
   the individuals within it.
   (J.D. Ratcliff, "The Case of the Vanishing
   Monsters," in The Editors of Reader's Digest
   Secrets of the Past (New York: Berkley Books,
   1980), p.65)

This inductive argument contains 2 premises and 1
conclusion. While premise 2 states that "there is
considerable evidence that..." it does not mention

what this evidence is. It is unsupported, as is
premise 1. Both need support, although probably the
second more than the first.

support space	main argument space	evaluation space
	1. Every animal has an ◄── established life-span.	support needed
	2. There is considerable ◄──── evidence that a species itself may well grow old and die just as do the individuals within it.	support needed
	∴ The dinosaurs simply died of "group old age."	

How much support an arguer should provide a premise
in an inductive argument depends very much on the
context in which he is arguing. In general, he should
strive to make his contention more plausible than its
negation, although, even here, the lengths he needs
to go to accomplish this will vary with the situation.
As has already been pointed out, it will very much
depend on the purposes or objectives he has in mind
in arguing, his assessment of audience expectations,
the information at hand, etc.

It should be recognized, however, how support for a
premise can vary. Suppose you are arguing as follows:

1. ...
2. ...
3. There is increased use of
   marijuana in City X's high
   schools.
4. ...
   ⋮
   ──────────────────────────
∴ ...

Suppose, moreover, you wish to support premise 3, as
you undoubtedly should. There are several ways of
going about this.

By way of a mini-premise you might point out the
following:

High school Y in City X surveyed 94% of
its students in 1979 and found that at
least 81% of them had used marijuana at
least once.
This mini-premise provides very weak support for
premise (3), for at least the following reasons:
(a) it doesn't show increased use, which
is, after all, what you're claiming.
(b) it examines only 1 high school in City
X, although premise (3) makes a more
general claim about all City X's high
schools. (If City X contains more than
1 high school, then we'd have to in-
quire if there is good reason to
suppose that the situation is the
same in those other high schools as
in high school Y)
(c) it doesn't indicate much about use.
(does "used once" count as "use"?)

Instead of the mini-premise above, you might try the
following one:
A survey of all existing City X high schools
indicated the following:
1959 - 2064 students reported using marijuana at least
once
1969 - 4141   "   "   "   "   "   "
1979 - 8301   "   "   "   "   "   "
In this mini-premise, we have some comparative figures
spanning three decades. Yet there are some problems:
(a) Has there been a corresponding increase
in the number of students in City X's
high schools between 1959 and 1979?
In other words, we need to know the total student
population in 1959, 1969, and 1979 for the high
schools in City X if we are to be able to judge if
there has in fact been an increased use of marijuana
in those schools during this period. Let us consider
three hypothetical situations concerning how the
total student body in the high schools of City X
increased during these two decades. They will shed
some considerable light on what the statistics cited
in the mini-premise really indicate.

Consider the following three circumstances:

366

date	usage	number of students		
		(1)	(2)	(3)
1959	2064	4541	4541	4541
1969	4141	9080	6814	13623
1979	8301	18166	10239	40869

In situation (1), the number of students reporting using marijuana doubled between 1959 and 1969 (so did the total number of students in the student body); between 1969 and 1979, it again doubled (as did the total number of students). In other words, in each year, the same proportion of students in the total student population used marijuana at least once. In this instance, the figures cited in the mini-premise do not support a proportional increase in the use of marijuana. Its proportional use has remained constant.

In situation (2), the number of students reporting using marijuana doubled between 1959 and 1969 (but the total number of students increased by only one and a half times); between 1969 and 1979, it again doubled (but again the total number of students increased only 1.5 times). In other words, in each succeeding year, the proportion of students using marijuana increased. Here the figures cited in the mini-premise would support a claim that there has been a proportional increase in the use of marijuana.

In situation (3), while usage doubles each decade, the total number of students triples. Consequently, there has been a proportional decrease in the use of marijuana-usage by students.

As we can readily see from these hypothetical figures concerning the total number of students, it is absolutely crucial for us to know this number if we are to understand and assess the figures cited in the mini-premise properly. There are, in addition, other problems with the mini-premise:
> (b) are the social pressures on students
>   to report marijuana-usage the same in
>   all three years sampled?
> (c) does "used once" count as "usage"?
> (d) are these 3 years typical?

To rectify some of these problems you might try a

367

different mini-premise. Consider, for instance, the
following candidate:

A survey of all existing high schools in
City X indicated the following:

1959 - 42% of students reported using marijuana
at least once
1969 - 61% "   "   "   "   "
1979 - 83% "   "   "   "   "

This is a superior mini-premise to the two previously
considered: it indicates percentage of usage and it
takes into account all high schools in City X. Some
problems, however, remain:

(a) are the social pressures on students to
report marijuana-usage the same in all
3 years sampled?
(b) does "used once" count as "usage"?
(c) are these 3 years typical?

In an inductive argument, premises can vary widely in
the amount of support they provide the conclusion. As
argument analysts we need to note very carefully what
is claimed in the inductive generalization, what is
provided in the inductive base, and to look at the
relationship between the two very critically.

(c) informative inductive base

As has already been indicated, the inductive base is
that from which an arguer reasons in an inductive
argument. In a good, carefully thought out inductive
argument the inductive base will be made clear and
sufficient details will have been provided so as to
support the inductive generalization in an informative manner. It should be sufficient so as to enable
us to see that what is brought forward as inductive
support does indeed support the more general point
being made.

Consider the following argument:
(e)   Interestingly enough, studies have shown
that once a person reaches 21, his ability
to remember drops off sharply. Therefore
effective rapid learning, it would appear,
takes place prior to age 21.

There are many flaws in this inductive argument. For
one thing, several of the key expressions in the
premise are vague: e.g. "ability to remember," and
"drops off sharply." Moreover, more needs to be said
(perhaps by way of an additional premise) about how
the ability to remember relates to effective rapid
learning. There is, however, another kind of defect
here.

The argument indicates the inductive base--"studies."
But that is all it indicates. We are not told:
- when those studies were carried out
- where those studies were carried out
- by whom those studies were carried out
- on whom (the subjects) those studies were
    carried out
- for how long those studies were carried out
In other words, we are not told any of the <u>details</u>
of the studies. The finding, moreover, is presented
in exceptionally vague terms. Furthermore, we are
provided with no means of going to the published
version of the studies so as to check up on these
matters. The inductive base is uninformative. (Indeed,
as it stands, the premise simply appeals to authority,
the authority of "studies.") The arguer needs to
provide much more support by giving us the details
of the various studies.

We would evaluate the argument as follows (focusing
here simply on the informativeness of the inductive
base):

support space	main argument space	evaluation space
studies	1. Once a person reaches 21, his ability to remember drops off sharply.	inductive base insufficiently informative (provide details, e.g. ...)
	∴ Effective rapid learning takes place prior to age 21.	

Consider this argument again:
(f) According to many studies done by Dr. G. Smack
     at the Marijuana Research Clinic in Sacramento,
     daily smoking of pot by males aged 18-28 sig-
     nificantly reduces the sperm count. Thus smoking

pot greatly reduces the male sex drive.

In this argument, the inductive base provides us with
some information. We are told where the studies were
carried out, by whom, and on whom. But we are not
told: when these studies were done, how much "pot"
was smoked daily, how long "pot" was smoked daily,
on how many males the studies were based, how long
the studies were carried out for, etc. The inductive
base is insufficiently informative.

support space	main argument space	evaluation space

Dr.Smack's studies
- M.R.Clinic,
  Sacramento
- daily smoking of
  pot
- males, 18-28
	1. Daily smoking of
	   pot by males aged
	   18-28 significantly
	   reduces the sperm
	   count.
		inductive base
		insufficiently
		informative (pro-
		vide details,e.g.
		...)

	.˙. Smoking pot greatly
	   reduces the male sex
	   drive.	

Consider next this argument:
(g) The last three batches of wine I've made from
     Tastee Grape Concentrate have turned to sour
     vinegar. Thus Tastee Grape Concentrate is an
     inferior product.

The inductive base is the arguer's experience with
the batches of Tastee Grape Concentrate. Before we
leap to the conclusion, however, we need to know
more details about the inductive base: e.g. were
directions followed? was sterile equipment used?
were precautions taken against contact with fruit
flies? etc. The inductive base is insufficiently
informative. It may very well be the case that the
troubles lie with the arguer's wine-making procedures
and not with the product.

support space	main argument space	evaluation space

	1. The last 3 batches of ←—— wine I've made from
	   T.G.C. turned to sour
	   vinegar
		inductive base
		insufficiently
		informative (pro-
		vide details;e.g.
		...)

370

 .·. T.G.C. is an inferior
  product

Consider one more argument:
(h) 3. <u>The prayer for others</u>. Such prayers are
  potent because, first of all, they are a wonder-
  ful way of getting ourselves off our hands. And
  they are powerful because they <u>can</u> change the
  lives of others.

   An elderly woman once told me how she had
  been dangerously ill in the hospital, and in
  pain. She had lost her courage and was fighting
  against tests she needed, because it seemed to
  her that she could bear no more pain. But one
  day a note came from her church--a place where
  prayer meetings had long since gone out of
  fashion--to tell her that her friends had
  formed a prayer circle and would pray all that
  night for her. "About one o'clock," she said,
  "I fell asleep and slept as soundly as a child."
  The next day she went cheerfully to take her
  tests and began a slow but steady convalescence.
   (Ardis Whitman, "Six Special Powers of
  Prayer," <u>Reader's Digest</u>, May 1980)

There are a number of difficulties here. For one
thing, in order to establish a link between prayer
and the patient's recovery here, we would need to
know more about this particular situation: e.g.
the patient's medication, possible sedation, possible
alternative sources of comfort and cheerfulness (e.g.
visiting friends, family, a book, patient's own inner
resources, etc.), etc. For another thing, in order to
establish a connection generally between prayer and
recovery, we would need to examine other cases where
a patient recovered without the benefit of prayer
and where the patient did not recover and yet had
the benefit of prayer. The inductive base is insufficiently informative.

support space	main argument space	evaluation space
	1. They are a wonderful way of getting our- selves off our hands.	

371

```
example of elderly ⎫◄──────────────────────── inductive base
woman, dangerously ⎪  ┌─2. They can change the     insufficiently
ill & losing hope, ⎬ ↗   lives of others.          informative (pro
is prayed for and  ⎪                                vide details: e.
recovers.          ⎭     ─────────────────────        ...)

                    ∴ Prayer for others is
                      potent.
```

(d) well-founded statistics

Not all inductive arguments present statistics, but
in those that do it is important that we be able to
see how these statistics were arrived at and on what
they are based. Good inductive arguments provide
details, thereby presenting well-founded statistical
information. Expert knowledge here would require, of
course, detailed study of statistical methods, a
matter that lies beyond the scope of this book. There
are, however, some facets of statistics of which even
the non-specialist should be aware. A few of these
are as follows:

(i) dubious statistics

Consider the following argument:
(i)   Since 1800 there have been 196,442 diets de-
      signed for weight loss. Of these, 196,438 have
      failed to produce long term effects for most
      of their dieters. The reason for this is that
      virtually all of these diets have worked on
      the principle of reducing caloric intake by
      one means or another. The Sure Fire Weight
      Loss Program (SFWLP) is different, however.
      Therefore, by following the Sure Fire Weight
      Loss Program, permanent weight loss will be
      assured.

This inductive argument contains three main premises,
the second main premise being supported by a mini-
premise ("The reason for this is...".). Aside from
several other difficulties (e.g. the unsupported
third premise), the statistics in premises (1) and
(2) are at best dubious. It is highly unlikely that
one can at this point identify and enumerate all the

diets since 1800 (in how many countries?), let alone
measure how many have failed to produce long term
weight loss. In evaluation space we would indicate
that such statistics are dubious.

(ii) absurdly precise statistics

One restaurant in Toronto used to advertise as follows:
(j)   In 1975 customers at Restaurant... consumed:
      6,551 miles of spaghetti, 185,601 meatballs,
      507,978 salads, 4,254 gals. of spaghetti sauce,
      10,216 lbs. of veal, and 13,246 lbs. of chicken.
      <Thus Restaurant ... is a popular (or fine)
      restaurant.>

The figures are, of course, absurdly precise. Even if
we generously do not construe 'consume' literally,
restaurant managing practices do not allow such precise quantification. In evaluation space we would
indicate that such statistics are absurdly precise.

Consider this argument:
(k)   In 1980 the average family of 2 adults and
      1.8 children needs at least $13,429.78 to
      maintain minimum levels of housing, food,
      and clothing. Thus the government must act
      immediately to enact a non-taxable Supple-
      mentary Grants Program for families whose
      combined income is less than this necessary
      amount.

Note that one basic key expression--"minumum levels
of..."--is not defined. But note also the absurdly
precise statistic of 1.8 children. When talking of
families (although not of average number of children
in families generally), this figure is simply absurd.
Note, too, the precise figure of $13,429.78, an
absurdly exact statistic given the range of life-
styles, health, occupations, and ages of those in
the families concerned. Again we would indicate that
such figures are absurdly precise.

(iii) improper comparisons

Many arguments present comparative statistics. In
such cases it is important (1) to make clear what
is being compared with what and (2) to make sure

that the items being compared are comparable. Comparisons often go astray on either of these requirements
Consider, for instance, the following argument:
(1)   In test after test, ... Toothpaste has proven
       effective in reducing cavities. In 1952, users
       had 28% fewer cavities; in 1963, 32% fewer
       cavities; in 1968, 24% fewer cavities; in
       1972, 26% fewer cavities; etc. Thus ... Tooth-
       paste is an essential component of dental
       hygiene.

The statistics in this inductive argument sound impressive until one asks: fewer cavities than what?
With what is this toothpaste being compared? Another
toothpaste? No toothpaste at all? Or what? The answer is not given: the arguer has not specified with
what this toothpaste is being compared. As a result,
we are in no position to judge the merits of these
statistics. The comparison, then, is improper because
it is incomplete. In evaluation space we would point
out that these statistics are improperly compared
(toothpaste compared with what?).

Consider next this argument:
(m)   In 1979 Americans making an income of $25,000
       would pay $6550 in taxes, whereas Canadians
       making the same amount would pay $7879. Thus
       Canadians pay a high price (approximately 20%)
       for independence from the U.S.A.

Assuming that it even makes sense to cost out political independence in such economic terms, what are
being compared are U.S. taxes and Canadian taxes.
The comparison is clear, but are they comparable
items? To answer this question, we would need to
research such matters as the following: are the
currencies at par? are the exemptions comparable?
are the benefits the same (do the people in one
country pay through taxes for benefits which people
in the other country pay for separately)? is the
structure of taxation the same (federal, state/
provincial, city, sales tax, etc.)? And so on. If
these matters are not the same, then we would have
an improper comparison.

In looking at several mini-premises concerning the
reported usage of marijuana in City X's high schools

in 1959, 1969, 1979 (see pages 366-368 above), we
asked if the social pressures on students to report
marijuana-usage were the same in all three years
sampled. In asking this we were asking if the comparisons were properly made. If the social pressures
have indeed changed (from, perhaps, the tendency to
hide marijuana-usage in 1959 to, perhaps, the tendency to over-emphasize it in 1979), then the comparisons are apt to be misleading. If the social
pressures are not the same, then the comparison
is improper.

A similar situation occurs in the study of rape. It
has been argued that statistics from the 1950's and
earlier (or from other cultures) are apt to be mis-
leadingly low because of social stigma on having
been raped and, consequently, of the extreme reluc-
tance to report rape in former decades. If this is
the case, then comparative statistics regarding
rape over the decades is very likely to be misleading.

In circumstances where social pressures have changed,
it is very difficult, if not impossible, to obtain
reliable comparable statistical figures. Similar
considerations beset the comparative statistical
study of such matters as suicide, abortion, and
euthanasia between our time and earlier times. It
also complicates cross-cultural comparative statistics.

(iv) omitted statistics

Many arguments omit relevant statistics needed to
place in perspective the significance of the figures
cited. An example of this is an argument already
considered
(n)   The last three batches of wine I've made from
      Tastee Grape Concentrate have turned to sour
      vinegar. Thus Tastee Grape Concentrate is an
      inferior product.
Three batches out of how many attempts at wine-making?
This is an important omitted statistic, for our evaluation of the significance of 3 batches will differ
if the arguer has made only 3 or 4 attempts rather
than 30 or 40 attempts. In evaluation space we should

indicate that a statistic has been omitted and the general nature of that statistic.

support space	main argument space	evaluation space
	1. The last 3 batches of◄—wine I've made from Tastee Grape Concentrate have turned to sour vinegar.	statistics omitted (3 batche out of how many attempts with the same product?)

∴ Tastee Grape Concentrate
is an inferior product.

Consider next this argument:
(o)   A grant of $78,000 is urgently needed to develop
a course in college-level English proficiency.
Two-thirds of the incoming students tested indicated a lower than average ability to read and
write college-level English.

This inductive argument contains a number of flaws.
For one thing, several key expressions are vague--
"lower than average ability," "college-level English."
Moreover, it is missing a premise, one that would
show that the sum of $78,000 would produce the much
needed course. In addition, it contains a defect of
another sort. Note carefully the inductive base: a
study on two-thirds of the incoming students tested.
This is phrased in a rather interesting manner, for
it fails to tell us just how many students were teste
Were all of them tested? most of them? some of them?
or perhaps only 3 students were tested, 2 of them
indicating deficiencies in English proficiency. The
last situation is not ruled out by what the premise
states, and yet if this were the case the support
would be much less than if all the students had been
tested. An important statistic has been omitted.

support space	main argument space	evaluation space
	1. Two-thirds of the ◄—incoming students tested indicated.. ..English	statistic omitted (2/3 of how many students?)

∴ A grant of $78,000
...college-level
English proficiency.

This concludes a very brief foray into statistical matters. It's enough, however, to indicate certain important aspects of the use of statistics in argumentation of which we ought to be wary. More advanced work in this area would consider problems with percentages, confusions concerning averages, appropriate methods for obtaining statistical results, interpreting the significance of statistical findings, sampling techniques, the use of charts to enhance or to suppress certain aspects of statistical results, calculation of probabilities, and so on.

(e) size of sample in inductive base

In inductive arguments, the inductive base is always more limited than the inductive generalization. This is simply another way of saying that the conclusion of an inductive argument always goes beyond the evidence presented in the premises. This is the case in all three kinds of reasoning which we have mentioned as characteristically inductive.

If the inductive base is a statement concerning what has been the case in the past, then it is limited because only selected, partial aspects of the past are examined in order to arrive at a generalization concerning what is likely to happen in the future. Similarly, if the inductive base consists of selected examples of a particular phenomenon, then it, too, is limited because examples, by definition, are simply restricted (but hopefully typical) instances of the phenomenon under consideration. Finally, if the inductive base is a statement concerning what was found to be the case in one or more studies, then it, too, is limited because studies cannot by their very nature examine all instances of what is being studied.

Because the inductive base is always limited, it is always possible that in the eventuality of further evidence, the conclusion put forward initially may be heavily challenged or even over-turned. This serves to indicate the provisional, tentative, probabilistic nature of the inductive conclusion, no matter how secure it may currently seem.

377

As has already been pointed out, it is important that we be provided with an informative inductive base, one that employs clear terms, and which supports--at least to some extent--the inductive generalization. Typical features of the inductive base that ought to be included have already been indicated: e.g., for studies, where, when, by whom, on whom, for how long, etc. the studies were carried out. Two additional features of the inductive base are also important to our understanding and assessment of the merits of an inductive argument: the size of the sample in the inductive base, and its representativeness. Let us consider sample size first.

"Sample size" refers to the number of things, items or persons discussed or examined in the inductive base and used to support the inductive generalization. The sample size may be one personal experience or the experiences of several, one example or several, a number of subjects tested or interviewed or who responded to a questionnaire, a number of items or objects tested or experimented on, etc.

It is important to note the size of the sample in the inductive base, the general principle being that other things being equal, the inductive base with the greater sample size is less apt to be misleading concerning the nature of the phenomenon being generalized about. The phrase "other things being equal" is, of course, important, for errors in procedure, counting, research design, etc. can throw off the reliability of even a large sample.

There is, moreover, no absolute, general answer to the theoretical question: how large must a sample size be to establish a particular inductive generalization? The inductive generalization always goes beyond the limited portion examined in the inductive base and so there is constantly the risk that the next item which could have been examined but wasn't will be somewhat different from those that were. But that's the nature of inductive reasoning: it involves risk. In the inductive base we endeavor to minimize the risk in as intelligent a fashion as possible.

Let us consider several inductive arguments with
sample size in mind:
(p) I've taken vitamin C now daily for 8 months and
     I haven't had a cold. Therefore vitamin C is
     effective in preventing colds.

We should note at the outset that the inductive base
is not particularly informative in this example. We
are given no information concerning any of the following: the number of colds this person had before
taking vitamin C daily; what else the person has
been taking or doing during these 8 months which
might also account for the absence of colds; what
counts or does not could as a "cold"; what might
have happened if the person had not taken vitamin
C, etc. Nor, of course, are we told the vitamin C
dosage.

Not only is the inductive base not especially informative, it is also highly limited in scope. The
sample size is 1--the experience of one person. It
is a very small sample size and one that is not
particularly supportive of the conclusion. It
would not even be supportive of a much narrower
claim that vitamin C is effective, at least for
the arguer, in preventing colds. We would point out
the very small sample size as follows:

support space	main argument space	evaluation space
	1.I've taken vitamin C ←	ind.base insufft.
	now daily for 8 months	informative.
	and I haven't had a ↖	
	cold.	small ind.base: 1
		personal experience

          .˙.vitamin C is effective
             in preventing colds.

A small sample size is simply that: a small sample
size. It is, perhaps, a bit better than no information
at all, but not much better. We should be wary and
sceptical of inductive generalizations based on such
limited samples.

This, of course, does not vitiate all arguments from
personal experience. There are many such arguments,

379

for example:

(i) I have used X laundry detergent daily
with no problems whatsoever. Therefore
laundry detergent X is a fine product.

(ii) I have always found Y to be honest and
trustworthy, a person of extreme integrity
and conscientiousness. Therefore Y would
make a perfectly reliable financial advisor
and estate manager.

(iii) I had cancer several years ago and after
praying all night I suddenly began to get
better until several months later the
doctors could find no trace of cancer at
all. Therefore miracles do happen, even
in this advanced age.

(iv) Even though I was fully prepared for the
experience, my abortion was a nightmare and
even now I wake up at nights thinking about
that horrible clinic. Therefore abortion is
a traumatic experience, even in the best of
circumstances.

(v) I have frequently shopped at ... Supermarket and have found the variety of food-
stuffs there and the prices satisfactory
and highly competitive. Therefore ... Supermarket is an excellent place at which to
shop.

(vi) I have found over and over again in my life
that things are rarely as bleak as they seem
It is important, therefore, in times of des-
pair and despondency, to remember that hope
will triumph in the end.

And so on. In all these cases, we should note that the
size of the inductive base is 1 and that it is theref
small. We should be wary and sceptical of such conclusions, no matter how sincere and vehement the
arguer reports his personal experience.

By noting the size of the inductive base as 1, we
indicate its exceptionally low level of support for
the inductive generalization. It is perhaps better

than no evidence at all (it at least allegedly
happened to one person!) but it is a long way from
providing substantial support which would warrant
our acceptance of the inductive generalization.

Suppose we have the following slightly augmented
version of argument (p):
>   I've taken vitamin C now daily for 8 months
>   and I haven't had a cold. So have 7 of my
>   friends. Therefore vitamin C is effective in
>   preventing colds.

Again the inductive base is not very informative:
the same sort of questions reoccur here as they did
with (p). Also its inductive base is still small: 8,
all personal experiences.

The same sorts of considerations also apply to examples. Examples are by their very nature limited and
restrictive. They are presumably selected and presented as typical or as illustrative of the inductive
generalization. (Indeed, their very strength rests
on the extent to which they are typical or representative of what is being claimed in the inductive
generalization.) They provide, however, a small
inductive base. Again this should be noted.

Consider, for instance, a mini-argument that was
considered in Chapter Five (see p.169 above). We
would evaluate this mini-argument as follows:

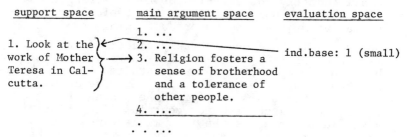

support space	main argument space	evaluation space
1. Look at the work of Mother Teresa in Calcutta.	1. ... 2. ... 3. Religion fosters a sense of brotherhood and a tolerance of other people. 4.	ind.base: 1 (small)

Studies, on the other hand, vary enormously in the
number of subjects, individuals, or items studied.
Many factors enter here: the availability of subjects
or items for study, various cost factors, time
factors, the general research design concerning what

is or is not an appropriate number of subjects for
testing, and so forth. Again, very generally, the
more subjects or items available for testing or
study, other things being equal, the less likely
the sample is apt to mislead us about the phenomenon
concerning which the inductive generalization is
made.

Some reports of studies fail to mention sample size.
This was the case, for example, in selection (i) in
Chapter Three (see p.97 above). The selection mentions the U.S. Surgeon General's Report, but it
does not cite the sample size. This is a serious
omission, and we would note it in evaluation space
(inductive base: not specified). Similarly, selection
(k) in Chapter Three (see p.102 above) omits the
sample size in Moynihan's study and also in Butler,
Wilson and others' studies on honeybees and ants.
Again this is a serious omission, for without this
information, we have no basis on which to judge the
adequacy of the finding.

Some studies examine only 1 item or sample, a very
small sample indeed. Selection (j) in Chapter Three
(see page 100 above) examined only one Boeing 707
flight. Consumers Union (see Consumer Reports)
routinely tests only one of each kind of product
from each manufacturer. Such studies with such
small inductive bases rely for their strength on
the extent to which the sample is typical or representative of the item or product being examined.

Other studies are considerably richer. In selection
(f) in Chapter Eight (see p.256 above), 366 adults
between the ages of 20-30 were studied. In all cases
we should note the size of sample in the inductive
base. We should also prefer, other things being
equal, those studies which contain a larger sample
size. They are apt to be less misleading, but even
here, regardless of sample size, there are risks.
Risks cannot be avoided in inductive reasoning,
only intelligently safeguarded against.

(f) representativeness of sample in inductive base

Very closely connected with sample size is the representativeness of the sample in the inductive base. In so far as it is possible to judge, the sample in the inductive base should be typical or representative of the phenomenon about which the inductive generalization is being made.

In a good inductive argument, the arguer will take steps to make a case that the sample in the inductive base is truly representative of whatever is being generalized about. Careful inductive reasoning takes pains to provide a good, typical inductive base. Such a base increases inductive strength. An inductive base that is unrepresentative, or of doubtful representativeness, or of unknown representativeness diminishes inductive strength.

One extreme is sheer unrepresentativeness. A study, for example, which purported to make some claim about women's career proclivities based solely on an examination of men aged 18-25 would not at all be representative. Similarly, a study which makes a general claim about the tendencies in all people to behave obediently to perceived authority figures based solely on men making less than $8000 a year would not be representative of all people. If we come across arguments containing unrepresentative samples in the inductive base, we should indicate this in evaluation space (inductive base: unrepresentative).

Doubtful representativeness is not at all uncommon. Selection (j) in Chapter Three (see p.100 above) examined only one Boeing 707 flight. On that very limited inductive base the argument went on to generalize about the distribution of smoke throughout airplanes. Before we accept this inductive conclusion, however, we need to know (1) how representative Boeing 707s are of all airplanes, and (2) how representative this Boeing 707 is of all Boeing 707s. Without this information being provided, the inductive base is of doubtful representativeness. We would indicate that in evaluation space (inductive base: doubtful representativeness).

Perhaps much more common in inductive reasoning is unknown representativeness. With reports of personal

experience, representativeness is often very difficult, if not impossible, to judge. How representative
is the person who experiences no colds after taking
vitamin C daily for 8 months? How representative are
his 7 friends who do likewise? How representative is
the person who recovers from cancer after praying?
Or the person who shops at ... Supermarket? And so
forth. Such questions are hard to answer. In such
cases we should simply indicate that the representativeness of such samples is unknown (inductive
base: representativeness unknown) or at least raise
the possibility that the representativeness is unknown (inductive base: representativeness?).

The same sorts of considerations apply also to examples, for here the strength of the examples lies in
the extent to which the arguer can support his claim
that these examples are indeed typical or representative of whatever he is generalizing about.

3. Summary

Step #9

In evaluating inductive arguments we cannot immediately and mechanically step in and say, "Ah hah!
This is a strong inductive argument" or "This is a
weak inductive argument." With this sort of argument
we do not have the same kind of procedures as we did
with deductive arguments. Instead we must look systematically at certain specific features of the argument, taking into account a number of guidelines.

Putting the various considerations together, Step #9
goes as follows:

> Step #9
> In an inductive argument, by considering
> the following
> (a) clear key expressions (see also Step#2)
> (b) supported premises (see also Step#1)
> (c) informative inductive base
> (d) well-founded statistics
>   (i) dubious statistics
>   (ii) absurdly precise statistics

384

      (iii) improper comparisons
      (iv) omitted statistics
  (e) size of sample in inductive base
  (f) representativeness of sample in
      inductive base
draw attention to those features of the
argument which serve to diminish its inductive strength.

It should be noted, of course, that this is by no
means an exhaustive list of considerations. See,
for instance, the additional matters referred to
above as included in more advanced study of inductive
reasoning. There are others: e.g. arguing from a
dubious or highly controversial explanatory or
theoretical basis (without arguing for its theoretical
merits). Examples of this include: arguing from a
Flat Earth theoretical perspective to dismiss space
pictures and global circumnavigation as hoaxes;
arguing from astrological horoscopes to indicate
what course of action should be followed by a particular individual on a particular day; and arguing
from the Bible on moral matters; etc. In each case
there may be considerable merit in arguing from a
Flat Earth perspective, from astrology, or from the
Bible, etc., but such theoretical frameworks need
discussion and justification.

Recall Quiz

(1)   What is an "inductive" argument?

(2)   To what does "the inductive base" refer? "in-
       ductive generalization"?

(3)   Indicate 3 different sorts of inductive bases.

(4)   In what 2 ways does the evaluation of inductive
       arguments differ from deductive arguments?

(5)   Why is it important to have clear key expressions
       in an inductive argument? supported premises?
       an informative inductive base? well-founded
       statistics? good sample size? representative
       samples?

(6) How are defects in inductive arguments annotated in evaluation space?

(7) What is Step #9?

Exercise #1

Identify the arguments contained in the following selections. Then critically evaluate them in terms of Step #9.

(1) According to recent figures released by the Bureau of National Statistics, only 1 out of every 5 marriages is truly happy. This is a shocking statistic and it shows that people are basically incapable of making marriage work.

(2) In my experience and those of several of my close friends, Dorfs are nothing but trouble. My Dorf's transmission broke down completely within the first 85 miles and even after that was fixed, the brakes went in 5,000 miles and the shocks in 8,000. John's Dorf dumped its oil on Interstate 75 while he was going 70 and this ruined his whole engine. George's Dorf was a lemon right from the start and spent most of its early life in the dealer's garage being fixed.

(3) Kraus and Kojak recently published figures in Science showing that 82% of all rubber plants grow best when acid rock music is played constantly for 18 hours a day. They urge that plant-lovers play such music daily so that their plants may enjoy the vibrations and grow as rapidly as possible.

(4) In 1890 only four million Americans had used marijuana according to recently released figures. By 1979 this number had jumped to eight million Americans. Thus there has been a significant increase in the number of Americans who use marijuana.

(5) Abortion is murder. Many religious authorities

386

agree with this contention. There are numerous examples: Pope John Paul II, Gregory Baum, Bishop Fulton Sheen, and Father Xavier all maintain that abortion is the killing of a human being.

(6)   SPERM PERK UP WITH CAFFEINE
Sperm swim twice as fast when they get a caffeine boost, according to an Israeli fertility expert quoted in Omni magazine.
Dr. Joseph Barkay of Central Emek Hospital in Afula, Israel, artificially inseminated 58 women with five parts semen to one part caffeine. There were 10 per cent more pregnancies in this group than in a control group.
(from a newspaper account of an article in Omni)

(7) In 1969 there were 46 reported rapes in City X, whereas in 1979 there were 182. Thus over a 10 year period rapes in City X have quadrupled.

(8) In City X, in 1979, there were 182 reported rapes. In City X, in 1979, the population stood at 2,100,000. Thus women in City X have a 0.00008% chance of being raped and rape is not a significant problem.

(9) For every child there is one guardian angel. The world can accommodate, at the maximum, only 98,550,441 children. Thus there are a maximum of 98,550,441 guardian angels, not all of whom are fully occupied in child-tending at any one time.

(10) I'm a Scorpio. The horoscope for Scorpios today reads: "Business plummets as associates call shots, get angry. Judgment off, and travel is hazardous. Taurus and number 0 figure prominently." Consequently I'll stay home today.

(11) Peace is illusory and the quest for peace doomed to failure. Humans are, after all, basically hostile beings, prone to conflict and violence as a way of life. The evidence for this is overwhelming: in all of recorded history there hasn't been a day without con-

387

flict. Indeed, since 2000 B.C. there have been 145,197 recorded wars.

(12) Product X reaches a higher level of pain relief than does its competitors. Therefore product X is a superior product.

(13) According to recent statistics, the Zlata Bll has outperformed all other cars in its class by 2:1. Thus Zlata Bll is a superior car.

(14)   SMOKING AFFECTS WOMEN

- More women are dying.

Mrs. Jean Nygren, a 34 year old mother of 2, is dead, the victim of lung cancer. She smoked two packs of cigarettes a day.

- More women are smoking.

In 1966 statistics showed that 11,444,987 girls aged 15-19 smoked; in 1977 this figure had swelled to 13,532,117.

- More women are dying earlier.
- More women are dying from diseases that once were comparatively rare for them: lung and heart diseases.

U.S. studies show that women smokers suffer nine times more deaths from coronary heart disease than do women nonsmokers and that the death rate among women from emphysema is five times as high for women with a history of smoking as for nonsmokers.

- It is evident, then, that smoking affects women.

(15) A study by psychologists Trygg Engen, of Brown University, and Brian Ross, of Catholic University, proved that the memory of odors is uniquely long-lived. When asked to remember visual details of pictures, most people could do so with nearly 100 percent accuracy after short periods of time. After three months, however, their ability dropped to about 50 percent accuracy. Subjects asked to remember smells, on the other hand, displayed only 80 percent accuracy over short periods. But this accuracy level did not drop even after a year's time.

      (Janet L. Hopson, "Scent: Our Hot-Blooded

Sense," in <u>Science Digest Special</u>, Summer 1980, p.52)

(16)   QUAKING COYOTES
About the "Newsline" item on animal behavior prior to earthquakes (February). We have six dogs and more cats than I care to think about. We noticed no odd behavior in them before the earthquake that shook our valley last August-- none more odd than usual, that is.

However, for about two weeks before the quake, we noticed, daily, far more coyotes traveling along and on the freeway than we have seen in our many years of residence here. The coyotes seemed to be confused, traveling erratically, as if they didn't know where they were going or why....This phenomenon did not occur before, nor has it occurred since the aftershocks died down.

Coyotes and other wild animals are not as accustomed to the earth shakings caused by trucks and jets...as domestic animals are.... Could it be that domestic animals are de- sensitized to the possibility of earthquakes by vehicle-caused tremors, while coyotes remain sensitive? Perhaps earthquake researchers would have more success if they would concentrate on the behavior of wild animals rather than that of domestic ones.

(letter by Merry Harris, Ocotillo, Calif., to <u>Psychology Today</u>, May 1980, p. 10).

(17) As a medical doctor with some 28 years'experience, I can say with some degree of assurance that I've personally found a very high level of job satisfaction indeed in my chosen profession. A medical career, therefore, is truly a reward- ing one.

<u>Exercise #2</u>

Identify the argument (or arguments) contained in either one of the following selections. Then evalu- ate it critically in terms of Step #9.

(a) Stanley Milgram, "Behavioral Study of Obedience,"

Journal of Abnormal and Social Psychology 67
(1963) and reprinted in the Bobbs-Merrill
Reprint series in the Social Sciences (#P 521).

(2) D.L. Rosenhan, "On Being Sane in Insane Places,
Science 179 (Jan.19, 1973), 250-28.

Exercise #3
Collect several print advertisements that use inductive reasoning. Identify the argument each contains and critically evaluate it in terms of Step #9.

Exercise #4
Collect several inductive arguments from any written
source. Identify each and critically evaluate it in
terms of Step #9.

Exercise #5
Using only inductive reasoning, prepare and present
an argument in standard essay style (of about 600
words maximum) that defends either one of the following conclusions:

(1) .·. to meet present and anticipated energy
needs, we ought to construct more nuclear
generating stations.

(2) .·. to meet present and anticipated energy
needs, we ought to consider alternatives to
nuclear generating stations (such as solar
power, wind power, etc.).

Exercise #6
As assigned by the course director, identify and
critically evaluate in terms of Step #9 the inductive
arguments contained on the following pages of this
text:

CHAPTER TWELVE

ARGUMENT EVALUATION: ORAL ARGUMENTS

1. Characteristics of Oral Argument: Speakers
    and Listeners

                  successful communication

An argument is not something an arguer creates for
his own amusement or pleasure. It is usually
forged in the heat of controversy, under considerable pressure, as a person attempts to structure
his point of view and put it forward effectively
and persuasively. Putting forward an argument
assumes that there are those who will hear,
reflect on, and respond to the argument which is
being presented. In other words, argumentation
involves not only an arguer but also those whom
the arguer is addressing ("the argument-recipients"
they might generally be dubbed). It is important,
then, that the arguer successfully communicate his
argument to the argument-recipients.

An argument is successfully communicated when the
person hearing or reading the argument correctly
grasps the argument which the arguer has actually
put forward. This means, of course, that the
argument-recipient must be able to differentiate
the different parts of the arguer's argument--i.e.,
the conclusion, the main premises, etc. In this
way the argument-recipient will accurately grasp
both "the what" and "the why" of the arguer's
point of view. When this happens, the arguer has
not only put forward an argument, he has actually
put it across to the argument-recipient(s).

For written arguments, the argument-recipient
ought to be able to grasp the full argument. On
the other hand, for oral arguments (where problems
of memory occur) all that is demanded is that the
argument-recipient grasp the argument for the most

391

<u>part</u>: certainly the conclusion, the main premises,
and the general lines of support for the main
premises (even though many details may not be
remembered).

Putting across an argument successfully does not
mean that the argument-recipient will necessarily
agree with the argument presented. But it does
mean that the argument responded to is the arguer's
and not some imagined or supposed argument the
argument-recipient vaguely thinks the arguer may
have presented. In the rational examination of
issues, it is tremendously important that arguments be presented and put across successfully.

For an argument to be successfully communicated,
there must be <u>a reciprocal relationship</u> between
the person presenting the argument and the person
receiving the argument.

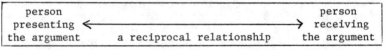

Putting across an argument successfully involves
a two-way process. For his part, the person
presenting the argument prepares and presents a
point of view in a structured manner. Similarly,
for his part, the person receiving the argument
must grasp the argument the speaker has put forward. This means (i) that he must want to grasp
the arguer's argument, and (ii) that he must be
able to discern its structure.

For there to be successful communication, the
process must work both ways:

    * The arguer, for instance, cannot guarantee
      that his argument will be grasped by the
      argument-recipient. It is within his power,
      however, to do all that he can to prepare
      and present the argument in such a way that
      it is capable of being grasped. This
      involves, of course, careful preparation
      and close attention to those facets of
      argumentation that facilitate the communi-
      cation of structure.

* Similarly, too, the arguer cannot make the argument-recipient want to grasp it. Here again, though, there is much the arguer can do. It is within the arguer's power, for example, to put forward the argument in a creative, imaginative, and persuasive fashion, one that would help whet the argument-recipient's attentiveness and interest.

* The argument-recipient, moreover, cannot compel the arguer to present the structure of his argument in an engaging, lucid, memorable manner (although, if the arguer doesn't, the listener is quite apt not to grasp his argument).

And so on. Successful communication depends on both parties involved in controversy. There must be a reciprocal relationship if the argument is to be successfully transferred from arguer to argument-recipient.

the medium of argument

Both parties, moreover, must be aware of and sensitive to the demands of the linguistic medium in which arguments are offered and challenged. The linguistic medium may be either written or oral:

medium:	the arguer is:	the argument-recipient is:
written	the writer	the reader
oral	the speaker	the listener

Each medium presents its own demands on both the arguer and the argument-recipient if successful communication is to occur. These should be carefully noted, especially the requirements of oral argument.

listener's obligations

The obligation on the part of the listener is to be attentive to the argument and to grasp as accurately as possible what the arguer is saying.

This is a matter which takes considerable practice, particularly with respect to oral arguments.
Oral arguments specifically require

* that the argument-recipient listen to
  the argument being presented:

* that he remember what the arguer says: and

* that he learn how to structure mentally
  what the arguer is saying <u>while</u> he is
  saying it.

In these three respects, an oral argument places
much greater demands upon the listener than do
written argument. In a written argument, after
all, the reader can take the time to go over the
argument as many times as is needed in order to
reconstruct its structure fully and accurately.
He can take the time to puzzle over the argument
if some portions of the argument throw him off.
This is not the case with oral argument where the
listener must grasp the structure of what the
arguer is saying while he is saying it.

speaker's obligations

The obligation on the arguer's part is evident.
If he is to communicate his argument successfully
to others, then he must take pains to prepare and
present as clear an argument as he can fashion.
This requires particular attention to structure
and to the facets of argumentation that facilitate
the communication of structure. The speaker must
assist the listener in this respect. This is
especially important in oral argument.

In written contexts, the writer has many ready-
made devices for communicating structure. These
include various numbering devices that make main
premises stand out. They also include visual
devices, such as paragraph structure, indentation,
using "*'s", etc. that serve to indicate to the
reader the various points being made. Paragraph
structure in particular is useful in signaling
to the reader when a shift is being made in the

points under discussion. There is, however, no
paragraph structure in oral argument, no indentation, no sound for '*', <u>etc</u>. A shift in topic,
or a movement from one point to another, has to
be indicated to the listener in other ways in oral
argument.

Similarly, in written argument, the arguer can
assume that the reader can go over and review the
argument, again and again, if portions of it were
not clear on first reading. The reader, too, can
devote his entire energies to search for structure, without having the burden of memory and
recall. And he can do so with some considerable
leisure, reading and re-reading various sections
of the argument which were at first puzzling or
baffling. None of these considerations applies
to arguments in an oral context. An argument is
said and its structure must be grasped as it is
being said. There is no review possible in oral
argument, and considerable demands are placed upon
memory and recall. In an oral context the listener either gets--or fails to get--the structure of
the argument on first hearing. As such the oral
nature of such arguments presents many opportunities for the listener to miss much of what is said
by the arguer.

For these reasons, then, it is imperative that the
arguer who prepares and presents an oral argument
pay particular attention to its structure if he
wishes it to be communicated successfully.

2. Problems in Identifying Oral Arguments

In contrast to written arguments, the oral nature
of oral arguments poses some particular problems
which affect accurate argument identification.
These are as follows:

(1) problems of style

In an oral argument, the medium in which the

argument is presented (spoken language) assumes
a much larger importance than does the medium of
written arguments. This feature places a much
greater burden on speaker and listener alike.
Such matters as the following become very important for the successful communication of the argument:

* the rate at which the speaker speaks.

* voice projection on the part of the speaker
  -- his degree of audibility.

* the speaker's delivery (e.g., pronounciation,
  mannerisms, intonation, variations in speed
  of delivery, liveliness, etc.).

* suitable pauses by the speaker, to allow
  listener to catch up, to reflect, or to
  grasp important points.

* appropriate expressiveness and emphasis on
  the speaker's part, so as to single out
  important points or to lend interest to the
  presentation.

etc.

The speaker who would successfully communicate an
argument to someone must be aware of such considerations and must present his argument with careful attention to matters of style.

(2) problems of communicating structure

In order to put across his argument in an oral
context, the speaker must also pay particular
attention to problems inherent in communicating
structure in this medium. The speaker should
realize that he cannot rely on visual clues (like
paragraph structure, indentation, signs like '*',
etc.) which abound in written contexts, and should
be sensitive to the strain even the most sympathe-
tic listener is under in paying attention to what
is said while simultaneously trying to grasp its
structure. The speaker therefore has to provide
explicit clues as to the structure of what he says,
while he is speaking. Such clues involve the

following:

* giving at the outset of the presentation a brief overview of the conclusion and main points to be covered.

* numbering the main points.

* repeating the main points at the end of the presentation.

* repeating points as the argument proceeds, for emphasis.

* pausing briefly after each main point, to allow it to sink in.

* organizing supporting considerations for main premises in a clear, easily understood manner.

* using locators.

etc.

The use of such clues by the speaker provides the listener with the essential means for making out the structure of what is being said while it is being said.

(3) problems of recall

The arguer in an oral context must also be aware of the great strain he is placing upon his listener's ability to remember and to recall the gist of what he has said. Unless he is sensitive to this feature of oral argument, the speaker runs the risk of the listener's not being able to remember anything he has said or else remembering it in a distorted or partial fashion. In either case successful communication of an argument has failed when this occurs. Bearing in mind the problems of listener recall, the arguer will pay close attention to such considerations as the following:

* speak short, pithy sentences, especially when stating the conclusion or main premises of the argument.

* avoid long lists of figures, examples,

authorities, considerations, etc.

* avoid long sentences that contain a lot
  of detail.

* repeat main points in a succinct fashion.

* develop a good delivery style, with good
  pacing, pauses, and emphasis in your voice.

* utilize clues that indicate to your listener the structure of what you are saying.

etc.

Long sentences with many figures, statistics, or
examples or long sentences with many dependent
clauses or qualifications, while fine in a written
context, will not be remembered in an oral context.
If you want to communicate your points, you won't
utter such sentences. When preparing an oral
argument, prepare it to be spoken. This involves
your being sensitive to the limitations of
memory.

3. Evaluating Oral Arguments

Since oral arguments are arguments, Steps #1
through #9 apply. There is, however, an additional step. Since such arguments are offered in an
oral medium, we should pay particular attention
to the three problem areas mentioned above, to
see if the arguer has faithfully discharged his
obligations in preparing and presenting his argument. They are key factors that affect substantially the extent to which an oral argument will be
successfully communicated. This takes us to Step
#10.

Step #10

Step #10
With respect to oral arguments, discuss the
extent to which the arguer has successfully
communicated his argument to his listeners.
In so doing, consider specifically the

strengths and weaknesses in the way in which
the speaker has coped with problems of style,
communicating structure, and recall.

When evaluating an oral argument, at some convenient place in right (evaluation) space of the
standard format there should be a brief discussion
of the argument as an oral argument, applying
Step #10. In many instances, because of space
limitations in evaluation space, this discussion
may have to be positioned in a space below the
argument as reconstructed. In evaluating an oral
argument in accordance with Step #10, your discussion should take the following form: write, in
evaluating space, the following.

This is an oral argument.
problems of style: strengths -
                    weaknesses -
problems of communicating structure: strengths -
                                      weaknesses -
problems of recall: strengths -
                    weaknesses -
summary: the speaker has (or, has not) successfully
communicated his argument.

Applying Step #10

Consider the following selection. It is intended
to be a transcript of an oral argument. Our task
is to identify and evaluate it. Instead of going
ahead and simply reading it, it might be helpful--
and fun--if you had someone read this selection out
loud while you attempt to identify its structure.
Ask the person to read it as if he were presenting
this argument in public himself. Hopefully you
can find a congenial friend at this point. So:
stop reading; listen.

(a) (the following is to be read out loud)
                 DANGERS OF TV
Since the onset of the TV generation in 1945,
almost every home in North America has acquired
at least one TV set. We find that on a typical
evening, more than half the population will be
watching TV for 4 hours or more--that's over

125 million people who are watching TV for that stretch of time! And many of these will be watching the same program. Over the past 30 years there has been a profound change in the way people experience the world. In our generation we have created a society that has substituted indirect experience of the world for direct experience of the world. In other words, we see the world, we see experience, we see reality, not directly, but through the tube, through celluloid film. That's a tremendous step in human evolution! It's also a neglected step. Make no mistake, TV is not a neutral device, no more than a gun. It's an instrument frought with danger. It can destroy its careless user.

In my talk tonight, fellow parents, I'm going to suggest a very difficult step. And yet, dear parents, it's a step we must take and must take soon if we're responsible parents who care deeply about the well-being of our children. What I'm advocating is this: that we as responsible parents, should not allow indiscriminate TV watching. Yes, that's my bombshell, that we, as responsible parents, should not allow indiscriminate TV watching. That's my point, and before you rise to turn me off, listen carefully to what I have to say.

First of all, if we, as responsible parents, allow indiscriminate TV watching, then we'll raise a generation of passive idiots. The reason for this is evident. TV is a major socializing agency in our society, for children ages 3-16. Yes, that's right, TV is the major socializing agency. According to a recent study by Arnold and Bates, who polled over 2500 children in their research, they found that the average 10 year old child in North America spends 33% of his time asleep; 22% of his time in school, 5% with family, and 40% of his time in front of the TV set. Yes, that's right, 40% of a day devoted to

400

watching TV. These statistics show that TV has become the major socializing force for children in our society today. This is truly shocking!

Secondly, we are raising a generation of passive idiots. The evidence is overwhelming. First of all, TV turns off our critical functions, for we don't have to think or reason when watching TV. Secondly, TV does not demand that we make decisions. Thirdly, TV doesn't demand that we do anything, except watch. Fourthly, when we simply watch, we take in, absorb, imbibe beliefs, values, attitudes--indeed a whole view of the world. Fifthly, when we take all this in, TV dictates who we are and what we are. Sixthly, when this happens, we've become passive idiots. The process is already well under way, and points all in one direction: we are raising a generation of passive idiots.

It's time we did something. For these two reasons, then, I contend that we, as responsible parents, should not allow indiscriminate TV watching.

That's the oral argument. How did your fare with your identification of it? Compare your work as you heard the argument with what you can now do by reading it. With the transcript before us, identifying the argument is relatively easy. It's usually easier, as this example illustrates, to identify a written argument than an oral one: we need not rely on memory or on our ability to pick up structural clues while the argument is being made. Besides, if we've missed anything, or if anything is not clear, we can go back over it in written form.

Referring to the written transcript, we see that it has the following general structure. Paragraph 1 provides background information, putting the argument into context. Paragraph 2 gives us the conclusion, namely

401

we, as responsible parents, should not allow
indiscriminate TV watching.

Paragraph 3 puts forward the first main premise
and its support; paragraph 4, the second main
premise and its support (6 mini-premises). The
last paragraph repeats the conclusion and mentions
that there were two reasons offered. The argument
in (a) is displayed as follows:

| support space | | main argument space |

A&B   found   1. TV is   1. If we, as responsible
Study   33%-asleep   the   parents, allow indis-
-2500   22%-school   major   criminate TV watching,
children   5%-family   social-   then we'll be raising
-av.   40%-TV   izing   a generation of
10yr old.   agency   passive idiots.
                              in our
                              society

We don't have to   1. TV turns
think...TV   off   2. We are raising a
                        critical   generation of passive
                        functions   idiots.
2. TV does not demand we make
   decisions
3. TV doesn't demand...except watch.
4. When we watch, we...the world.
5. When we take...what we are.
6. When this happens...passive idiots.

                        .˙. We, as responsible
                            parents, should not
                            allow indiscriminate
                            TV watching.

In any full scale evaluation, we would, of course,
apply Steps #1 to #9. We won't do this here--
our immediate focus is on Step #10--but several
things should be mentioned. The main argument is
deductive (do you recall its pattern? Is it valid
or invalid?). Both mini-arguments are inductive,
and both need more support (especially the
contentions in the second mini-argument). Also
some key terms (e.g. "passive idiots," "indiscriminate TV watching," etc.) are vague.

In applying Step #10, we would first note that
we are dealing with an oral argument. Then we
would consider how the arguer has handled the
problems of (1) style, (2) communicating structure,
and (3) recall. Considerations of style depend
very much on how the argument was presented. Here
one would comment on its pace (hurried? moderate?
too slow?) its delivery (clear? slurred? lively?
monotonous? hard-to-hear? etc), use of pauses to
let main points sink in, use of emphasis, and so
forth.

In terms of communicating structure, we can usefully point out several merits:
- the conclusion is stated twice (once at
  the beginning of the argument, once at
  the end)
- the mini-premise on behalf of main premise
  1 is repeated.
- the important statistic of 40% is repeated
  in the first mini-argument
- the two main premises are numbered
- the mini-premises in the second mini-
  argument are numbered.
On the negative side, the introductory background
is rather long and wordy. Also the second mini-
argument needs much more discussion--each mini-
premise is rather contentious.

As for recall, the repetition already mentioned
helps, as would suitable pauses, emphasis and
liveliness in style. On the negative side, 6
mini-premises presented one right after the
other (as in the second mini-argument) is not
conductive to good recall. More discussion here
might help them sink in. Also many may find that
the rapid succession of numbers in the first mini-
argument: 2500, 10, 33, 22, 5, and 40 difficult to
remember.

4. Two Types of Oral Argument: Discussions and
   Debates

There are many kinds of oral arguments, but two

are of particular importance: discussions and
debates. Oral arguments are found especially in
the contexts of public discussion and public
debate. While closely related, these two kinds
of oral argument differ, and it is important to
note how they differ and the ways in which argument plays a role within each of them.

discussion

Discussion involves the cooperative reflection on
problems and issues so as to facilitate better
understanding or so as to formulate some course
of action. In discussion, a problem is initially
presented and analyzed. The problem may be, for
instance, how to control inflation by means of
appropriate legislation, or how to design a safer
car with higher gas mileage. After the problem
has been clearly identified, then various alternative solutions are proposed and critically examined by the participants in the discussion. In
terms of the example of inflation, for instance,
some participants may suggest increased governmental spending through winter works projects or
through various ways of providing incentives for
the consumer to spend. Others may suggest devising a balanced budget. And so on. Finally,
after considerable deliberation, the stage may be
reached in which a solution to the problem is
agreed upon.

In the process of discussion, argument plays an
important role in several areas. Argument is
involved, for example, in presenting considerations that support the various individual solutions
to the problem. In this instance, the argument
that is developed supports the claim that a particular solution ought to be adopted for such-and-
such reasons. Different reasons would be offered,
for example, by those who think increased governmental spending would solve the inflation problem
than by those who favor decreased governmental
spending. In addition, argument enters into the
process of discussion in developing considerations
that support the preference of one solution over

another. In this case the argument is comparative in nature. That is, the reasoning involved here contends that a particular solution is better than another for such-and-such reasons.

In discussion, then, the starting point is the problem, the goal sought is the solution, and argument plays an essential role in rational decision-making. Discussions, however, form only one part of oral argument.

debate

Debate differs considerably from discussion, although it, too, assigns tremendous importance to the development and evaluation of different arguments. Debate essentially consists of the orderly presentation of arguments both for and against a particular proposition (conclusion). Debate often concerns, for instance, presenting the lines of argument that support or fail to support whether some particular policy ought to be adopted, or whether some specific item of legislation ought to be adopted, or whether some specific item of legislation ought to be enacted by some governmental body, or whether someone is or is not guilty of some crime. In other words, debate has as its focus the presentation of arguments centering upon the claim whether some particular policy (governmental bill, action, etc.) p ought or ought not to be done (implemented, passed, etc.). The affirmative side supports the view that p ought to be done; the negative side, that p ought not to be done.

The emphasis in debate, then, is not upon the cooperative search for a solution to a particular problem but upon the production of a partisan line of argument that can be offered for a conclusion already determined. What is to be discovered in debate is not the conclusion but the considerations that support the conclusion in question. The conclusion is the proposition being debated. It may be, for instance, RESOLVED: that the

405

Federal Government ought to increase spending in order to overcome the current problem of inflation. The affirmative side of the debate presents arguments that support this proposition; the negative side, that the Federal Government ought not to do so. What is to be tested in debate are not the relative merits of competing solutions to a problem but the relative strengths of lines of argument that are offered on behalf of the proposition in question by the affirmative and negative sides.

Debate is to be found in many contexts. It may be employed by an individual mulling over in his own mind what he ought to do in some particular situation. Or it may be used by an individual or group seeking to obtain a decision from others. In this latter context, debate is found especially in legislative, legal, and academic contexts, as well as within meetings of all types generally.

In legislative and legal contexts, debate is (usually) public and it is formal. That is, it has a specific agreed-upon structure. Such a structure is adopted in order to provide some assurance that considered reasoning will take place, that all the arguments will be heard, and that a decision will take place in an informed and judicious manner. Such formal procedures are adopted, for instance, by lawyers in the arena of a courtroom, by political representatives deliberating in legislatures, by clergy in ecclesiastical assemblies, by participants at meetings, and, in general, by all bodies concerned with policy-setting and decision-making. Debate, consequently, relies on a format in which the disputants take their turn, have their say, and in which there is some third party (e.g. the judge, the jury, parliament as a whole, everyone present at the meeting, etc.) to decide the outcome of the debate.

One style of debate that is of particular interest to the study of argument is the academic debate. This represents a kind of intellectual game which serves as an adjunct to the curriculum of many universities and which is designed to provide

trained in the preparation and presentation of
oral argument. In the standard format for
collegiate and inter-collegiate academic debate,
there are five main components:

    (1) a statement to be debated ("the proposi-
        tion")
    (2) an affirmative team (who support the
        proposition)
    (3) a negative team (who deny the proposi-
        tion)
    (4) a format indicating the speaking time
        alloted to each member of the opposing
        teams and the sequence of participants.
    (5) a judge (e.g. panel, audience, etc.) who
        evaluates the debate and who renders a
        verdict about the merits of the debate.

In whatever context it occurs, debate exhibits the
following important characteristics:

    (1) Debate involves advocacy.

In debate, the participants advocate the merits of
one particular side over another. They are not
neutral, but partisan. This represents an important difference between debate and discussion, for
in the latter the participants need not be partisan nor be advocating one solution over another.

    (2) Debate involves controversy.

Issues which have already been settled are not
debatable, _e.g._, whether the earth is round,
whether man will ever fly, _etc_. Such matters are
no longer open to contest, _for_ consensus has
already been reached by informed people on these
matters.

    (3) Debate involves the challenging of
        arguments.

In debate, no argument, however well prepared and
well presented, is free from challenge. Debate
takes place in the context of a spirited, lively,
interested opposition. It flourishes in a hostile
environment.

> (4) Debate provides an arena for the public examination of an issue.

Debate accomplishes this by operating within a format which allows the pros and cons of a particular proposed policy to be subjected to scrutiny. It allows for interest and enthusiasm generated by commitment to a point of view and encourages skill in advocacy and partisanship.

> (5) Debate facilitates decision-making.

The debate format takes advantage of the enthusiasm and intellectual prowess generated by commitment and partisanship, but it does not base the decisions on such qualities. Rather debate contributes to decision-making in two major ways:

> (a) by providing a ritualized structure in terms of which the strengths of various lines of argument can be put to the test by means of challenge, counter-considerations, rebuttal and refutation.

> (b) by providing a means of rendering a decision after the debate has been held: e.g. by voting (as in legislative contexts, meetings generally, etc.), or by judicial pronouncements (as in legal contexts), or by judging the merits of the respective cases (as in academic debating).

Exercise #1: An In-Class Debate

(The following may be modified in various ways, or omitted entirely, to suit various course emphases and teaching formats.)

object
As a way of gaining experience in preparing and presenting an argument in an oral context, as well as gaining experience in listening to and evaluating oral arguments critically, debates will be held during the latter portion of the course. The sort of debate to be held represents a variant

of collegiate debating adapted to classroom use.
Each student in the class will participate in one
debate held during class time. The point of the
exercise is to provide experience in the successful communication of arguments in an oral context.

format

At various times during the latter part of the
course, debate sessions will be scheduled as a
regular feature of the course. Each debate
session will last approximately 15-20 minutes.
The format of each debate session is that of a
"one-on-one" type of debate. There will be 2
speakers:
>   (1) an affirmative speaker, who will uphold the
>   position stated in the proposition to be
>   debated, and
>   (2) a negative speaker, who will develop a line
>   of argument that denies the position stated
>   in the proposition.

The affirmative speaker will speak first. Each
debater will speak for a maximum of 5-5½ minutes.
A speaker will be cut off at the end of 5½ minutes,
for the task is to prepare and present an argument
within the set time-frame. After the two debat-
ers have finished, questioning will be opened up
to the class. Each debater is expected to defend
the position he has put forward.

There will be no formal rebuttal whereby one
speaker attacks the other. If time permits, the
class will collectively consider the merits and
flaws in the arguments presented by the two
speakers.

debater's task

The task each debater is assigned is to prepare,
present, and successfully communicate as good an
oral argument as possible on behalf of the conclusion being argued for. Particular attention
should be paid to the problems of style, communicating structure, and recall mentioned in this
chapter.

In the debate, the debater may make use of notes, books, and, of course, a prepared text. The debater should remember that he is attempting to put across an argument, so he should avoid just reading a prepared script.

After presenting his argument, each debater will submit a written transcript of his oral argument for grading. If the speaker has been cut off at the 5½ minute mark, only that portion of the transcript that was presented orally will be read for grading. The work will be judged as an argument, taking into account the appropriate steps of argument evaluation, i.e. Steps #1 through #10. The debater's response to questions will also be taken into account.

listeners' task
In this debate exercise the audience has a specific task designed to provide opportunities for learning how to identify and evaluate arguments in an oral context.

For each debate, half the class will identify and evaluate the argument the affirmative speaker presents; the other half, the negative. As the debate proceeds, listeners should make rough notes that will assist their reconstruction of the argument offered by the speaker.

After the speakers have finished, members of the group are expected to participate in the discussion of the topic under consideration, by asking questions of the speakers. These questions should be directed to specific speakers. They should not be requests simply to repeat information or points already stated. Rather the question period is designed for the group to draw speakers out, to ask for more information, to seek alternate options, to consider why this line of argumentation was put forward rather than another, and so forth.

Before the next class, listeners will complete a "debate evaluation sheet" for the assigned debater.

On this sheet, using standard format, listeners
will identify and evaluate the argument offered by
the debater, taking into account Steps #1-#10.
The debate evaluation sheet appears as follows
(not actual size):

```
┌─────────────────────────────────────────────────────────┐
│ debater:_____                             │
│                                                         │
│ topic:_____aff. neg. date:_____   │
│                                                         │
│ support space    main argument space    evaluation space│
│                                                         │
│                                                         │
│                  evaluator's name:_____     │
└─────────────────────────────────────────────────────────┘
```

These sheets are to be completed as homework and
handed in at the next class following the debate.
These sheets will not be marked, but they will be
looked at and a record will be kept of those submitted. They will be returned to the debater. In
this way the debater will be provided with a
written record of how his argument was understood
and evaluated by the group to whom he presented
his argument.

topics
The topics suggested for debate are controversial.
For the most part they involve matters of policy,
that is, they recommend that something ought or
ought not to be done by some particular group or
agency. They involve matters whose solution is by
no means obviously or decisively true. They are
therefore questions about which reasonable people
may differ.

To the extent possible in setting up a debate
schedule for classroom purposes, you are free to
select the topic, and side, you wish to debate on.
Your preference must, of course, be matched by
someone wishing to present the opposite side. A
list of suggested debate topics will be provided
by the course director. You are free to select
other topics. You are also free to consult with

411

others in the class to see if someone else would like to debate the same topic, but the other side, of the topic you'd prefer to tackle.

In selecting a topic, your primary consideration should be the topic and side for which you think you could prepare and present a good argument, one that contains both evidential and persuasive worth. You should not simply take the side you personally believe in, or think most people (in the class, in society generally, etc.) would accept. You are not being judged on truth, personal conviction, or widespread popularity. Your task is the preparation and presentation of a good oral argument.

Once the debate schedule has been set up, begin planning immediately.

5. How to Prepare a Debate for Presentation

It is one thing to prepare an argument for presentation in a written format; it is quite another to prepare one for an oral context. In each case demands are made on the arguer to make good use of the particular sort of linguistic medium in which his line of thought is articulated.

Presenting an argument in an oral context requires good structural organization of the argument: a crisp, clear conclusion; succinct main premises that are made to stand out; support for main premises thoughtfully composed. It also requires a sensitivity on the part of the arguer to the strains under which listeners are placed in following an oral argument. Style becomes tremendously important, for how the argument is presented affects considerably what is remembered of it. Structure and style: both are essential for successful communication in an oral context.

While there are many tips on how to prepare and present an oral argument, there is no substitute

for actual experience. It is only then that
matters of structure and oral style begin to loom
as personally pertinent--as something one needs
to master and not just to read about. Exercise
#1 is especially important in this respect.

By way of preparation strategy, the following
points are suggested. Rather than tackling this
matter for all forms of oral argument, this section will focus instead just on preparation for
debate, i.e. on partisan argumentation. Many of
the same principles apply, however, to all sorts
of oral arguments.

    (1) Be sure you are clear in your own mind
        what you are defending.

Suppose the proposition under debate is the following:
    RESOLVED: that the Government enact legisla-
    tion permitting doctors to practice euthanasia
    on terminally-ill patients.
The affirmative side defends the conclusion that
the Government enact legislation permitting
doctors to practice euthanasia on terminally-ill
patients.

Because a change in existing policy is being proposed, the affirmative side should state what the
existing policy is and why it should be changed
in the direction proposed. You could argue the
need to change, the advantages of changing, the
disadvantages of the present system, etc. In so
doing, at some point along the way, you should
make clear what 'euthanasia' means, what doctors
are involved, what constitutes a terminal illness,
the rights of the patient, his family, and so on.

The negative side contends that the Government
ought not to move in this direction. Many options
are open concerning how this sort of conclusion
can be approached. You could expound on the
merits of the present policy (thereby undercutting
any need to change). Or you could show the negative features of the proposed changes (thereby

indicating the undesirability of moving in that specific direction). Or you could defend some alternative policy to euthanasia that would accomplish the same objectives or have the same merits as the policy proposed by the affirmative speaker.

> (2) Read material on the topic, picking out
>   arguments both pro and con.

Check books on the topic in various libraries (city, college, university), magazine articles, library files of newspaper clippings (often these are arranged by topic), indices to periodical literature, etc., noting the various sorts of arguments that have been presented on the topic by others.

Note arguments both for and against the position you are defending. In this way you will gain a sense of the sorts of considerations you can advance as well as an indication of the probable line of argumentation your opponents are apt to take. You can also work out possible responses to their lines of thought as well. Ask friends, spouses, etc. where they stand on the issue, and why. Brainstorm. Be imaginative. Think of various possible ways of approaching the issue. List all sorts of pertinent considerations. Think about the topic from a variety of angles.

> (3) Select considerations that would build
>   a strong argument for your position.

Begin to construct your own argument for the conclusion you are defending. Be wary of plagiarism: don't just lift arguments, words and all, from the material you read. Use the articles as resource material, as indicating various lines of thought people have used in connection with the topic under examination.

Select several main points that are central to your case and begin organizing your presentation around these. It may prove helpful to you at this point to sketch out the gist of your argument using standard format for identifying arguments indicated in this text. This should provide you with an overview of your argument. It also gives you a basis for criticizing--and fixing up--your argument as you construct it.

(4) Write out your argument.

Write out your argument as you imagine you would speak it. Examine it critically. Revise and refine it. This process will take several drafts at least. No good oral argument springs right from the mind on to the paper right off the bat!

(5) Speak your argument out loud.

Once your argument has been organized and drafted, practice speaking it out loud. Here you can be your severest critic: as you speak, imagine that you, too, are the listener and consider whether you as arguer have paid sufficient attention to the problems of style, communicating structure, and recall. Remember that your task is not simply to read a written argument but to present an oral argument. There's a vast difference.

After having spoken your argument out loud several times, consider such matters as the following:
- is your delivery clear, sufficiently loud, lucid (with no stumbling or awkward pauses), confident? Does it indicate that you are in command of your line of thought and that you know where you are going in your argument?
- did you vary your pace, slowing down at various points for emphasis, variety, interest, etc.?
- did you pause every now and then, to let important points sink in? (It may be helpful to mark in pauses in your transcript)
- have you constructed and presented an interesting, engaging argument, one that someone would like to listen to? Do you present it in a lively fashion, as if you cared about what you are saying and wanted

to convince someone?
- do you provide enough emphasis? (Here you may want to underline words or phrases in your transcript)
- is the conclusion clear? Is it simply worded? Does it stand out?
- are the main premises clear? Are they simply worded? Do they stand out?
- have you supported your main premises in a careful and clear manner?
- are there sufficient locators to help your listeners grasp the structure of what you are saying?
- do you need to repeat certain points? Do you need to provide an initial overview? a recap of main points?
- do you avoid long lists of figures that would only serve to confuse a listener?
- do you look at your audience (or do you have your head buried in your transcript)?
- do you avoid rhetorical questions, questions like "who is to say that...?" or "is there anyone in his right mind who would oppose..?" (such questions, which admit of a variety of possible answers, some facetious, distract the listener and often fail to make the point the arguer wants made and could have made by a simple statement)
- do you avoid mannerisms which distract listeners from what you are saying?

In sum, is it clear what your position is, and why you support it? And is it likely, so far as it is in your power to control, that your audience is apt to listen to and remember what you have said?

Successful communication depends on your creative and analytic abilities to blend matters of structure with matters of style. As a good argument, it should have both solid evidential worth and effective persuasive worth.

(6) Remember the time limit.

Most debate presentations have a definite time

416

limit which should not be exceeded. Most are mercifully short. Obviously, in a short space of time, you will not be able to deal exhaustively with all the considerations you would like to introduce. Clearly you must select, and select well, what you plan to present. Stick to several main points, developing and supporting these in an able fashion. Do not even try to cover all possible arguments that could be cited on behalf of your point of view--there simply isn't time.

If you try to introduce everything, you will find yourself rushed when you present your argument. You will then speed through your argument, so as to get everything in. The end result of this, however, is that while you have spoken everything you want spoken, your audience will be enraged at the callous treatment and they will remember nothing (other than the fact that you zipped through your presentation).

    (7) Finally, remember that you are giving an _oral_ presentation in which you are attempting to communicate a good argument successfully to an audience.

Practice putting an argument across orally. Be sure in practicing to speak it out loud--perhaps even before a receptive audience (like a friend, spouse, etc.). Don't just mumble it to yourself. Don't just read it silently, thinking that it'll come out all right when the time comes to present it.

Also be sure to remember your audience. After all, you are trying to communicate to them. You want to convince them of the truth of some position. You want them to accept a point of view. Speak as though what you have to say matters. Don't just hide behind a prepared transcript. Put your argument _across._

Recall Quiz

(1) When is an argument "successfully communicated"? In the successful communication of an

417

argument, what must an argument-recipient be able to do?

(2)   In what specific ways does successful communication involve a reciprocal relationship or a two-way process between arguer and argument-recipient?

(3)   In an oral argument, what obligations are there on the part of the listener that help successful communication?

(4)   In an oral argument, what obligations are there on the part of the speaker that help successful communication?

(5)   What 3 problems are there that affect accurate identification of an argument in an oral context?

(6)   With what matters are problems of style concerned? Problems of communicating structure? Problems of recall?

(7)   What is Step #10 in argument evaluation?

(8)   In applying Step #10 to an oral argument, what sort of comments are placed in the evaluation space of the standard format?

(9)   How do discussion and debate differ?

(10)   As used in the context of debate, what is a "proposition"?

(11)   What are 5 important characteristics of debate?

(12)   What is suggested by way of preparation strategy for presenting a debate?

Exercise #2
The class will be divided into an equal number of teams for a formal debate (or series of formal debates, depending on class size and format).

The format of the debate, the rules, and the proposition to be debated will be provided by the course director.

Each team will meet together to plan their collect-

ive approach. The debate may be taped or videotaped for purposes of classroom discussion.

Exercise #3: Applying Step #10

The course director will provide a series of taped
and/or videotaped oral presentations (e.g. from
radio, TV, lectures, community groups, etc.) for
classroom discussion on applying Step #10 to oral
arguments.

Exercise #4: Presenting Oral Arguments

If not already assigned, exercise #2 at the end
of chapters two and three may be done at this
point as an in-class debate and judged strictly
in terms of Step #10.

CHAPTER THIRTEEN

GRAND FINALE

1. A Review

of the text

In sum, this text has developed a format for identifying and evaluating arguments. It has given you
considerable practice in spotting and criticizing
the arguments of others. It has also provided you
with opportunities for preparing and presenting
arguments of your own, in both written and oral
formats.

Before you leave this text and pass back into the
real world of controversy and discussion, you should
take time to review the structure with which you
have been provided and which you can now bring to
bear in all its fullness on the arguments you meet.

of the format

The format, you will recall, went as follows:

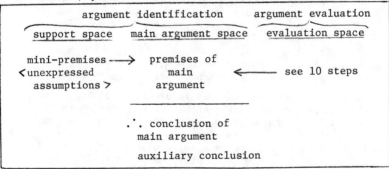

of the 10 Steps

The following 10 Steps in argument evaluation have

been presented:

#1 Look at the premises in the argument and draw attention to those that need support or more support.

#2 Look at the language used in the premises and conclusion and with respect to the basic key words and expressions needed to make sense of the argument, draw attention to words and phrases which
    (a) are vague
    (b) are ambiguous
    (c) exhibit an unhelpful use of language
    (d) represent an undiscussed controversial definition

#3 Look for missing premises (needed to establish the conclusion)

#4 Look for absent qualifiers in the premises and conclusion.

#5 Look at the premises offered by the arguer to ascertain if any are bogus. If any are, then recommend deletion of the premise and state the reason. A premise may be bogus for any of the following reasons:
    (a) because it is <u>ad hominem</u> (AH), e.g.
        (i) by character assassination
        (ii) by attacking origins
        (iii) by attacking affiliations
        (iv) by suggesting guilt by association
    (b) because it begs the question (BQ)
    (c) because it appeals to authority (AA)
        (e.g. the authority of an author, leader, group or in-stitution, society generally, a book, etc.)
    (d) because it represents an irrelevant reason (IR)
        (i) appeal to force
        (ii) appeal to pity
        (iii) appeal to "two wrongs make a right"
    (e) because it represents an appeal to ignorance (Ig)

#6 Look at the genuine premises to ascertain if they give sufficient support to the conclusion. A genuine premise may fail to give sufficient support to the conclusion for any of the following reasons:
    (a) because it represents a false dilemma (FD)
    (b) because it exhibits slippery slope reasoning (SS)
    (c) because it leads to a hasty conclusion (HC)

#7 Look at the argument in relation to other arguments in the controversy (either by the same arguer or by others) to ensure:

(a) that no misrepresentation has occurred
(b) that the arguer has not attacked"a straw man"position
(c) that the arguer has not been inconsistent, e.g.
    (i) through contradiction
    (ii) through words changing meaning
    (iii) through change in details

#8 In a deductive argument, determine if the argument is valid or invalid
    (a) by truth table method
    (b) by detecting common patterns of deductive argument

#9 In an inductive argument, by considering the following
    (a) clear key expressions (see also Step #2)
    (b) supported premises (see also Step #1)
    (c) informative inductive base
    (d) well-founded statistics
       (i) dubious statistics
       (ii) absurdly precise statistics
       (iii) improper comparisons
       (iv) omitted statistics
    (e) size of sample in inductive base
    (f) representativeness of sample in inductive base
    draw attention to those features of the argument which serve to diminish its inductive strength.

#10 With respect to oral arguments, discuss the extent to which the arguer has successfully communicated his argument to his listeners. In so doing, consider specifically the strengths and weaknesses in the way in which the speaker has coped with the problems of style, communicating structure, and recall.

2. Applying the 10 Steps

note

For the sake of systematic exposition in Part Two of this text, we have, for the most part, simply focused on one step at a time, discussing it, and then applying it to specific arguments. This is somewhat artificial, although useful in learning argument evaluation. Arguments, however, do not just exhibit one and only one flaw: they tend, on the contrary, to portray a number of defects. It is time now to turn our attention to applying all 10 Steps in argument evaluation. In so doing, several matters should be carefully noted:

(1) In a complete evaluation
   - Steps #1 through #6 apply to all arguments
   - Steps #7 through #10 are restricted steps
     - Step #7: applies only to argument exchanges
     - Step #8: applies only to deductive arguments
     - Step #9: applies only to inductive arguments
     - Step #10: applies only to oral arguments

(2) The Steps apply to main arguments and also to mini-arguments.

evaluation strategy

Complete evaluation of an argument requires that we look systematically at each component of the argument, remembering the 10 Steps at our disposal. The following evaluation strategy is suggested:
   (1) identify the argument
   (2) focus on the main argument
     - apply Steps #1 through #6 inclusive
     - apply Step #8 if deductive, #9 if inductive
   (3) focus on each mini-argument separately. For each
     - apply Steps #1 through #6 inclusive
     - apply Step #8 if deductive; #9 if inductive
   (4) apply Step #10 if the argument is oral.
   (5) apply Step #7 if the argument occurs as part of an exchange of arguments.

argument repair/argument response

At the beginning of Part Two of this text we discussed several different purposes of argument evaluation. These included:
   - indicating where arguments are defective
   - indicating why arguments are defective
   - indicating ways of improving flawed arguments
   - avoiding flaws in our own arguments
   - responding effectively to arguments (by attacking their weak spots)
Having the full range of different kinds of defectiveness before us, we are now in a better position

to carry out these objectives.

At this point you know where and why arguments are defective. You know generally how various sorts of defects can be repaired. Furthermore, by engaging in argument evaluation you can quickly and systematically zero in on an argument's significant flaws, thereby having an excellent basis for discussing and responding to points other arguers have raised. In addition, hopefully you have built up an awareness, a consciousness of argument strengths and weaknesses, that should carry over into your own attempts at argument construction and presentation.

some examples

The following examples show how various arguments exhibit a variety of defects. As practice, work along with the text in this section. For each of the following selections, identify the argument it contains and then critically evaluate it in terms of all applicable 10 Steps.

(a)   If saccharin is a harmful food additive, then it will be banned by the government. Saccharin is indeed a harmful food additive. Consequently it will be banned by the government.

This is a "bare-bones" sort of argument--2 main premises and a conclusion. It is reminiscent of where we began the study of argument back in chapter one. Identifying its structure is now easy. In terms of argument evaluation, Steps #1 and #2 pick up flaws. The argument is deductive, so Step #8 applies.

support space	main argument space	evaluation space
	1. If saccharin is a <u>harmful food additive,</u> then it will be banned by the government.	← support needed — vague key expression
	2. Saccharin is indeed a <u>harmful food additive.</u>	← support needed — vague key expression
	∴ It will be banned by the government	← this is a deductive argument. Valid (MP)

425

As this argument reminds us, even a deductive argument can exhibit some serious flaws.

(b) No one has shown that saccharin in the diet significantly harms humans. No one, after all, has shown that saccharin is not safe for human consumption. Consequently saccharin will not be banned by the government.

This argument contains 1 main premise (supported by 1 mini-premise) and a conclusion. In going through the list of Steps, we note the following:
- Step #2 - "significantly harms" is a vague key expression
- Step #5 - mini-premise 1 and its conclusion (i.e. main premise 1) beg the question. Because mini-premise 1 is bogus, we recommend its deletion. (So main premise 1 now needs support--but before we say this, we note something else)
- Step #5 - main premise 1 represents an appeal to ignorance. As a bogus premise, we recommend its deletion. So we have, on inspection, no argument at all.

support space	main argument space	evaluation space
1. No one has shown that saccharin is not safe for human consumption.	1. No one has shown that saccharin in the diet signifi- cantly harms human.	Delete: mini-premise is bogus because BQ Delete: premise is bogus because Ig vague key expression
	∴ Saccharin will not be banned by the government	not a genuine argument: all premises are bogus.

(c) Rosenhan's article ("On Being Sane in Insane Places," Science 179 (1973), pp.250-258) on insanity is full of hot air: it's complete and utter assinine nonsense.

Why, if we were to accept Rosenhan's position, we'd allow loonies, crazies and other weirdos loose on the street where they would harm themselves, menace others, increase violent crime,

426

and eventually wreck civilized society.

Moreover, if you're going to turn the insane
loose, why not also turn prisoners loose on
society?

History, moreover, shows us plainly that per-
missive attitudes towards the mentally sick
and the criminally minded undermine and destroy
the very fabric of society.

It's also reassuring to note, too, that Dr.Job,
a psychiatrist with 32 years' experience, tells
us that he can readily recognize those who are
mentally ill.

I suggest, then, that we by-pass Rosenhan's
article and turn to more profitable reading.

As we should quickly recognize, this "argument" pays
very little attention to Rosenhan's article. In evaluating it, we should turn our attention particularly
to Steps #5 and #6 to see what they indicate about
the argument.

support space	main argument space	evaluation space
	1. R's article is full ◄─── of...assinine nonsense.	Delete: premise is bogus because AH.
	2. If we were to accept ◄─── R's position, we'd allow loonies, ~~crazies and~~ ─── other weirdos...where they would...wreck civ- ilized society.	SS (support needed) unhelpful use of language
	3. If you're going to ◄─── turn...why not also turn....	Delete: premise is bogus because IR.
	4. History shows...very ◄─── fabric of society.	Delete: premise is bogus because AA (history)
	5. Dr. J. tells us... ◄─── mentally ill.	Delete: prenuse is bogus because AA
	∴ We should by-pass R's ◄─── article and turn to more profitable reading	Ind.argument: 4 premises deleted; strength rests on 1 flawed premise.

The argument contained in (c) is so weak and so flawed that it comes close to being a bogus argument: there's not much that can be done to salvage premise 2, the only premise not deleted. As a response to Rosenhan's interesting and provocative article, it is totally inadequate.

(d)   SANTA'S DILEMMA 1980
        Santa's dilemma goes as follows:
        First of all, Santa Claus is to visit all the good boys and girls in the world.
        Secondly, if Santa Claus is to visit all the good boys and girls in the world, then he must go either by reindeer or by rocket ship.
        Thirdly, Santa Claus can't go by reindeer. The evidence here is overwhelming. There are, in 1980, 94,500,427 good boys and girls in the world. With an average of 2.4 children per household, this would mean that Santa must stop at 39,375,177 households. With a 1-minute stop at each household, this would require 656,252.95 hours (which is equal to 27,343.872 days or 74.914717 years).
        Therefore Santa Claus must go by rocket ship.

The structure of this argument is readily apparent: 3 main premises (the third one being supported by a mini-argument) and a conclusion. The main argument is deductive, the mini-argument inductive.

support space	main argument space	evaluation space
	1. S.C. is to visit all the good boys & girls in the world.	← support needed vague key expr.
	2. If S.C. is to visit ...,then he must go either by reindeer or by rocket ship.	← FD (other options available); suppor needed
1.In 1980 there are 94,500,427 good...world.		← dubious statistic
2.With an avg. ...stop at 39,375,177...	3. S.C. can't go by reindeer	← ind.mini-argument (absurd statistics absurdly precise statistic
3.This wld require 656,252.95hrs...		missing mini-

428

premise?(this
schedule would be
impossible for
reindeer)

∴ S.C. must go by rocket ← this is a deductive
ship.   argument. It is
                             valid (see below).

$$\{(v) . [v \supset (r \lor s)] . (\sim r)\} \supset s$$

(1)	(2)	(3)	(4)	(5)	(6)	(7)	(8)	(9)	(10)
v	r	s	v	r v s	v ⊃(rvs)	~r	4.6.7	s	8⊃9
T	T	T	T	T	T	F	F	T	T
T	T	F	T	T	T	F	F	F	T
T	F	T	T	T	T	T	T	T	T
T	F	F	T	F	F	T	F	F	T
F	T	T	F	T	T	F	F	T	T
F	T	F	F	T	T	F	F	F	T
F	F	T	F	T	T	T	F	T	T
F	F	F	F	F	T	T	F	F	T

The following argument is an oral one (if possible,
find a friend to read it out loud to you).
(e)   It's time for tough talk. I'm going to give
it to you straight, in plain terms.
         In my experience as a prison guard for over
10 years, there's been far too much molly-
coddling of prisoners. They eat well, have no
responsibilities, have access to TV and books,
get lots of treats and frills, and are generally provided for in a manner far in excess of
what many law-abiding folk can manage. Why I'd
say that 85% of them live better in prison than
at home.
         I utterly reject the gutless, spineless, do-
gooders such as social workers and liberal
clergy who rant on and on about rehabilitation,
stressing the need for more programs, more this
and that, and, of course, more money.No one has
shown that rehabilitation works. Most people
don't favor rehabilitation. Besides, studies
have shown that rehabilitation isn't possible.

Also there's no more money: the well is dry.

It shouldn't be forgotten, too, that as prison guards we're paid a measly salary for our hours and responsibilities. After all, we're not paid much for our duties.

Prisons are places of punishment. Most of the guards in cell block D would agree with me on this. I dare say, too, that 80% of the decent folk in this country would back us up.

Therefore I urge this Commission to adopt much stricter measures concerning what prisoners can and cannot do.

support space	main argument space	evaluation space
1.They eat well.. ..get lots of treats & frills.. ..can manage. 2.85% of them live..at home.	1.In my exp. as a prison guard...of prisoners	support needed vague key expr. ind.base: 1 (small representative?) dubious statistic
1.No one...works. 2.Most people... 3.Studies have shown.... 4.There's no more money...dry.	2.I utterly reject gutless,spineless, ...rant on and on.. ..more programs... more money.	delete: Ig delete: AA ind.base insuff. informative (provide details) support needed unhelpful uses of language
1.We're not paid much for our duties	3.As prison guards we're paid a measly salary for our hours....	delete: BQ delete: IR
1.Most guards in cell block D wld agree.... 2.80% of the decent folk....	4.Prisons are places of punishment	ind.base: small (representative?) dubious statistic needs support delete: AA
	∴.I urge this commission ...cannot do.	ind.argument. Rests on 3 largely unsupported premises

430

This is an oral argument
problems of style (this depends very much of how the
    argument was spoken and presented)
problems of communicating structure -- few locators used,
    main premises too long for the most part, no overview,
    no summary, not sure where argument is headed since
    conclusion is stated only at the end, no repetition of
    main points, probably too many mini-premises to be
    remembered in such a short time, etc.
problems of recall -- few locators, no overview or
    summary or initial statement of conclusion, premises
    not clearly identified as such, etc.

Recall Quiz

(1) What are the 10 Steps in argument evaluation?

(2) What Steps apply to all arguments? What Steps
    are restricted? To what are the restricted
    Steps restricted?

(3) What evaluation strategy is suggested?

(4) What is the point of argument evaluation?

Exercise #1

In the following selections, carefully indicate
what is wrong with the evaluation in right space.

support space   main argument space   evaluation space

(a)   1.No one has shown ←——delete: IR
                       that astrology
                       doesn't work.← ————— vague key expr.
                     _____
                     ∴ The horoscope is a ← hasty conclusion
                       good predictor of
                       human behavior. ———— ambiguous expr.

(b)   1. I have a choice: I ←—FD
                       can either pay my
                       income tax or not
                       pay my income tax.

                     2. If I pay my income ←—support needed

431

tax, then I'll be
supporting <u>an immoral
system.</u> ↰⎯⎯ undiscussed
controversial defn.

3. I'll not support an
immoral system. ⎯⎯ hasty conclusion

⎯⎯⎯⎯⎯⎯⎯⎯⎯⎯

∴ I'll not pay my in-← ind.argument (rests
come tax. on 3 unsupported
premises)

(c)   1.If I go to Acapulco,
I'll get Montezuma's ← support needed
Revenge.

2.I'll not go to ⎯⎯ hasty conclusion
Acapulco.

⎯⎯⎯⎯⎯⎯⎯⎯⎯⎯

∴ I won't get Monte- ← this is a deductive
zuma's Revenge argument. It is
valid (MT)

(d)   1.The benefits of mari- ←delete: misrepre-
juana ought not to be sentation (m.isn't
overlooked: at its like this at all)
best it gives an
experience of <u>true</u> undiscussed con-
<u>serendipity.</u> troversial defn.

1.It cures the
humdrum
2.It represents an →2.In my experience, ← ind.base: 1
alternative to serendipity is not
the usual. <u>something to be</u> ← ambiguous expr.
3.It uplifts the <u>sneezed at.</u> ⎯⎯ more support
spirit. needed
⎯⎯⎯⎯ ambiguous expr.

⎯⎯⎯⎯⎯⎯⎯⎯⎯⎯

∴ Marijuana is not
something to be
underrated.

(e)   1.Rosenhan says there← delete: IR
is no way of telling
who is and who is

432

not insane. ←————— hasty conclusion

←————— unhelpful use of
language

2. This study confirms ←— more support
the findings of many   needed
other studies.

∴ There is no way of ←— deductive argument.
telling who is and   valid (MP)
who is not insane.

(f) (the following is from a speech)

1. In 1967 avg.age
was...; in 1979
...; in 2000 will
be...
(spoke too fast;
cldn't get details)
→ 1. Av.age of.Americans ←— needs support
is increasing at an
astonishing rate.   vague key expression

1. in education
2. in advertising
3. in business
generally
4. in...
(spoke too fast;
cldn't get details)
2. Because of this ←——— needs support
there will be fewer
senior jobs open   ind.base: small,
for most workers   unrepresentative
and many will have
to content them-
selves with never
reaching the top.

1. no accumulated
funds
2. no young people
paying in...
3. but, in some ways,
there will be...
(spoke too fast;
cldn't get details)
3. Also because of ←——— needs support
this, pension plans
in the year 2000   qualifier omitted
will be in con-   (shouldn't it be
siderable difficulty. "not many"?)

∴ We must start plann- ←— ind.argument (rests
ing for an economic   on 3 unsupported
crisis when the   premises)
present 30-40yr olds
reach retirement age

This is an oral argument. It is a good one. The arguer
has successfully communicated the structure of his
argument. Good work!

433

Exercise #2
Using standard format, identify and critically
evaluate the following arguments in terms of all
applicable 10 Steps.

page 31, (2)	page 106, (2)
page 31, (3)	page 110, (8)
page 32, (5)	page 145, (1)
page 32, (7)	page 254, (d)
page 50, (f)	page 255, (e)
page 52, (g)	page 354, (c)
page 65, (3)	page 387, (11)
page 100,(j)	page 399, (a)

FOR FURTHER READING

The following are just some of the readily available works that examine the study of argument.

1. on the study of argument generally

Copi, Irving M. Introduction to Logic. 5th ed. New York: Macmillan, 1978.
Kahane, Howard. Logic and Philosophy. 3rd ed. Belmont: Wadsworth, 1973.

2. on argument identification

Beardsley, Monroe C. Thinking Straight. 4th ed. Englewood Cliffs: Prentice-Hall, 1975.
Scriven, Michael. Reasoning. New York: McGraw-Hill, 1976.
Thomas, Stephen N. Practical Reasoning in Natural Language. Englewood Cliffs: Prentice-Hall, 1977.

3. on language as the medium of argument

Beardsley, Monroe C. Thinking Straight.
Copi, Irving M. Introduction to Logic.
Engel, S. Morris. With Good Reason. New York: St. Martin's Press, 1976.
Hospers, John. An Introduction to Philosophical Analysis. 2nd ed. Englewood Cliffs: Prentice-Hall, 1967. see ch. 1.

4. on fallacies

Copi, Irving M. Introduction to Logic.
Engel, S. Morris. With Good Reason.
Johnson, Ralph H.& J.Anthony Blair, Logical Self-Defense. New York: McGraw-Hill, 1977.
Kahane, Howard. Logic and Philosophy.
Michalos, Alex C. Improving Your Reasoning. Englewood Cliffs: Prentice-Hall, 1970.

5. on deductive argument

Copi, Irving M. Introduction to Logic.
Copi, Irving M. Symbolic Logic. 5th ed. New York: Macmillan, 1979.

Kahane, Howard. <u>Logic and Philosophy</u>.

6. on inductive argument

Copi, Irving M. <u>Introduction to Logic</u>.
Giere, Ronald N. <u>Understanding Scientific Reason-
    ing</u>. New York: Holt,Rinehart & Winston, 1979.
Kahane, Howard. <u>Logic and Philosophy</u>.
Skyrms, Brian. <u>Choice and Chance: An Introduction
    to Inductive Logic</u>. 2nd. ed. Encino and Belmont:
    Dickenson, 1975.

7. on oral arguments, debating

Capaldi, Nicholas. <u>The Art of Deception</u>. New
    York: Donald W. Brown, 1971.
Freeley, Austin J. <u>Argumentation and Debate</u>.
    4th ed. Belmont: Wadsworth, 1976.

8. on argument strategies, etc.

David J. Crossley & Peter A. Wilson. <u>How to Argue</u>.
    New York: Random House, 1979.
Gilbert, Michael A. <u>How To Win an Argument</u>. New
    York: McGraw-Hill, 1979.

436